Economic Principles for Education

'Clearly, the more students, within reason, Dixon could get "interested" in his subject, the better for him; equally clearly, too large a number of "interested" students would mean that the number studying Welch's own special subject would fall to a degree that Welch might be expected to resent. With an Honours class of nineteen and a Department of six, three students seemed a safe number to try for.'

Kingsley Amis
Lucky Jim (1954)

'Have those public endowments contributed in general to promote the end of their institution? Have they contributed to encourage the diligence, and to improve the abilities of the teachers? Have they directed the course of education towards objects more useful, both to the individual and to the public, than those to which it would naturally have gone of its own accord?'

Adam Smith
An Inquiry into the Nature and Causes of the Wealth of Nations (1776)

Economic Principles for Education

Theory and Evidence

Clive R. Belfield
University of Birmingham, UK

Edward Elgar
Cheltenham, UK • Northampton, MA, USA

Published by
Edward Elgar Publishing Limited
Glensanda House
Montpellier Parade
Cheltenham
Glos GL50 1UA
UK

Edward Elgar Publishing, Inc.
136 West Street
Suite 202
Northampton
Massachusetts 01060
USA

A catalogue record for this book
is available from the British Library

Library of Congress Cataloguing in Publication Data

Belfield, C.R.
    Economic principles for education : theory and evidence / Clive R. Belfield.
    Includes bibliographical references and index.
    1. Education—Economic aspects. 2. Human capital. I. Title.

   LC65 .B45 2000
   338.4'737—dc21

00–057656

ISBN 1 84064 444 3
Printed and bound in Great Britain by MPG Books Ltd, Bodmin, Cornwall

Contents

List of Figures   *vii*
List of Tables   *viii*
Preface   *ix*
Acknowledgements   *x*

**1. THE APPLICATION OF ECONOMICS
   TO EDUCATION**   1
    1.1 An Economic Description of Education   1
    1.2 Economic Methods   6

2. HUMAN CAPITAL AND EDUCATION   16
    2.1 Introduction   16
    2.2 The Basic Human Capital Model   17
    2.3 Investment Appraisal   27
    2.4 Over-education   35
    2.5 Information Costs and Education   40
    2.6 Issues and Conclusions   46

3. THE THEORY OF ENROLMENT CHOICE   48
    3.1 Introduction   48
    3.2 Uncertainty and Risk   49
    3.3 The Demand for Education   54
    3.4 Allocations of Education   59
    3.5 Issues and Conclusions   70

4. THE THEORY OF THE ENTERPRISE   72
    4.1 Introduction   72
    4.2 Production Function Models   73
    4.3 Cost and Revenue Functions   84
    4.4 Issues and Conclusions   94

5. EVIDENCE ON EDUCATION ENTERPRISES   96
    5.1 Resource Effects   96
    5.2 Evidence on Resource Effects   97
    5.3 Specification of Resource Models   103
    5.4 Scale Effects   108
    5.5 Issues and Conclusions   117

6. FACTOR INPUTS   120
    6.1 Concepts   120
    6.2 Teacher Inputs   121
    6.3 Other Inputs   133
    6.4 Factor Complementarity   140
    6.5 Issues and Conclusions   142

7. THE THEORY OF THE MARKET   144
    7.1 Introduction   144
    7.2 Market Structures   145
    7.3 Evidence About the Market   149
    7.4 Exchange Mechanisms   154
    7.5 Issues and Conclusions   161

8. THE ROLE OF GOVERNMENT IN EDUCATION   163
    8.1 Introduction   163
    8.2 The Government in Education   164
    8.3 How Government Funds Education   166
    8.4 The Costs of Government Provision   179
    8.5 Issues and Conclusions   190

9. AGGREGATE EFFECTS OF EDUCATION   193
    9.1 Concepts   193
    9.2 Social Effects   194
    9.3 Economic Growth Effects   200
    9.4 Macro-economic Effects Reconsidered   203
    9.5 Issues and Conclusions   207

10. EDUCATION POLICY USING ECONOMICS
    10.1 Economic Concepts in Education   209
    10.2 Directions for Policy   213

Notes   218
References   222
Index   250

Figures

1.1 Cost-effectiveness of Education Programmes   8

2.1 Life-cycle Human Capital Framework   17
2.2A Wage Effects when Quotas are Relaxed: High-skilled Workers 24
2.2B Wage Effects when Quotas are Relaxed: Low-skilled Workers 24
2.3 Directed Technological Change and Wage Premia   26

3.1 Wealth Effects and the Demand for Education   51
3.2 Efficiency Effects from Enrolment Criteria   60

4.1 An Efficiency Matrix for Four College Types   73
4.2 Output Functions for Education Enterprises   77
4.3A Perfect Information Curriculum Standards   80
4.3B Binary Curriculum Standards   80
4.4 Cost Functions in Education   86

6.1 Proportion of Operating Costs Paid to Labour   122
6.2 Teacher Supply with Government Intervention   127
6.3 Mixed and Streamed Student Enrolment   139

8.1 Government Prescriptions on Demand   183

Tables

1.1 Total Education Expenditure as a Percentage of GNP, 1996   3
1.2 Mean School Years and Participation Rates, 1960–90   4

2.1 Mincerian Rates of Return to Schooling   29

3.1 Highest Qualification at Age 33 by Father's Occupation   61

5.1 Effects of Teacher–Pupil Ratio and Expenditure Per-pupil on
      Student Performance   97
5.2 Economies of Scale and Scope in US Higher Education   111
5.3 Economies of Scale and Scope in UK Higher Education   112
5.4 Exam Results by Sizes of Secondary Schools in England   114

6.1 Distribution of Expenditure of State Schools
      in England, 1996–97   121
6.2 Teacher Salary to Average Worker Earnings Ratios   125
6.3 Allen Elasticities of Factor Substitution   141

8.1 Performance across Sectors of the UK Economy   189

9.1 Estimates of the Annual Value/Impact of Additional Schooling   199

Preface

This book, *Economic Principles for Education: Theory and Evidence*, has been written for two sorts of reader. Primarily, it is for undergraduates interested in how economic theories and principles can be applied within a particular sector. So the text includes models, concepts, frameworks and diagrams. But the book is also for general readers interested in gaining an economist's perspective on education. So there is evidence, inference and some speculative exhortation. It is hoped that readers are sufficiently sceptical of all the arguments presented here that they can decide for themselves which are convincing.

There is plenty of excellent literature on the economics of education – as will hopefully be evident below – but, mostly published across a range of academic journals, it is not accessible as a collection. For anyone but the specialist or fanatic, it is difficult to appreciate the depth and breadth of the invasion economics has made into the study of education.

This book intends to redress that difficulty: using evidence from a range of countries (but mainly the UK and the US), it summarises and synthesises economic research on education. In this respect, this book builds on previous Economics of Education texts by Mark Blaug, by Cohn and Geske and by Geraint Johnes. These earlier texts covered similar ground to this one, but for different economic circumstances and with different institutional contexts. Within this tradition, this book is intended to illustrate the most attractive facet of the discipline of economics: supple analysis embedded in a set of core principles.

Acknowledgements

I would like to acknowledge the great help of colleagues: Stan Siebert, Arnaud Chevalier, Geraint Johnes, Mark Blaug, Hywel Thomas, Alison Bullock, John Heywood, Xiangdong Wei, John Addison and Celia Brown.

The author is grateful for the permission to reproduce material from the following sources: Victor Gollancz; American Economic Association; Blackwell Publishers; Taylor & Francis Ltd (www.tandf.co.uk/journals); Elsevier Science; Cambridge University Press; and MIT Press.

1. The Application of Economics to Education

1.1 AN ECONOMIC DESCRIPTION OF EDUCATION

1.1.1 The Basic Concepts

Education – the process of learning new skills, of finding out new information or of understanding various phenomena – can be analysed by theories of cognition, theories of behaviour and through most Social Science disciplines. For the purposes of this book, education may be regarded as a way of generating, accumulating and maintaining human capital (Becker, 1985). Human capital – an individual's embodied skills above their raw labour ability – can be obtained in many forms: schooling and training are the educational forms of interest here, but alternative forms may be experience or simply watching those who already have a larger stock of human capital. Typically, such accumulation takes a long time and it may be measured using educational credentials, such as certificates, years of schooling or examination grades. But although exams are sometimes an end in themselves, the deployment of human capital typically has external effects in the labour market, in the household or in broader society. Educated people are typically more skilled, allowing them to earn more; but they may also be more health-conscious, allowing them to enjoy life more, or more civic-minded, contributing to society's goals. In choosing how to deploy their human capital to any of these ends, individuals are making decisions about resources, economic decisions.

Economics is a discipline which brings a particular mode of thinking to everyday activities. The fundamental assumption of economics is that the resources available to achieve any objective are scarce (when set against wants). This scarcity then affects how people behave – and so why they become educated – as well as how education is delivered through schools, colleges or in training. Such scarcity can be countered by the efficient utilisation of resources: a given objective is efficiently achieved if the lowest possible amount of resource has been used; and if resources are saved in

1

achieving one objective, they can be put toward achieving another separate one. Economists should therefore compare the actuality of education systems to the potential opportunities with the resources available, recognising that all resources have alternative uses or opportunity costs.

The aim of this introductory chapter, therefore, is to analyse education using economic principles and to do so in a way that provides strong justification for the sub-discipline of the economics of education. This requires a full response to the question: what roles can economists perform in analysing education?

1.1.2   The Roles of Economists

A first (and popular) role for the economist of education relates to the labour market. Education is a primary determinant of wages, included in most estimates of earnings, and for many drives the demand for learning and for training. From apprenticeships to higher education (and indeed, over-education), the labour market and education are interlinked at this micro-economic level. Aggregating up the individual labour effects, education may have macro-economic effects and raise economic growth.

Second, economists have a role in formulating behavioural and demand theory, studying how education changes behaviour and alters information sets. This applies to individuals, households and communities, across all domains: at work, in consumption and during leisure. To the extent that education is efficacious, and the human capital model articulates how it could be, people will demand it and this demand function – by population cohorts, for qualification levels and for course programmes – may be modelled.

A third role is in the study of educational organisations such as schools or universities: this encompasses their technologies, use of factor inputs and their objective, cost and revenue functions. The supply of education provision will depend on all these aspects and the theory of the enterprise can be applied to describing such provision.

A fourth role for economists is as market analysts. The equilibration of the supply of and demand for education will depend on how the market is constituted: schools may be competitive or cartelised and education may be traded either through vouchers, loans or allocated by fiat. The efficiency and equity of these market structures and exchange mechanisms merits attention.

Finally, economists have an important role as accountants. Education has become an increasingly important activity within all economies: from early years kindergarten instruction to continuing education and training, the accumulation of skills spans a lifetime, absorbing substantial scarce resources. So the scrutiny of publicly funded expenditures on education, as well as non-market time of potential workers, is a significant research area in which economists can play an important role.

Table 1.1   Total Education Expenditure as a Percentage of GNP, 1996

	Education expenditure as a % of GNP
China	2.3
India	3.4
Japan	3.6
Germany	4.8
United Kingdom	5.4
United States	5.4
Australia	5.6
France	6.1
Canada	7.0
Norway	7.5
South Africa	7.9
Denmark	8.2
Sweden	8.3
World	4.8
Low/middle income countries	
East Asia & Pacific	2.7
Europe and Central Asia	5.4
Latin America and Caribbean	3.7
Middle East and North Africa	5.2
South Asia	3.0
Sub-Saharan Africa	4.3

Source: World Bank Indicators (1999)

For exposition, Table 1.1 shows education expenditures as a proportion of GNP across different countries as of 1996. The average expenditure is around 5% of GNP, but this varies considerably: China spends about half as much as the average country and, even within Western economies, the

Scandinavian countries spend at least two percentage points more than the average. There are also substantial differences across continents.

These figures typically exclude indirect (or private) costs of schooling and the opportunity costs of students' time (see also OECD, 1997). The overall trend in expenditures (if not in enrolments) has been reasonably stable (or even declining) over the last decade. UK expenditure, for example, rose by 2.8% in real terms over the five years 1993–97, a figure below generally accepted long run trend rates of economic growth (and suggestive of disinvestment by government in education, perhaps compensated by increases in private markets). Moreover, such aggregate figures obscure competing priorities within the education sector. Looking at UK expenditures during the 1990s, investment in children under five was significantly increased, with declining investment in the upper tiers of the education system. These changes reflect a significantly altered government investment strategy.

Table 1.2   Mean School Years and Participation Rates, 1960–90

	Mean school years		% with no education (age 15+)		
	1960	1990	1960	1990	*n*
Mideast and North Africa	1.22	4.47	81.0	41.0	*10*
South Asia	1.51	3.85	74.2	55.2	*7*
Sub-Saharan Africa	1.73	2.93	68.9	48.3	*23*
East Asia and the Pacific	2.83	6.08	52.5	15.4	*10*
Latin America and Caribbean	3.26	5.24	37.9	17.3	*23*
OECD	7.05	9.02	5.0	4.5	*23*
Former centrally planned economies	7.54	9.98	2.5	1.6	*9*

Source: Barro and Lee (1996)

Relatedly, Table 1.2 shows mean school years and participation rates in education across countries between 1960 and 1990. Substantial increases in mean school years are evident, broadly doubling within developing economies and increasing by around one-third in the OECD and former centrally planned economies. The coverage of education has also been extended: across all the developing economies, the proportions of population aged 15 or over with no education fell sharply. Substantial upgrading has also occurred in Western economies: for the UK over the period 1973–95, the proportion of workers with no qualifications fell by around 60% and the numbers of degree holders rose at least threefold. Generally, these figures indicate a substantial increase in the world's stock of education (even as the distribution of education remains skewed towards males and the link between education funding and enrolment fluctuates). This greater stock of education without an obvious (or proportionate) increase in education expenditures suggests large scale changes in the production function for education.

Translating such stock and expenditure aggregates into per-student expenditures, the average for the OECD in 1995 was around $3595 in primary, $4971 in secondary and $12 018 in higher education (Dutta et al., 1999, 357). Within these averages, there is a substantial spread: expenditure on university students in the US is approximately 2.5 times that in the UK, where grant spending per full-time equivalent student fell by around one third between 1993 and 1998 (DfEE/OFSTED, 1998). For these OECD nations, the ratio of higher education to primary education per-student expenditure appears reasonably consistent at 2–2.5 (this figure is derived both with the 1995 data and Tsang's (1988) cost ratios from the 1980s). As an alternative metric, spending per-pupil as a proportion of per capita GDP is broadly equal across primary and secondary schooling within the OECD (Barro and Lee, 1996; 1990 data). Across the developing economies, however, the relative investment across sectors is less balanced: secondary education receives around 2.6 times the per-pupil resource of primary education. Less clear – but equally important – is the relationship between government and private expenditure on education, that is, how substitutable and relatively efficient they are at generating human capital. In this chapter it is sufficient to refer to the probably substantial effects of all these changes in participation and resourcing and note that, in mapping these disbursements and resource usage, economics plays an essential role.

To fulfil each of these above roles, economists have access to copious amounts of data, typically cross-sectional and sample surveys. Data on educational activities have grown in volume and become more accessible to research: in the UK, league tables, inspection grades and Research Assessment Exercises are available for study; costs data are also available. These data offer a solid foundation for hypothesis testing and so are ripe for the economist both as an accountant and in the general role of the empirically minded social scientist.

So there are plenty of avenues for applying economic analysis and the economist's way of thinking to education. Perhaps this can be inferred from the substantial growth in the economics of education. None the less, there are two ostensible impediments. First, there is the grass-roots preoccupation of economists with markets: supply, demand and equilibrium. Yet there are few (competitive) markets in education and many educationalists are resistant to this impersonal trope (Grace, 1994). And where they do exist, such markets do not seem to work in standard ways: few might be described as competitive and many are heavily regulated or commanded. Second, formal economics is a world of homogeneous goods, of limited uncertainty with tractable utility functions and standardised production technologies. Little of this seems directly pertinent to education, where consumption and investment are interlinked, where service provision is not homogeneous, where societal imperatives may dominate concerns over efficiency and where uncertainty and ignorance may be common. Education and learning may not easily be quantified and agents do not operate in perfect markets with complete certainty about future events. Hence there may be some resistance to applying predominantly quantitative, model-building tools and apparatus to a context-rich endeavour such as education. These two discrepancies should be recognised and they are addressed throughout the text – primarily through discussion of methodological issues. However, they are not found to be of critical importance: quantification is often possible for making decisions and agents do appear to act using the fullest available, albeit uncertain, expectations set.[1]

In summary, this array of roles for the economist is reassuring: the returns to applying economics to education might appear to be high and economics may positively contribute to education policy. To show how this is possible, the next section describes the economic methods used to study education. These tools appear multivarious, but in fact can be reduced to two very simple ideas: the study of efficiency and cost–benefit analysis.

1.2   ECONOMIC METHODS

1.2.1   Efficiency Studies

Efficiency involves getting the most out of the resources available and therefore has two sides: what is 'got out' compared to what is 'put in'. Both sides need to be considered: efficiency can be improved either if more is obtained from the same inputs or if the same amount is obtained but with less inputs. Efficiency can therefore be assessed internally, in terms of input resources to gain a given educational outcome, and externally, in terms of subsequent outputs achieved from a given resource dose of education. Behrman (1996, 345) distinguishes the three main forms of efficiency. First, allocative (internal) efficiency is where inputs are distributed toward the production of various outcomes in order that the values of marginal products for each input are the same across all uses. So university faculty should be optimally deployed both on teaching and research, for instance.

Second, input-choice efficiency occurs where inputs are selected so that their marginal contribution equals social marginal cost. Here wages paid to teacher input should be compared with factor prices of infrastructure inputs in generating desired educational outcomes. Finally, output (external) efficiency applies when the quantities of outcomes are such that social marginal cost equals social marginal benefit. So the numbers of enrolments or costs of provision of medical education, for instance, should be sufficient to meet a society's health preferences. Ensuring all such efficiencies is of central concern; each of these forms is addressed in detail in later chapters.

One way of examining internal efficiency is via cost-effectiveness analysis (or more simply, but along the same lines, unit cost analysis). Cost-effectiveness analysis relates costs to outcomes in a numerical form: this may be a ratio, equivalent to a unit cost per outcome, but the functional form for analysis is general (see Thomas, 1990, for per A-level grade costs). Simply, cost-effectiveness ratios can be calculated, relating costs to total academic achievement:

Cost-effectiveness Ratio = Total Costs/Total Achievement   (1.1)

Such analysis may be applied to a range of programmes – teacher training, education media and different modes of instruction – and a distinction should be made between incremental changes, that is, extra, marginal funding for an existing programme, and whole-funding, that is, the cost-effectiveness of an entire programme. Typically, cost-effectiveness analysis is used to decide how to, rather than whether to, implement a given policy goal; it therefore helps in deciding which version of an educational programme should be funded (assuming that outcomes can be effectively compared across versions). Figure 1.1 sketches the basic relationship: programme A is the reference programme and any programmes in quarter X would definitely be rejected; any programmes in quarter Y would definitely be preferred (assuming the transition costs from programme A to X or Y are trivial). A financing constraint needs to be imposed to decide on the relative merits of programmes in the remaining quarters.

Although this is a proper test of efficiency in comparing inputs with outputs, data are often insufficiently available for such testing. For cost-effectiveness analysis, a definition of effectiveness is needed: outcomes may be defined as programme completion; employment; student learning; student satisfaction; and/or college placement. There is no obvious reason to choose one over another. The appropriate choice of outcome may depend on: how widespread the benefits of programme participation are; what the impacts are for those who benefit the most from participation; how the gains depend on students' initial characteristics; and how individual students choose between programmes. For any given outcome, an effect size may be calculated: such effect sizes, calculated as the standardised mean difference between two programmes, represent a metric for comparing outcomes.

Figure 1.1 Cost-effectiveness of Education Programmes

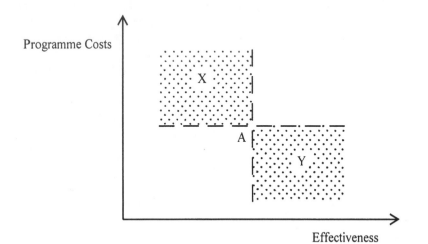

As well, accurate cost data are needed and Tsang's (1988) review of cost studies highlights many deficiencies and difficulties. These include: the problems of measuring capital costs and estimating rates of depreciation; double-counting of some costs, particularly transfer payments; and the definition of the educational unit when an activity is a joint one (that is, whether cost-effectiveness should be considered for the individual or the school). Many cost analyses use expenditures rather than opportunity costs, with the costs of students' and parents' time often omitted from the analysis; transition costs, for example, divestment of physical capital, should be considered; and generally few cost studies have robust and full data available on actual expenditures (being reliant on accounting conventions). Breneman (1998, 364–367), for example, describes the difficulties of getting consistent and reliable cost information on US remediation programmes; Harbison and Hanushek (1992) chart similar problems for evaluating Brazilian education. Inouye et al. (1997) compare the costs of five US elementary school programmes to improve reading: they find per-pupil costs of these incremental programmes to vary between $114 and $5508 (1990 dollars). Because of incomparable effectiveness measures across the five programmes, however, they do not estimate cost-effectiveness ratios.

Instead, a more modest cost-consequences analysis serves to map the costs of programmes, including indirect costs imposed on other agents as a result of the programme (for instance, the closure of a neighbourhood school raises school commuting costs to local families). For example, Slavin et al. (1996) use a matched pair analysis for schools in their evaluation of the US Success for All education programme (see also Slavin, 1999, for the effectiveness of education interventions to improve the attainment of disadvantaged children). They calculate the additional costs of the programme, its effect sizes and indicate potential areas for cost reduction, but no assessment of cost-effectiveness is made. At best then, this approach allows cost savings to be identified.

A second area for research on internal and external efficiency is through modelling of the education production function. Production function studies model schools, colleges or universities as institutions which 'manufacture' educational outcomes, so as to discover which types of resource and which allocations have the greatest effect on outcomes and how input-choice and allocative efficiency could be improved. Whereas in industrial sectors performance may be measured *inter alia* by firm surpluses or sales value per-employee, point-estimate academic performance measures may be similarly tractable in the case of education enterprises (as well as readily available, both in cross-section and over time). One performance measure is the academic achievement of students. For example, in the aggregate across the period 1993–98, there was a substantial increase in the numbers and standards of qualifications obtained by school-leavers in the UK (with academic outcomes raised by around one-sixth and vocational ones fourfold, DfEE, 1998b). Combining this evidence with that on broadly static per-unit resources in UK education, there appears (assuming equivalence across the education credentials over time) to have been a substantial increase in efficiency – much higher academic outcomes with unchanged (or even declining) resources.

Production function models explore these relationships, but at a much more detailed level, yielding more information about the education process than cost-effectiveness analysis and typically looking at whether or not increasing resources (for example, lowering class size) results in superior educational outcomes. This modelling of the production function may be tested via regression analysis, although (non-parametric) data envelopment analysis can also be utilised. Complementary organisational case studies may be used to explain the logic behind mergers of colleges or schools and to estimate economies of scale and scope and the optimal sizes of institutions.

A third area for research into efficiency is in market analysis, demand and supply studies. The market for education programmes and services is equilibrated through demand and supply, and study of each of these may yield insights into agents' behaviour. On the demand side, student enrolment, participation and effort levels can be investigated. Of particular

interest are how levels of public subsidy affect the demand for education
and how capital market constraints may preclude optimal outcomes. On the
supply side, many education providers are run by governments and
subsidised, but they may still co-operate, collude or compete to provide
education. The structure, conduct and performance of these providers is
important and the mode of interaction of suppliers with demanders can be
assessed for its efficiency.

1.2.2 Cost–Benefit Analysis

A second general research method in the economics of education is cost–
benefit analysis (see Brent, 1996; Levin, 1995; Hough, 1994). This
compares the costs of undertaking an education programme with the benefits
of that programme using pecuniary values. Conventionally, cost–benefit
analysis is used to identify whether or not a policy is worth undertaking,
rather than how it should be undertaken. The fundamental rule is simple: if
the benefits of a programme exceed the costs, then that programme is worth
undertaking. (If the costs are regarded as inputs, and the benefits are the
outputs, then a cost–benefit approach is analogous to a study of efficiency.)
Yet this fundamental rule is much more difficult to put into practice. Such
analyses require, *inter alia*, identification of the costs, including opportunity
costs; specification of the benefits expressed in money terms; a justifiable
discount rate, because costs and benefits are likely to be incurred at different
times; and an explicit statement of which perspective the analysis is to be
viewed from (as many programmes affect more than just the students in
class).

   As well as difficulties in measuring costs and benefits, the incidence of
education itself may be only imperfectly observed. For modelling, years of
schooling are typically used, although one year of schooling is unlikely to be
uniform across different population cohorts or academic levels. School
quality measures should be incorporated in simple quantity estimates,
particularly if the intention is to model education as an input into the
production of other social outcomes. The bias from this measurement error
(depending on the variance of the error in measuring schooling relative to
the variance of observed schooling) may be substantial. Similarly, the
differences in prior ability or home endowment across groups may only be
imperfectly observed and so modelled (notwithstanding value-added
adjustments).

   Furthermore, cost–benefit analysis itself may be difficult to
operationalise (Herrnstein, 1997). There may be a saliency mismatch: it is
hard to envisage some of the costs or some of the benefits and this may
falsely diminish their significance. With education, some of the benefits
(improved health or a better understanding of cultural differences, for

example) are particularly hard to quantify and so may be overlooked in any cost–benefit calculation. A scale mismatch may also occur: the costs of undertaking a single act may differ significantly from repeated or sequential endeavours. One example here is to recognise that the benefits from five years of study at school are not simply five times the benefit of one year. Notwithstanding these mismatches, cost–benefit analysis offers a critical evaluative criterion for deciding on educational investments and resource redistribution; three examples elaborate this criterion.

One way of examining costs and benefits is through rate of return appraisal (Psacharopoulos, 1995). This is discussed in more detail in Chapter 2, but the aim is to estimate an internal rate of return, that is, that return which equalises the discounted costs and benefits of undertaking a programme of education. Typically, this rate is compared to a critical discount rate for funding projects, such as a government test discount rate or bank lending rates. If the internal rate of return to education exceeds the rate of return to alternative investments, that is, if the benefits exceed the costs, then education should be undertaken. This measure is used to estimate, for example, the gains from going beyond compulsory education for the individual and the gains from government subsidised places. Comparing expected rates of return across a range of educational investments should lead to an optimal investment strategy.

A second application might be to look at the costs and benefits of discrete changes in education provision. Bishop (1996a, 150) estimates the costs and benefits from changing the volume of school provision. Lengthening the school year in the US from 180 to 200 days and adding 45 minutes instruction to each school day would raise total expenditure by 15–20%. Set against these costs, the long term educational benefits may be substantial: as well as more learning, students would 'forget' less over the summer vacation. Savings in child care would also offset this extra cost significantly (and the extra time investment may be substituting for leisure, which may have a lower value). On broad-brush cost calculations, Bishop (1996a) estimates that the net present value of benefits would be around five times the costs, plausibly making a longer school year a worthwhile investment. A similar use of this approach is Krueger's (1999, 530–531) discussion of the costs and benefits of reducing class sizes based on experimental evidence. These types of innovative restructuring of the education system merit serious consideration and comparison against other reorganisations; cost–benefit analysis is the way to approach this.

A third variant to estimating the costs and benefits of alternative investment strategies is to look at external efficiency through growth models. With positive externalities, that is, effects of education which spill over to other agents, then education may raise aggregate economic growth beyond its effect on the educated individual; growth accounting models may estimate such effects (Blundell et al., 1999). At a more disaggregated level, education institutions are important sites of economic activity: they attract students into a region and the faculty's and students' expenditures are typically on locally produced goods. The economic impact may be estimated using multiplier analysis, where injections into and leakages outside the region are compared through a coefficient linking the total change in economic activity to the initial investment. If this coefficient is greater than one, positive multiplicative effects are evident (Bleaney et al., 1992).

1.2.3   Economic Methodology

Both of the above lines of enquiry – studying efficiency and cost–benefit analysis – are primarily quantitative and draw on cross-sectional survey data.   Not many experimental trials have been undertaken on school education; Boruch (1997, 5–6) lists fewer than ten (although there are more in medical education). This is despite a general recognition that one of the key problems in estimating the benefits of education is selectivity bias of enrolees: students only enrol on courses they expect to be effective; this makes inference about non-participants difficult. Although there are many advances in selection correction statistics, the fact that people choose the education that is the best for them limits the power of inference about marginal expansions of education provision.   For example, it is not straightforward to infer the effects of expanding higher education to include ten percentage points more of a population cohort, based on parameters estimated with a student cohort of 30%. The marginal 10% of students may have different preferences or abilities and the current education provision may not be replicable with the same costs structure.

In particular, measurement error may be substantial if there is heterogeneity in students' abilities and in their environments. It will not therefore be easy to establish that the education has caused the resulting outcomes. In order to identify causality, it is important to distinguish the separate effects of environments on students' achievements. Manski (1995, 128–129) divides these into endogenous, context and correlated effects. Endogenous effects are those where the individual behaves in a way that depends on the prevalence of behaviour in that group – so if a student's peers are high-achieving, that is likely to affect that individual's own achievement. Context effects are those where achievement depends on the background of a class – so achievement may be influenced by the socio-economic or gender composition of the group. Correlated effects are those where individuals are influenced by the same factors – students may have similar outcomes because they are taught by the same teachers or attend the same institution, for example. These effects need to be distinguished.

Experimental trials, rather than sample surveys, would clarify the benefits of education, abstracting out many covariates. Yet experimental trials (and perhaps natural experiments) are no panacea. Manski (1995, 53–55) describes why experimental regimes may not operate so effectively in education, unlike their role in research on health. Fundamentally, it must be possible to translate an experimental programme into an actual programme. There are several reasons why this translation might not be straightforward. Primarily, people like to choose their education and have more heterogeneous tastes, much more so than for health treatment (complicating the identification of intention-to-treat effects). Hence Krueger (1999, 499) details significant endogenous student movement across classes and schools during the Tennessee STAR trial, as does Rouse (1998b, 561) for the Milwaukee school choice programme. Lectures may be pedagogically better than independent study, for example, but only for those people who prefer lectures, and these people may not be easily identifiable. Inference from marginal probabilities is problematic, what Manski (1997) refers to as the 'mixing problem'. Given only the different graduation rates of two education programmes, it is not straightforward to infer a new graduation rate based on a different mix of these two programmes. Because some students will fare better with one programme rather than the other, the expected graduation rate cannot be bounded without a set of further assumptions about students' ability and the relationship between the two programmes.

Furthermore, many education programmes last several years, during which period many of the original contexts may have altered. Experimental trials are often small-scale and may have unknown effects when applied across a whole cohort. As well as for reasons adverted to above, the effects of education programmes are especially difficult to observe if the benefits of education stem from learning things others have not or if there are general equilibrium or market effects from an educational programme (Heckman et al., 1999). For example, Inouye et al. (1997) describe the inability of some US school districts to replicate a successful reading improvement programme undertaken previously within another school district. In this case, non-replicability may have arisen because of differences in contexts. Finally, if the focus of research should be on what works and what happens in schools, then experiments to reveal underlying causal relationships may be less pertinent; descriptive surveys and accounts of actual practices and behaviours may have greater explanatory power. For all these reasons, therefore, a range of methodological issues (not just those that rigorously adjust for enrolment quality) need to be attended to in discussions of the evidence.

Notwithstanding the difficulties of using sample surveys (and experiments), there is significant literature – both empirical and theoretical –

which has applied economic principles to education.   This empirical research illustrates how, in practical ways, questions about education provision, process and performance can be answered and theories tested.   In this respect, it matters little which country the evidence relates to: economic behaviour and specific solutions will depend on context and environment, but economic principles should not.   Using all available evidence together with economic theory offers causal simplicity.   Economic principles are uniform, stable and compositional and this allows a picture to be constructed around a few accepted concepts.

1.2.4   An Economic Taxonomy for Education

With reference to the possible roles for the economist looking at education and the available evidence base, it is possible to stylise the economics of education. The stylisation offered here grafts the economics of education on to mainstream, core micro- and macro-economics.[2] Here this stylisation work is explained and its merits outlined; the subsequent chapters endeavour to reinforce the case.

There is reasonable uniformity in standard economics textbooks.   After an overview of the principles of the market economy, six key areas are covered.   Topics on 'Household Behaviour and Consumer Choice' include discussion of consumption bundles and demand; budget constraints and choice under uncertainty – these are covered below in Chapters 2 and 3. Topics on 'The Firm and Its Goals' include the optimisation function of the firm; technology and production; and the cost function – these are covered in Chapters 4 and 5. 'Factor Markets' include the demand for factors of production in competitive, monopolistic or monopsonistic markets, trade unions and bargaining – this is Chapter 6.   'The Theory of the Market' includes sections on perfect competition, monopoly and strategic oligopoly (and game theory). 'General Equilibrium' includes the theory of exchange and contracting, as well as property rights. Chapter 7 addresses both these. 'Welfare Economics' includes study of externalities; equity; public goods and government – together, these elements are considered in Chapter 8. Building on these externalities and on the individualised human capital model, the macro-economics of education can also be underpinned with micro-economic foundations – such aggregated effects are considered in Chapter 9. An additional chapter on policy is appended, with a conclusion.

There are a number of benefits to this stylisation, which relates the discipline to a common and, for economists, familiar framework. Primarily, it prevents the economics of education from being a solely empirical discipline (or a collection of topics), where the attempt is to measure elements of the process of education.   Inquiry can then be theory-led, integrating the research within mainstream economics and permitting use of many more economic instruments and tools in a coherent manner.[3] By appealing to shared principles and non-disputed models and frameworks, such as the theory of the market, it may ensure fairness across rival explanations (Runde, 1998).

The fundamental, basic model assumes that individuals have embodied labour skills which can be augmented through education; this human capital model is the subject of the next chapter.

2. Human Capital and Education

2.1 INTRODUCTION

The human capital model may be regarded as the foundation for linking education and the labour market. If education or training is to be undertaken, it has to pay off in some way, and typically this is through increased earnings or more certain employment associated with greater human capital. This nexus is a fundamental part of much economic activity; and a useful context for the issues raised here is embodied in Table 1.2 above, showing the substantial world-wide increases in both the coverage and the amount of education. Broadly, the subject of this chapter is why these increases have happened, and what the economic consequences are for individuals. But also, the discussion here relates the human capital model to investment decisions for individuals and policy choices for governments.

The chapter begins with the basic human capital model, developed in Section 2.2, and the returns to such capital, generated either through education or training. From evidence presented in Section 2.3, the rate of return appears to be significantly positive, suggesting that education is a worthwhile endeavour for many individuals. The evidence on the economic benefits from training are less persuasive, perhaps because of the greater difficulties in measurement. However, these positive returns to education (and training) do not preclude mal-investment, particularly if the effects of education are uncertain or there are government subsidies. Consequently, much debate has focused on the incidence of and effects from over-education as education levels rise. This phenomenon is discussed in Section 2.4. Such debate has been buttressed by arguments that education does not augment human capital but merely serves to signal innately capable workers and thus reduces information costs for firms. These arguments appear in a variety of guises, and are discussed in Section 2.5. Alongside this discussion is an assessment of the relative explanatory power of human capital and screening models; adjudication of the evidence broadly favours the human capital model. Issues and extensions to this model are considered in a final section.

2.2   THE BASIC HUMAN CAPITAL MODEL

2.2.1   Education as Human Capital

Education may serve to enhance human capital. Thinking of education either at school, college or university as an investment, generating a stream of benefits over time, yields powerful insights.[4] The more one learns, the more productive one can be and over a lifetime individuals should accumulate human capital and then run it down (Becker, 1985). This can be illustrated pictorially using McMahon's (1998) framework, with lifetime earnings of two individuals of different education levels.

Figure 2.1 Life-cycle Human Capital Framework

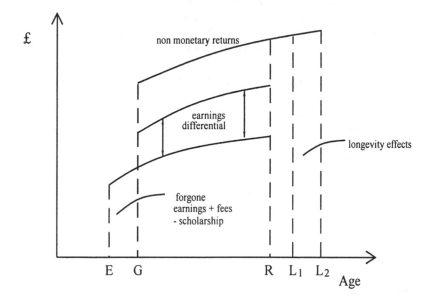

Figure 2.1 illustrates the returns to education over the life-cycle (0 to L_1 or L_2). From enrolment E, an individual incurs direct costs of tuition fees (which may be offset by scholarships, grants or part-time work) and forgone earnings. On graduation G, the individual typically obtains an earnings premium over those with lesser education, extending until retirement R. In addition, individuals obtain non-monetary returns, extending beyond retirement and possibly to include an increase in longevity ($L_E > L_U$) if there are health effects from education. The earnings profile reflects net earnings, rather than capacity earnings, and typically peaks prior to the individual's retirement from the labour force. The life-cycle model of education can be

modelled dynamically, as individuals allocate time across leisure and work (Mincer, 1997); these dynamic models essentially follow the same intuition as the simple presentation in Figure 2.1, but allow for a more robust and formal derivation of the concave earnings function.   The life-cycle framework also illustrates where the costs and benefits of education accrue; and discussion in this and following chapters adds detail and evidence to the life-cycle model.   How individuals' investment decisions can be supported by government policy is investigated in later chapters.

Such human capital models have predictive power, explaining positive effects of years of education (and training) on earnings, employment and labour market participation (hours or weeks per year worked).   They also explain how earnings grow against age but at a decreasing rate, because individuals' human capital is running down (Polachek, 1995).   For two groups, high school leavers and graduates, the spread of incomes should be very high among the young, narrow as the educated eventually graduate from college and then widen again (Mincer, 1997, s47).   Further, the life-cycle model in Figure 2.1 shows why capital constraints may be important: forgone earnings during education may be large, but they are also immediate and certain; these costs are in contrast to the earnings differential, which is less certain and deferred.

Using this model, a rate of return to education can be estimated.   The internal rate of return to investment in an educational qualification is that rate which equalises the net present value of the costs of education to its benefits.   The costs are the earnings forgone during study and the costs incurred for necessary learning inputs.   The benefits are the earnings premia (suitably discounted) for those with the educational qualification over those without it.   Of interest here is the private rate of return, that is, the rate of return to the individual from an investment in education.   (Other rates – social and fiscal – are considered in subsequent chapters.)

Several concepts need to be formally separated at this stage.   Generally, human capital can be accumulated through education, but both of these entities will depend on an individual's ability and prior attainment.   The above life-cycle presentation does not include an adjustment for selection of education by the more able, however.   Rather, Moll (1998) presents a model of the demand for schooling as a way of increasing wages, where ability is incorporated:

$$Y = \mu_i \exp(\beta E + \gamma B + \alpha C + \varepsilon_i)$$

(2.1)

Here Y is the wage, which depends on schooling E, ability B and cognitive attainment C, with ε_i a random influence and μ_i an unmeasured individual wage-generating factor such as motivation or physical capabilities.

Cognitive attainment here represents human capital, with schooling encompassing more general skills and signalling effects in the labour market. Cognitive attainment will depend on schooling and ability:

$$C = \lambda_0 + \lambda_1 E + \lambda_2 B \tag{2.2}$$

Individuals invest in schooling to maximise wealth W (over an infinite horizon with a discount rate of r), with income forgone as the cost of schooling. As higher ability students may gain more satisfaction from schooling, any net cost is reduced by δB. Hence the individual's optimisation function is:

$$\text{maximise } W(E) = \int_0^\infty (Y - \delta B)e^{-r(E + t)}dt \tag{2.3}$$

The first order condition for a maximum is where the rate of change of wealth with respect to education is zero:

$$\partial W(E)/\partial E = e^{-rE}\left\{ (\partial Y/\partial E)r^{-1} - (Y - \delta B)\right\} = 0 \tag{2.4}$$

This first order condition simplifies to:

$$\partial Y/\partial E = r(Y - \delta\beta) \tag{2.5}$$

Individuals will invest in schooling up to the point where the present value of the gains from marginal schooling, across the infinite horizon, is equal to the net income forgone per unit of time spent on schooling. Differentiating the initial earnings equation (2.1) with respect to schooling:

$$\partial Y/\partial E = Y(\beta + \alpha\lambda_1) \tag{2.6}$$

Combining equations (2.5) and (2.6) and solving for Y:

$$Y = \frac{r}{r - \beta - \alpha\lambda_1}\delta B \tag{2.7}$$

Substituting for Y from the initial earnings equation (2.1) and the cognitive attainment equation (2.2) and solving for E, Moll (1998) yields the determinants of the optimal amount of education:

$$E^* = \frac{1}{\beta + \lambda_1 \alpha} \left[\ln(\frac{r}{r - \beta - \alpha\lambda_1}) + \ln(\delta B) - (\gamma + \alpha\lambda_2)B - \alpha\lambda_0 - \ln\mu_i - \varepsilon_i \right] \qquad (2.8)$$

Motivation μ_i is negatively correlated with E^*, the optimal amount of education, because it will be positively correlated with receiving an early, acceptable job offer. Also, the higher the discount rate, the lower the accumulation of education. Most importantly, the optimal amount of schooling depends on ability B, and this needs to be adjusted for (Garen, 1984). This ability–schooling relationship could be negative or positive, depending on the sizes of the consumption coefficient, the direct and indirect effect of ability on earnings and on cognitive attainment (δ, γ, α and λ_2). But it is likely to be positive, with higher ability students obtaining more education. So if B is not available, then the education coefficient in the initial earnings equation (2.1) is likely to be biased, probably upward. Consequently, all income gains cannot be attributed to education.

2.2.2   Training as Human Capital

Discussion above has been on the economics of schooling or formal education. A related area involves study of the training needs of firms and the importance of skills obtained during work (at the policy level, Keep and Mayhew, 1999, survey the travails of vocational education and training in the UK over the past decade in failing to deliver the right sorts and sufficient amounts of skills). Training is a form of education, but one which is here distinguished from formal education by dint of being directly relevant to work tasks: it therefore has benefits for individuals, but also for firms. As well, there is no pedagogic theory underpinning such training; its provision is strictly ergonomic and less likely to have a syllabus. Examples here are on-the-job training, training either by managers or co-workers or by watching others (which is probably about 85% of all training, Barron et al., 1997). However, training clearly involves learning and unavoidably some education will look like training – medical internship degrees, for instance – and some training looks like education – professional development courses may be an example.

Ashton and Green (1996, 45–50) have modelled the demand for training both for individuals and firms. As in the human capital model, individuals are maximising lifetime wealth through training investments. Consequently, individuals' training is likely to vary positively with: lower unit cost; lower initial skill levels; lower current age; greater distances to retirement; and fewer credit constraints. These lead on to predictions of more training for new recruits and public sector workers (with lesser mobility); and for larger companies and those with more strategic planning. National summaries of training activity – whether or not an individual undertook training within the last four weeks – support this framework: public sector workers with low mobility are found to have high training rates, as are those working in sectors with high research and development components (DfEE, 1998a). For the firm, the general demand for training is a function of: the cost to the firm of training; the rate of technical progress (to include the production function, the external supply of skilled labour and the quit function of trained workers); and the rate at which the firm discounts profit.

This relationship between skills and acquired income depends on the type of training being undertaken and how skills are rewarded in the labour market. Training models are actually more general than those for schooling in that there is an explicit relationship between the type of learning and who funds it. One way to fund training, for example, is if trainee workers receive lower earnings during the period of training (thus causing the age–earnings curve of trained workers to be steeper than that for non-trainees). Alternatively, firms may fund training and obtain the benefits. The appropriate funding source is likely to be contingent on the type of training, that is, whether the training is general (usable at any firm), specific (only usable at the current firm) or transferable (defined by its portability across firms).

Specific training may be invested in either by the firm or the worker (Becker, 1985). In contrast, firms are not willing to pay for general training, because if they tried to appropriate any of the returns from such training, then the workers would quit to higher paying jobs elsewhere. Hence only workers are ready to pay for general training. Turning to the evidence, Barron et al. (1997) find wages are not appreciably lower during training, although this may be attributable to more able workers being trained. Greenhalgh and Mavrotas (1995, 1996) model vocational training across the cycle in the UK and find this typically paid for by the employer. Acemoglu and Pischke (1999, F114–116) suggest that training in forms such as mentoring or advice may be hard for workers to observe, so firms may designate standard tasks as 'training'; and, if wages are compressed at higher skill levels, firms may pay for some general training. Finally, Boal and Ransom (1997) explain firm-sponsored general training with reference to monopsonistic labour markets.

Transferable training – often claimed as a superior alternative to higher level academic schooling – is neither general nor specific (Stevens, 1994). Only applicable within a few firms, this transferable training is neither monopsonistic (only useful to one firm) nor perfectly competitive (as with general training). Instead, the extent of this training depends on the value of skills across a range of companies, imperfections in the labour market, and on the degree of worker mobility. Stevens (1999) suggests that the fear of having workers poached may lead firms to over-invest in firm-specific training so as to lock in their workers; but conversely constraints on job mobility may make firms more willing to invest in worker training. Hence training (along with education) may suffer from labour market and capital constraints which reduce the amount undertaken to a sub-optimal level (or distort the type of training). Contracts, apprenticeships and strong internal labour markets may, however, ameliorate this.

2.2.3   Concerns Over the Human Capital Model

There are a number of problems with drawing simple inferences from the human capital model (Polachek, 1995). These do not invalidate the existence of human capital markets, but they do render such markets somewhat more complex than simple goods markets. First, individuals are assumed to be risk-neutral, whereas many are likely to be risk-averse against committing themselves to five-plus years of post-compulsory education (unless perhaps everyone else is doing the same). Such risk aversion may hinder individuals' following an optimal investment path. Second, the human capital rental rate is assumed to be uniform, although borrowing constraints are important (and these are not explicitly incorporated in the life-cycle model in Figure 2.1). Third, individuals are assumed to work fully over their lifetime, whereas income earnings paths for given individuals may not reflect this (particularly if leisure is a normal good and increasing with education). Fourth, rates of time preference are assumed to be uniform; yet individuals are likely to vary in their willingness to defer consumption and in their expectations of their future lifetime earnings. Fifth, individuals' human capital production functions are assumed to be homogeneous. Human capital is assumed to be of standard quality – there is no difference in the type or in the atrophy rate (even as intermittent labour market participants should choose human capital with the lowest rate of atrophy). Relatedly, not much is known about the rate of depreciation of education. One of the few estimates calculates skill depreciation at a rate of 11–17% per year (Groot, 1998), suggesting that effects of education do not endure over the full life-cycle and that Figure 2.1 is very much a simplification of an optimal investment strategy.

Some individuals may have greater innate or developed ability or more powerful incentives and these facets may be hard to measure (Siebert, 1985). The 'alpha factor' is the so-called element of the returns to education which is a function of this prior ability and may absorb between 40–80% of any earnings premium. Selectivity of individuals to become, say, graduates, means that it is hard to identify what proportion of the return to graduation is attributable to the individual and which to the education itself. Although the net effects on any empirical estimates of the returns to human capital may not be large: Moll (1998, 267) contraposes the over-estimate of returns because of ability bias with (under-estimate) errors in measuring schooling and differences in discount rates. Moreover, higher ability individuals may simply invest in more education until their rate of return is equal to that of lower ability students.

As well, investment in human capital need not be monotonically decreasing with age or experience (again as might be derived from Figure 2.1). Polachek's (1975, 457) model depicts the marginal costs and revenues from investing in human capital: plausibly, marginal cost would be increasing in education amounts and the marginal revenue from each investment in education is likely to shift down as the worker gains experience (with diminishing returns to learning in the current period). This gives a downward-sloping gross investment function in terms of experience (with no depreciation of human capital). However, there may be credentialist steps to promotion or random shocks to the benefits of human capital accumulation through skill-biased technology change. If so, then the marginal revenue curves need not monotonically shift down with experience (or in terms of age, if there is intermittent labour market participation). The gross human capital investment function may therefore have a positive slope at some experience levels.

As well as these micro-economic effects, aggregate effects also need to be incorporated into the individual human capital model. Although the Mincerian earnings function is highly general, it does not readily permit distinction between supply and demand influences on education–earnings premia; yet these need to be considered for analysis and for development of policy.

To illustrate this, a rise in the numbers staying in school may be assumed, where this is caused by a relaxation of government quotas on access. As the supply of high-educated workers increases then their average wages will fall; for low-educated workers (whose supply will therefore have fallen), wages should rise (at least in the short run). Figure 2.2A and B shows this, with an increase in the supply of high-educated workers from $S1_E$ to $S2_E$ and a corresponding decrease in low-educated workers from $S1_U$ to $S2_U$. However, the increased supply enrolment of high-educated workers still represents a good investment if the gap between the wages of the high- and low-educated workers ($W2_E - W2_U$) exceeds the discounted cost of study. The relaxation of quotas has reduced the rents obtained with the initial wage premium ($W1_E - W1_U$), although it is likely that high-educated workers' wages adjust downward only slowly, perhaps with unemployment rather than lower wages. Critical to these interconnected labour markets is the assumption about why such a supply change occurred. In the above example it was because of an imposed barrier on access (one possible, but not the only, explanation for high rates of return to education). But if supply has changed because of newly formed expectations about the returns to education or improvements in the technology of learning, then different outcomes will obtain.

Figure 2.2A Wage Effects when Quotas are Relaxed: High-skilled Workers

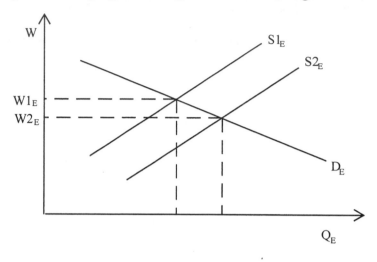

Figure 2.2B Wage Effects when Quotas are Relaxed: Low-skilled Workers

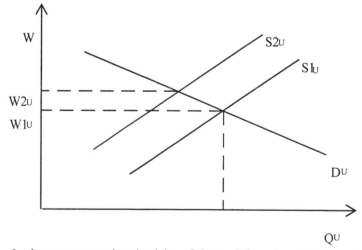

In the aggregate, the elasticity of demand for educated labour by firms will depend on the extent to which educated labour can be substituted for other inputs in production, particularly low-educated labour. The elasticity of substitution σ between the two types of educated and uneducated worker is:

$$\sigma = - (\% \text{ change in } Q_E/Q_U)/(\% \text{ change in } W_E/W_U) \qquad (2.9)$$

Here W_E is the wage paid to educated labour and W_U the wage paid to uneducated labour of quantities Q_E and Q_U respectively. Such elasticities may be calculated by looking at the relative salaries of college versus school leavers against the proportions of college enrolments (Freeman, 1995). If this elasticity is large, then enterprises can readily substitute differently skilled labour. A big increase in the supply of graduates relative to non-graduates will therefore have little effect on their relative wages and so have only a dampened effect on the distribution of earnings. Conventionally, this elasticity will be greater in the long run, as cohort enrolments change.

A more potent long run effect is considered by Acemoglu (1998). The above reasoning suggests that the wage premium to more educated workers should have fallen with the increases in enrolment over the previous two decades. Yet the evidence for the US shows the reverse has in fact occurred – the college wage premium has been increasing since 1979 – and Acemoglu (1998) contends that this is because of workers' skills and firms' production technologies being complementary. Once invented, technologies are non-rivalrous and can be used within most enterprises at low marginal cost. If enrolments increase and so the numbers of skilled workers, then the market for these technologies increases.

The short and long run effects of such technological developments are given in Figure 2.3 (taken from Acemoglu, 1998). With an increase in the relative supply of highly skilled workers (a shift along the horizontal axis), the short run effect is for the college wage premium to fall from $(W_E - W_U)_1$ to $(W_E - W_U)_2$, intersecting with the short run relative demand SRD_1. However, in the long run the relative demand curve shifts out to SRD_2 because of the 'directed technology effect', the expansion in the market for using these technologies. The college wage premium therefore rises to $(W_E - W_U)_3$, with a long run relative demand for skills locus LRD. This long run effect suggests (a) the importance of the flexibility of highly skilled workers to new industrial technologies; and (b) the economy's capital stock will affect the demand for highly educated labour. On the latter, there is some evidence that, as the capital stock ages, there is a fall in the relative demand for highly educated workers (Bartel and Lichtenberg, 1987). As well, this directed technology effect may also highlight the different human capital requirements across countries (and hence explain 'brain drain' migration patterns). More generally, these cyclical (or general equilibrium) effects militate either against estimating the individual rate of return in isolation or against assuming that simple supply-side effects will dominate.

Figure 2.3 Directed Technological Change and Wage Premia

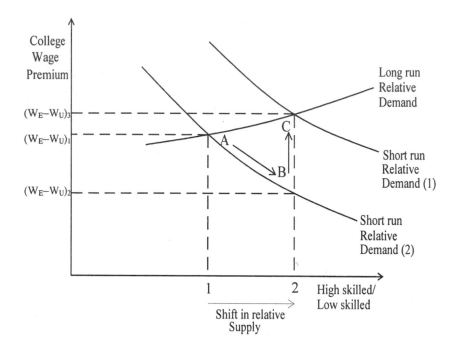

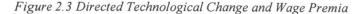

In sum, the above arguments are not criticisms of the human capital model as such; they read more as cautions against ready inference about key economic variables such as the path of investment or the trend of returns. However, the human capital model may be opposed more directly (Blaug, 1976). Human capital returns are typically expressed in terms of earnings, yet added to these should be consideration of the social and external benefits of education: if these are substantial, as well as education having a consumption value, many individuals may be undertaking education without their needing it to fully augment their human capital. At a more fundamental level, there may be concerns over what is the opportunity cost to education investment: for children, forgone earnings may not be appropriate. Lastly, invidious screening and signalling may be important ways in which education (a) helps individuals at the expense of others and (b) improves matching of jobs to workers. Neither of which represents an augmentation to one's augmenting human capital. Before considering this phenomenon, the rate of return is calculated and estimates of the rate of return to education are summarised.

2.3   INVESTMENT APPRAISAL

2.3.1   Calculation of the Rate of Return to Education

Estimates abound on the returns to education and a variety of measurement methods have been used (in part reflecting the difficulties in measuring returns). Cohn and Addison (1998, 254–55) present three methods for calculating the rate of return r, of which the most basic is the short cut method:

$$r = (\ln Y_E - \ln Y_{E-Ed})/Ed \qquad (2.10)$$

Here Y_E and Y_{E-Ed} are mean earnings for an individual completing E and E – Ed years of education.

A more common (and more sophisticated) estimation is via Mincerian earnings premia, where the log of earnings is regressed on years of education E, experience EXP and experience squared (Johnes, 1993a, 29):

$$\ln Y = \alpha + \beta E + \delta EXP + \gamma EXP^2 \qquad (2.11)$$

From estimates of this earnings function, holding the EXP variables constant at their mean values, an increase in education E of one year increases earnings at a rate β:

$$\ln Y_{E+1} - \ln Y_E = \beta \approx (Y_{E+1} - Y_E)/Y_E \qquad (2.12)$$

Assuming that Y_E as forgone earnings represents the costs of undertaking education, then β approximately represents the private rate of return as the ratio of extra earnings $Y_{E+1} - Y_E$ over base earnings Y_E. This calculation should be made across uniform years of education, not education courses: for example, costs differ across groups of graduates – a degree course in medicine is two years longer than for social sciences – and this may drive the earnings premia. Estimates using this method are not exactly equivalent to rates of return; not only because they omit the actual costs of education (such as fees), but also because these are estimates of the returns from an earnings equation, not a schooling equation (and so selection of years of schooling are neglected). Individuals may choose, for example, to undertake education up to a threshold value of β. Also, this method is increasingly less appropriate as income forgone diverges from the actual opportunity costs of education and as the proportions of tuition costs paid by students vary. It is also less accurate with increases in the ratio of education-augmented earnings to base education earnings.

The third measurement method is to use full cost information, estimating lifetime earnings functions and using direct costs. This method directly accounts for the costs and benefits identified in Figure 2.1 and sets these equal:

$$\sum_{t=c+1}^{T} (Y_E - Y_{E-c})(1+r)^{-t} = \sum_{t=0}^{t=c} TC_t (1+r)^{-t} \qquad (2.13)$$

The left-hand side is the discounted earnings premia ($Y_E - Y_{E-c}$) for a person with c years of extra education from graduation in period c + 1 to retirement in period T. These benefits are to be equated to the costs TC_t incurred during the extra years of schooling. The internal rate of return is the value of r which equates the present values of these costs and benefits. This full method is not sensitive to the caveats applied to the Mincerian estimation technique, although it is very demanding in terms of data. When used extrapolatively, it critically depends on the parameters used to predict future earnings differences.

2.3.2   Estimates of the Rate of Return to Education

Based on the above calculation methods, much research has been devoted to estimating the rate of return to education qualifications and to calculating earnings premia. Rates of return or wage differentials might be distinguishable in three ways: the return to an additional year of schooling; the return from possessing a given level of education; and the return to an additional increment of education quality within a given level of education (the 'intensive' margin). Typically, the returns given beyond schooling are for a given education programme such as a degree. For returns across those with below-university schooling, years of education are more commonly used. The evidence base on rates of return yields findings which are reasonably robust.

Using the National Child Development Study, with which ability adjustments are possible, Dearden's (1998) evidence shows the returns to an additional year of full time education in the UK are 5–6% for males and 9–10% for females. Similar evidence for many other countries – using Mincerian, not full, rates of return – is extensively detailed by Cohn and Addison (1998), a sample of which is reproduced in Table 2.1. These estimates show returns which are all significantly positive and broadly close to 10%. Although the table presents evidence from industrialised, market-based economies, these educational effects even appear in non-marketised, productive realms. For example, Moock and Addou (1995) summarise evidence on how agricultural productivity is improved with greater education; Katz (1999) finds positive wage effects in the highly controlled labour market of the former Soviet Union.

Table 2.1   Mincerian Rates of Return to Schooling

Country	Rates of return to schooling (%)
Italy	2.3
Japan	4.4–13.2
Denmark	4.8
Sweden	5.0
Norway	5.4
Netherlands	5.7
Finland	7.3
Germany	7.7
Australia	8.0
United States of America	8.4–17.9
Canada	8.9–11.5
France	10.0
United Kingdom	15.3
Mexico	16.1

Source: Cohn and Addison (1998)

Yet as education is compulsory up to age 16 in most industrialised economies, reflecting a social consensus, most attention has focused on the returns to higher education. (Kane and Rouse, 1995, do chart the positive returns to a two year community college degree in the US, but there are few estimates of the rate of return specifically for tertiary or further education.) More clearly, the returns to higher education arise from large earnings premia, which are immediate and persist over the life-cycle; from lower unemployment; and from higher labour market participation. Overall, a reasonable estimate of the private rate of return for the 'average graduate' in the UK between 1980 and 1990 would be 10–15% (Bosworth et al., 1996; Blundell et al., 1997; Lissenburgh and Bryson, 1995; although for higher rates and across regions, see Bennett et al., 1995; for the US, see Ashenfelter and Rouse, 1999). This figure is higher than the yield on most other economic activities and does not incorporate the stream of social or consumption benefits from education.

For OECD countries, because only the lowest of such rates of return are close to the (long-term) opportunity cost of capital and/or the government test discount rate, expansion of education is presumed to be a good investment (particularly for females, OECD, 1997). Overall, the evidence of a positive relationship between education and earnings appears to be compelling. If the opportunity cost for education is taken as the long run rate of interest in financial markets or a government test discount rate (for example, the US Office of Management and Budget's rate of 7%), then most of the rates presented in Table 2.1 would pass a cost–benefit test (indeed, under-education seems more plausible on this evidence). For most individuals, education appears to be worth doing for at least 12 years, if not 16–18. Following this stylised fact, though, three main issues and one methodological concern merit investigation.

First, the decision for enrolees must of course be more specific: individuals want to find the type of education which maximises their rate of return and the estimates given above are ranges. Within the graduate cohort, rates of return are higher for females, despite lower absolute salaries, reflecting the reduced earnings inequalities at higher levels of education (see Bennett et al., 1995).[5] Higher classes of degree are correlated with higher earnings (perhaps suggestive of returns to effort by undergraduates), as is mode of study. More importantly, there are variations by subject: graduates in medicine, dentistry and law earn the most (for the UK, see Dolton and Makepeace, 1990ab; Belfield et al., 1997), perhaps reflecting the high extent of regulation in these markets. Similar evidence is presented for the US by Grogger and Eide (1995, 294), who find starting salaries for engineering graduates to be highest (absent those for clinical subjects), followed by sciences and social sciences and then by humanities (controlling for occupational effects).

Second, there is the obvious difficulty in inferring future rates of return from current or historical earnings profiles, and then using that evidence to identify whether participation rates should be raised. The future returns will of course depend not only on these supply effects, but also on changes in demand, such as skill-biased technology change. Ashworth's (1997) calculations set the auxiliary assumptions, including a measure for 2% growth, with 4% graduate unemployment, a zero loan and with the alpha factor ability adjustment at 60%. In this scenario, the private rate of return for an average UK graduate after the 1992 expansion of higher education is high, at 17.2%. For the marginal graduate after expansion, however, faced with £12 000 loan and 7% unemployment probability, the rate of return is - 2.6%. It is this marginal graduate whose rate of return is critical for policy-makers, when deciding on (expansion of) enrolment levels. On this evidence, expansion of higher education may therefore be a poor investment for those who are induced to enrol by new participation opportunities.

Looking at the changing pattern over time, the UK average rate for the 1990s appears slightly, but not appreciably, lower than the private rates calculated in 1988 for an earlier cohort (DES, 1988). Using an alpha value of 60%, the average male rate of return compared to that for all A-level completers was then 22% (based on General Household Survey data). This estimate varied between social sciences (26%); engineering (25.5%); sciences (19.5%); and arts (8.5%). A fall in returns may indeed occur because of an increased supply of graduates. But equally important are the lower subsidies to universities which have reduced the returns to education (although these subsidies are themselves endogenous to anticipated changes in the gains to education). Conversely, the increased supply of graduates may be because expectations of future returns have risen.

Other international evidence on trends in returns shows a mixed picture. Palme and Wright (1998) have directly investigated earnings premia for Sweden over the period 1968–91. They find that such premia declined significantly over the period, with those to higher education falling by a factor of three. In contrast, and for a much less constrained labour market, returns to skills and education rose during the 1980s and early 1990s in the US (Cohn and Hughes, 1994; Ashenfelter and Rouse, 1999). For most developing countries, rates of return appear to have declined during the 1980s and early 1990s for primary and tertiary education, but risen for higher education (Psacharopoulos, 1995).

Third, there may be concerns over what is the proper opportunity cost of education. McMahon (1991) has calculated the internal rate of return for the US from 1967 to 1988, finding a modest rising trend between these two decades but also finding that returns to non-housing physical capital appear slightly higher than the returns to human capital (with returns to housing being much lower than both). As noted above, the criterion for expansion of education enrolments is to look at the returns to the marginal enrolment, and less is known about this. Yet, given a reasonably flexible education system, the rate of return to human capital should adjust to that on similarly risky physical capital, or more simply to the prevailing market interest rate (Siebert, 1985, 30). Logically, Blaug (1992, 216–219) interprets the human capital model as predicting that rates of return to education should be equalised across types of education. In their survey using US population data, Ashenfelter and Rouse (1999) do find few differences across ability levels in rates of return. Yet this notion of interest rate parity, which has not been extensively addressed, is likely to be undermined by two factors: constraints on access, which appear to be particularly prevalent in the UK (Cohn and Addison, 1998; Zweifel and Eichenberger, 1992); and government intervention, in that funding calibrations may influence the covariance of costs and benefits, compressing rates of return to education.

In addition to these three cavils about reasoning using empirical rates of return, methodological aspects should be considered. A minor concern is that rates of return derived from different estimation approaches may not be directly comparable. There are numerous ways in which such estimates can vary arising from: assumptions and projections about economic conditions (these will affect assumptions about the growth of salaries into the future); the particular group of educated individuals being measured (which group of graduates being compared to which group of non-graduates); and the method used to generate the earnings distribution and path over time (typically, current and past salaries are used to predict the future earnings of recent graduates). The estimates cited above are based on projections of earnings into the future, which may be subject to extrapolative errors. As well, few rates of return explicitly refer to capital constraints, despite their importance as the main barrier to educational uptake; implicitly, capital constraints may be the reason for higher rates of return to education, compared to other investments.

However, the fundamental methodological problem remains that individuals make endogenous choices about their education, reflecting differences in developed ability or personal tastes. Several approaches have been tried to resolve these two problems. One is to 'instrument' the likelihood of undertaking education, that is, find an alternative variable to represent the probability or possibility of enrolment. One example is to draw on variation in schooling availability: if transport costs are high for some groups, this may reduce the opportunity to undertake education (in a way that is independent of either ability or tastes). Bedi and Gaston (1999) use this instrumental variable approach to estimate the returns to education in Honduras, contingent on schooling being available for the student (proxied by the number of school teachers per capita). Schooling availability is unlikely to be influential in Western economics though (cf. Kane and Rouse, 1995).

An alternative approach is to examine legislative changes which alter the pattern of enrolment and may be considered as 'imposed choices' or natural experiments. Harmon and Walker (1995) use the UK change in the school leaving age introduced in 1973, which compelled many more students into education. Angrist and Krueger (1991) look at the season of birth effect in the US: children born in the first quarter of the year can leave compulsory schooling with fewer months of education than children born in later quarters, yielding an education–earnings spread from differently imposed compulsory schooling. Empirically, neither experiment yields rates of return substantially different from those using ordinary estimation techniques; Harmon and Walker's (1995) instrumented estimates are actually higher (at 15%) than those using ordinary estimation methods. Hence the simpler estimation methods may be more or less valid, at least in the context of the decision rule identified above.

A third approach, which may be more generally applicable, is to estimate returns based on samples of people with similar family background or genetic characteristics but different amounts of education. These samples may be father and sons, siblings or twins. Here the similarity is in terms of the correlated effects of family background or the context effects of genes (Altonji and Dunn, 1996b). Recently, and with newly available data, a number of estimates have been made using these comparison groups (Ashenfelter and Krueger, 1991; Bound and Solon, 1999). Miller et al. (1997) use evidence on Australian twins to estimate the rate of return to schooling. They estimate the returns to one year of schooling for males (females) of 7.1% (5.7%) and calculate that this is comprised of: 2.3% (2.8%) due to the true returns to schooling; 4.2% (0.8%) due to the effects of family background; and 0.7% (2.1%) due to the influence of genetic factors. Hence the pure returns to schooling appear to be better for females than males, but the family background effect is stronger for males than females (which may be attributable to specialised allocation of education-rearing resources within the household). However, such twins-based approaches may only have limited generalisability to a population cohort and may be difficult for governments to re-estimate periodically, when calibrating fees.

Finally, rates of return are often presented in endogenous form. Many rates are presented in terms of outputs such as the returns to a particular occupation; yet for rates of return to be informative either for individuals' decisions or for government policy, they should be couched in terms of inputs (see Groot, 1994). The important issue is not whether lawyers earn more than accountants, but whether three years studying law yields a greater return than studying accountancy, or whether a distance-learning pedagogy produces higher returns than a lecture-based one (as in Altonji's, 1995, modelling of the effects of student course work on earnings). Rates of return should be considered in terms of initial investment, not outcomes.

2.3.3   The Effects of Training

As the human capital model underlies both the acquisition of education and training, effects similar to those for education should be expected for training also (Mincer, 1997). However, for training – either government-sponsored or at the workplace – the evidence is less clear and evaluations of training have not proved definitive (see the inconclusive benefits of training reported by Green et al., 1996; Bassi, 1984).

Specifically, training programmes may raise individuals' earnings or employment or firms' profits. For the firm, the effects of training may be manifest in higher profits, greater productivity or other process variables. These effects are described in Ashton and Green (1996), Blundell et al. (1996) and Booth and Snower (1996). For the individual, the effects of training appear to vary, being greatest for those with the least labour market experience. Makepeace's (1996) study of the UK Youth Training Scheme shows a weakly positive wage effect, although an increased wage may not be the most important change for such trainees: many training programmes are directed at improving general employment prospects (labour market participation) rather than earnings. Outcome measures for such workforce programmes therefore emphasise an increase in the numbers of hours which individuals are working (Greenberg, 1997). More clearly, Cohn and Addison (1998) report US estimates of the rate of return to training which range from at most 13% for apprenticeships down to 0% for training by previous employers; Heckman (1999) offers similarly sceptical evidence on the returns. OECD (1997, 64) tabulates the outcomes of 20 government training programmes across ten economies: some are not found to be significantly effective; none are evaluated by the use of cost-effectiveness analysis.

Although the above evidence is plausible, the methodological problems of self-selection arise here also: typically only the equilibrium of training (that is, the intersection of demand and supply) is observed. Oosterbeek (1998b) finds some evidence of sub-optimal amounts of training (around one-seventh of workers who want training do not get it) and that firms are not bothered whether or not they train the educated or the uneducated, but that the more educated are more willing to learn or to volunteer. As well, measures of training are typically very poor, with low correlation between firm and worker declarations of the incidence of training (Barron et al., 1997). Generally, the distinction between producing something and learning how to produce it may easily be confounded.

Measurement error should also be considered. There are problems of scale, as on-the-job training is often only a small part of regular work routines. Also, cost–benefit analysis of training may be difficult, because the costs of training may be split across workers and firms, so individualised earnings premia from training will be incomplete measures of the benefits.[6] At the macro-level, the general equilibrium effects on wages of large scale government training will depend on: whether or not they are directed toward assisting new workers who have lost their jobs rather than providing training for new entrants; and whether they improve or worsen the welfare of the unemployed. To these problems should be added the uncertainty about how exactly training does enhance earnings. Together, these impediments go some way to explaining why few cost-effectiveness or cost–benefit analyses of training interventions have been undertaken, with aggregate impact analysis (studying economic conditions rather than outcomes) used instead.

2.4   OVER-EDUCATION

2.4.1   Defining Over-education

With rapid recent expansion of participation in higher education in most Western economies, there are concerns that some graduates may find a degree to be a poor investment (although these concerns do appear to be perennial, Lange, 1998). Some new graduates may find work for which they are over-educated or at which they are under-utilised. If the optimal amount of education is hard to estimate and a lot of education is publicly subsidised, high levels of over-education may indeed be expected, even as the average rate of return is positive.

Over-education and skills mismatch may be considered in terms of either the human capital needed by workers or the search efficiency of educated workers. Using graduates as an example, the first case suggests that such graduates might be mismatched because the aggregate stock of human capital is too high, causing some to be employed in occupations for which a degree is not required. In the second case, where over-education depends on search inefficiency, there may be sufficient graduate jobs available but graduates cannot find them (perhaps because the degree certificate is insufficiently informative, credible or discriminating). Either source of external inefficiency is important: as evidenced below, the over-educated have inferior labour market performance (both in terms of earnings and job satisfaction, Groot, 1996; Groot and van der Brink, 1997). Although over-education is ultimately an individual's 'problem', if education is publicly funded then the state is in effect subsidising an unproductive activity.

To establish the scale of over-education three main measures have been utilised. The objective measure involves professional job analysts ascertaining the level and type of education required in particular occupations. Over-education may be defined in terms of the minimum formal qualifications required for entering the job (Dolton and Vignoles, 2000). Another option is the subjective measure of a worker's assessment of his or her own job.[7] Here the extent of over-education is determined by comparing the required level of education with that actually attained and these two measures may cover either the skills to do the job; qualifications to get the job; or the average qualifications of people doing that job. An alternative third measure is the standard deviation measure, perhaps utilised as a short-cut when no direct information exists on the required education levels. This measure, which typically gives the lowest estimates of over-education, involves taking the average of the actual levels of education for those in a particular occupation, with over-education defined as a level of actual education more than one standard deviation above the mean. A simple variant of this compares actual educational attainment with either the mean or modal level of education within each occupation.

The consequences for earnings of over-education are usually estimated using one of two approaches. The first approach builds upon a standard Mincerian earnings function incorporating terms for required education, over-education and under-education. Earnings Y are then a function of both demand (required education) and supply (attained education), with required education as the default term:

$$\ln Y = \gamma_0 + \gamma_1 E^r + \gamma_2 E^s + \gamma_3 E^u + \gamma_4 Z + \varepsilon \qquad (2.14)$$

This specification includes a vector of individual and socio-economic characteristics Z and an error term ε. (These characteristics may need to include ability, as the over-educated and appropriately educated may not be homogeneous, see Battu et al., 2000.) Here, actual educational qualifications E are decomposed into required E^r, surplus E^s and deficit E^u qualifications in relation to those necessary to obtain the job where:

$$E = E^r + E^s - E^u \qquad (2.15)$$
$$E^s = E - E^r \text{ if } E > E^r, \text{ or } 0 \text{ otherwise} \qquad (2.16)$$
$$E^u = E^r - E \text{ if } E^r > E, \text{ or } 0 \text{ otherwise} \qquad (2.17)$$

A second approach – where the incidence but not the extent of workers' over-education is measured – simply incorporates a dummy variable for whether the individual is over-educated OE or not in a standard Mincerian earnings equation:

$$\ln Y = \alpha_0 + \alpha_1 OE + \alpha_2 EXP + \alpha_3 EXP^2 + \varepsilon \qquad (2.18)$$

Using this formulation, the coefficient on the over-education term typically tends to be negative, that is, being over-educated reduces earnings. This coefficient represents the (average) penalty for not fully utilising one's education because these workers are being compared to their appropriately educated peers.

Such categorical variables might be a useful first order proxy for the individualised scale of over-education: if it is not possible to accurately identify who is over-educated, identifying their degrees of over-education may be even more difficult. Also, there may be good reasons for using individuals as the unit of account for measuring over-education: if the intention is to relate over-education to participation rates in higher education or to funding arrangements, government may wish to use persons over-educated rather than proportions. For measuring the efficiency of the labour market or for identifying priority areas for retraining, the educational extent of over-education may be more useful, even as policies are nevertheless targeted at individuals.

Finally, an alternative definition would be to regard over-education as applying to those workers where an investment in education has yielded returns less than the returns to the next best alternative investment. Even as the previous methods identify the particular workers who have the lowest rates of return, this does not necessarily establish that these workers are over-educated. For instance, Mason's (1996) rigid definition of over-education has two components: first, there are no salary differences between graduates and non-graduates; and second, the jobs have not been substantially adapted to suit graduates' skills (for a critical discussion, see Keep and Mayhew, 1996). With non-zero costs of study and non-positive earnings differentials, this rigid definition has the rate of return as definitely negative. This definition therefore identifies only a sub-set of the over-educated. A fuller definition – but one which may be preferable to those described above – is that an over-educated worker is someone for whom the rate of return to education (be it positive or negative) is less than the opportunity cost, such as investments in work experience or leisure time.

2.4.2   Evidence on the Scale of Over-education

Using the above methods, evidence suggests that the average percentage of individuals within the labour force who are found to be over-educated, using any of the estimation techniques, is around 15–40%. Estimates of over-education among the US workforce range up to 40% (Cohn and Khan, 1995; Hersch, 1995). Similar figures are found for Europe at 16% for Holland, 17% for Spain and 31% for Britain (Hartog and Oosterbeek, 1998; Alba-Ramirez, 1993; Sloane et al., 1996). Hence, many workers, including graduates, are employed in jobs for which their current qualifications appear not to be required. However, this education may be required outside the workplace and so need not be an indicator of inefficiency.

Given the greater amount of subsidy, some studies focus on graduates alone. For Britain, evidence from the 1980 National Survey of Graduates and Diplomates, found that 38% of graduates were over-educated in their first job and 30% six years later in 1986 (Dolton and Vignoles, 1997). From the 1995 Labour Force Survey, over-education for graduates is estimated at between 27% and 38% (Alpin et al., 1998); from a 1996 survey of 15 000 UK graduates, around 40% of graduates say they are in jobs which do not require degrees (Battu et al., 1999). This seems a reasonable consensus estimate, although again inference about enrolments should be cautious. For example, there is less information on whether over-education is temporary or not, that is, whether firms or workers adapt to the increased skills in the workforce.

Fundamentally, it might be expected that job tasks converge to education levels: firms will manipulate their production function so as to optimise the additional skills of their graduate employees. In contrast, Keep and Mayhew (1996) argue that the skills of the over-educated may decay, preserving or exacerbating any initial difference in status. Notwithstanding this possibility, such convergence might occur either for particular graduates (as tenure increases, job characteristics for all graduates tend to equivalence) or for economies over time (compared to last year's cohort, this year's cohort of over-educated graduates have jobs closer in characteristics to those of appropriately educated graduates). This general convergence principle has been explored by looking at earnings, job satisfaction, managerial duties and promotion prospects across time and across cohorts of UK graduates by Battu et al. (2000). Their evidence suggests that the proportions and characteristics of over-educated graduates appears stable over the cohort lifetime: over-education does not appear to be a temporary phenomenon when looked at in time-series at the economy level.

Other evidence suggests the economy has absorbed greater numbers of graduates without substantial economic distortions. So although there has been a large expansion in the numbers of graduates in the UK over the last ten years, there is no clear evidence that over-education has increased. The clearest example is for UK graduates where, despite a 75% increase in the proportion of graduates in the workforce over the period and a much greater change in flows, the percentages of graduates in jobs which do not require degrees appear to have risen only trivially. On these data, an argument that over-education has grown over time (as per evidence from Lindley, 1991, or Alpin et al., 1998) cannot be sustained.[8] Thus, as the overall proportion of over-educated graduates is stable, graduates may supplant education for experience, may face discrimination or may lower career expectations. Hence the concept 'proportion mismatched' may lose relevance as graduates age, plausibly suggestive: of the waning influence of higher education on productiveness and employability; and of the notion of degree to work matching as pertinent only to a particular time during one's career.

As with rate of return estimates, there is a need to relate outcomes to inputs. Over-education is correlated with a number of characteristics of education provision. For higher education, subject-related differences stand out: graduates from engineering, mathematics, sciences, law and medicine are more likely to be in work which requires a degree. Relating the quality of education to the amount of over-education, universities of higher quality are less likely to generate over-educated graduates. Some modes of study – mature and/or part-time study – appear to be less conducive to yielding 'matched' work. These matching effects are typically immediate, persistent and dominate degree class effects. At graduate level, prior characteristics seem not to matter significantly: few family background effects appear to be strong in driving over-education.

2.4.3   Evidence on the Effects of Over-education

Over-education affects both the individual and the firm. Those who have been or are in matched work report significantly higher levels of job satisfaction than the remainder of graduates – strengthening the argument that degree requirement is a proxy for unobservable job quality differences. Mismatch mainly affects earnings, with the returns to required education typically exceeding the returns to attained education. However, the returns to over-education are generally found to be positive, though less than the returns available to those whose higher education matches that required. So in a job that requires 12 years of education, a worker with 16 years of education earns more than a worker with the required 12 years of education but less than those workers matched to jobs requiring 16 years of education. It is possible that the lower job satisfaction of over-educated workers could reduce their earnings absolutely below those of appropriately educated workers in the same job, but this is not typically found (see Cohn, 1992).

Empirically, the returns to having the appropriate amount of education are a couple of percentage points higher than those considered in Section 2.3.2 above, with the returns to each year of over-education some percentage points lower. So Cohn et al. (1999) report returns for the US and Hong Kong: earnings premia for each year of over-education are around 5–10%. For UK graduates, Battu et al. (1999) find the earnings premium for those who are matched is 8–20%, with the premium being a couple of percentage points higher for female than male graduates (which may be explained by participation decisions). Although Battu et al. (1999) find a persistent graduate earnings differential over time, Dolton and Vignoles (1997) find the effect of over-education on earnings falls over the initial six years after graduation.

As well as individuals, over-education is likely to affect labour productivity and so firms' profits, with indirect effects through worker turnover, mobility and training (Sloane et al., 1996; Groot, 1993; McGoldrick and Robst, 1996). Overall, firms should be paying their workers (whatever their degree of over-education) their marginal product, and so the effect on productivity should be neutral. But if a worker is allocated to tasks for which he or she is over-educated, this is likely to lower job satisfaction. Over-educated workers are less likely to work at their maximum capability; under-utilising their skills causes productivity and so output to fall.

More directly, Tsang (1987) has shown how the allocation of over-educated workers can be analysed within a cost–benefit framework, using data from subsidiaries of the Bell company. Because over-education has a negative effect on job satisfaction, this reduces firm output. The firm therefore has two options: decrease over-education either by changing the allocation of workers to tasks or by reducing the educational standards of the company. If the firm opts to reallocate workers so as to reduce the average levels of over-education by one year of schooling, job satisfaction will increase. Tsang estimates this will add around 8% to output, assuming that there are no costs to such a reallocation. Alternatively, if the firm decides to reduce education levels by one year, labour quality will fall (with some small effects if wages remain equal to marginal product) and job satisfaction will rise (directly, because more educated workers report lower job satisfaction, and indirectly, because more educated workers are more likely to be over-educated). This second strategy will generate a net benefit to the company but probably of a magnitude less than the 8% output gain of the first strategy. The optimal strategy will therefore depend on the costs of implementing the first strategy.

This discussion of over-education has raised a number of issues. First, both the firm and individual have a role to play in bargaining to ensure that jobs and workers are codetermined, and so looking only at the supplied education is incomplete. Second, there remain questions about how temporary over-education is; whether or not markets can reduce it quickly enough; or whether these measures are simply identifying the lowest-yielding or bottom quartile of the earnings–education relationship. Third, the extent to which over-educated and under-educated individuals may be substituting different levels of experience is unknown. Finally, if the rate of return to education is still significantly positive and greater than the alternative uses of human resources, perhaps in the aggregate there is under-education instead with too few people studying (for a critical discussion, see Johnes, 1993b).

2.5   INFORMATION COSTS AND EDUCATION

2.5.1   Screening, Signalling and Sorting

Although the human capital model is well established, education may have another use in revealing individuals' innate productiveness or character. The contention here is that education only signals better workers to hire or screens employees for firms to allocate to tasks (Arrow, 1973). Students therefore attend school for longer to show that they would be the best workers rather than to accumulate human capital. This screening and signalling argument suggests the direct benefits of education are low:

individuals only obtain education because they think employers will hire those with the 'right' qualifications. Spence's (1973) model, adapted by Varian (1999), shows how this signalling effect might operate. Workers are dichotomised into high and low ability, with respective marginal products of MP_H and MP_L. If both workers and firms are fully informed about labour quality, then firms should pay wages such that:

$$W_H = MP_H > W_L = MP_L \qquad (2.19)$$

If firms are not informed about worker ability they will offer all workers an average wage equal to the expected productivity of any given worker. This wage will be:

$$W_A = p.MP_H + (1 - p).MP_L \qquad (2.20)$$

Here p is the proportion of highly able workers in the economy. Importantly, W_A is less than W_H, so able workers may be unwilling to work at the average wage. A market in 'lemon' workers may arise as W_A exceeds W_L, collapsing the market as wage offers and labour supply iteratively diminish. More likely, the able workers will be prepared to pay for a signal to indicate to firms that they are worth W_H. This signal may take the form of an education certificate where the costs per unit of education to each group are C_H and C_L. If the costs of education to the more able are the same as those to the less able, then firms are still likely to offer W_A because low ability workers will be able to signal as readily as high ability workers. More plausibly, the costs to the more able should be lower than those for the less able, perhaps thinking of the costs as the duration needed to complete the course. Consequently, high ability workers would be able to signal their greater ability to firms and so receive W_H. High ability workers will undertake such education under two conditions:

$$W_H - W_L > C_H \qquad (2.21)$$

$$C_L > W_H - W_L \qquad (2.22)$$

The first condition (2.21) establishes that the benefits of education must be greater than the costs – such benefits may be particularly strong if there are barriers to entry in credentialist labour markets which the certificate can override. The second condition (2.22) establishes that the costs of education to the less able are greater than wage differential. These conditions also imply C_L is greater than C_H.

This simple model assumes that education has no effect on productivity, with significant costs to firing unable workers (where W_A is greater than

MP_L). The significance of the model depends on the relative costs of the education to each group and on the extent to which the individual has any private information which can be hidden from employers. Although workers may try to hide their private information, firms may use low wages during a probationary work period to uncover the true marginal product. The model also allows distinctions between screening types. Weak screening occurs when employers pay a higher starting salary to the more educated relative to the less educated, but eventually revise upward (downward) the salaries of able (less able) workers from W_A to W_H (W_L). Strong screening occurs when employers continue to pay higher salaries to the more educated, even after observing them on the job.

Following the model through, if individuals are willing to incur the costs of education to signal their greater productiveness, then a separating equilibrium occurs. This separating equilibrium may be considered inefficient from a social point of view: each able worker finds it in his/her best interests to pay for acquiring the signal because of the private increases in wage, even though it does not improve his/her productivity. In reducing information costs, screening only does so across education levels and the gains from education are only for years which discriminate between students. Notwithstanding, education as a signal does reduce information costs (preventing lemon markets) and may indeed be the most cost-effective way of doing this.

The ideas behind screening and signalling are simple and several versions have developed. Weiss (1995, 134) gives a comprehensive definition of screening by firms and signalling by workers, in that both phenomena involve sorting individuals: 'sorting models extend human capital theory models by allowing for some productivity differences that firms do not observe to be correlated with the costs or benefits of schooling'. This definition allows both human capital and sorting elements to be identified mutually rather than exclusively.

Because education is linked with a variety of other traits, it proves difficult to disentangle education from innate characteristics. Thus the extra wages for someone with one more year of education measures the combined effect of (a) one additional year of learning and (b) the effect of being identified as the type of person who has one additional year of learning. This dual effect should influence how wage equations are interpreted. For the coefficients on wage equations for years of schooling (given as β in equation (2.11)) to be only productivity-enhancing, then wages must be assumed to be proportionate to productivity; this is a plausible assumption. But also, attributes that are not observed by firms and that also affect productivity must be assumed to be uncorrelated with schooling; this is much less plausible. Reasonably, Weiss (1995) argues that some individuals have (unobserved) traits which make schooling less costly to them, such as perseverance or conscientiousness, but which also enhance their productivity. Education is beneficial for private individuals through both channels; these individuals are gaining from augmented human capital and from sorting effects. The relative weight of these two aspects is open to determination, however. Finally, the sorting model does not necessarily imply that education is yielding no social returns: society gains from a better match of workers to jobs, even if the human capital effect is muted.

2.5.2   Evidence for Sorting versus Human Capital Models

It is plausible that education acts as a low cost way of generating tatonnement in the labour market through screening and signalling. A strong sorting effect may also explain why the rate of return to education appears to exceed returns to the cognitive skills taught in school. Despite this, there is little exclusive evidence to support this model. Instead, a number of varied empirical tests of screening and signalling versus human capital have been undertaken. These point compellingly to the strength of the human capital model.

Groot and Oosterbeek (1994) present a series of careful tests, drawing on the particularities of the Dutch education system. They disaggregate actual years of education into five possible components: set against years which are effective in progression through schooling, some individuals will either skip years, take extra years which do not directly lead to progression, repeat the same academic year and/or drop out before reaching their qualifications. Each component has a different effect across the human capital model, adjusted for ability, or across the screening model, unadjusted for ability.

First, the human capital model predicts that skipped years will have a non-positive effect on earnings; the screening model predicts that skipped years – as a sign of greater ability – should have a positive effect on earnings. The evidence shows a negative effect of skipped years on earnings, supportive of the human capital model. Second, inefficient years should have a non-negative effect according to the human capital model, but no effect under the screening model, because these years convey no information about ability to the employer. The evidence shows no effect, perhaps supportive of the screening model. Third, repeated years should have a non-negative, possibly positive effect according to the human capital model; the screening model predicts that repeated years, as an obvious signal of low ability, should have a negative effect on earnings. Groot and Oosterbeek's (1994) data show no effect of repeated years on earnings, again supportive of the human capital model. Finally, years in education but without a qualification (drop-out years) should boost earnings in the human capital model, but not so in the screening model. This last measure pertains to 'sheepskin' effects on earnings.

Sheepskin effects on earnings refer to the jump in the rate of return from the graduating year of high school relative to the returns associated with the earlier years. This jump suggests that individuals are being rewarded for the signal of a graduation certificate, in addition to the human capital of the extra year of education. Groot and Oosterbeek's (1994) findings here are in line with those of Heywood (1994) and support the human capital model: years of education which do not yield a qualification do have a positive effect on earnings.

But sheepskin effects also support the screening and signalling models; Jaeger and Page (1996) find significant sheepskin effects for the US, with the implication that the returns to non-credential years are lower. Also for the US, Heywood (1994) finds sheepskin effects are evident after 8, 12 and 16 years of education: obtaining these particular award-bearing years of schooling adds significantly to earnings, surplus to the effect on earnings for any other years of education (the college diploma year adds 9.3% to earnings for private sector workers, for example). However, looking at a more regulated sector of the economy, the unionised public sector, sheepskin effects are not evident; the magnitude of sheepskin rewards to education appears to rely on the hiring practices and employment bargains made by firms in the private sector. Revisiting this analysis, Belman and Heywood (1997) find sheepskin effects fall to insignificance as workers age and become more experienced (even though signalling effects should not attenuate over time if employers only use signals which are of any use to them). A direct test by Tyler et al. (2000) exploits differential pass rates for the US General Educational Development (GED) equivalency credential. Workers with a GED in states where the pass mark is low can be thought of as equivalent to workers without a GED in states where the pass mark is high: the former possess a labour market signal, the latter do not. Tyler et al. (2000) find that workers with a GED obtain an earnings premium of between 10% and 19% over those of the same ability but without a GED; strong evidence of a signalling effect. Overall, then, the weak version of signalling and screening at least appears to be upheld.

Another test of the screening model is offered by Kroch and Sjoblom (1994). They describe how education quantity has risen over time cohorts (that is, the generation born in the 1960s obtained more education than that born in the 1940s), not necessarily concomitant with ability within cohorts. If screening and signalling arguments are important, then an individual's educational rank in his/her cohort should be more informative of his/her earnings than his/her years of education compared to other cohorts. Using a set of earnings equations with absolute and relative measures of education, they find little evidence that the educational rank of someone is related to the earnings rank. Absolute education is more important than one's position in the educational distribution in driving earnings.

In addition, Johnes (1998) evaluates the screening and signalling model by examining the effect on wages of three critical variables. First, the interaction term between self-employment and schooling is used (holding education constant), on the logic that education can only influence a self-employed person's earnings through its effect on human capital. Second, the coefficient on an interaction term between education and age should decline as the firm acquires information about the worker. Third, higher average levels of schooling of workers in the individual's labour market should have a negative effect on own earnings, because these levels reduce the individual's educational rank order. For each of these three tests, there is no strong support for sorting models.

Variously, other findings also appear to be less compatible with the screening and signalling model. For example, self-employed workers with more education earn more; although Grubb (1993) compares wages of screened against unscreened positions and finds support for screening for vocational qualifications (but against for academic ones). In turn, the self-employed may invest in more education because they use credentials as a sign of quality for their consumers. Tucker (1987) has in turn rejected that hypothesis, arguing that the earnings of the highly skilled self-employed differenced against employees' earnings are not any greater in these credentialist service sector occupations (but for support, see Brown and Sessions, 1998).

There is also a strong correlation between the subject of study in higher education and the subsequent occupation, although this may reflect tastes (Arabsheibani and Rees, 1998); and vocational subjects generate higher returns than non-vocational. Looking at salaries over the longer term, it is hard to maintain the screening hypothesis: as firms learn more about workers they should adjust down the benefits to education, leading to age–earnings profiles which converge. Looking at evidence in the workplace, training appears to have an effect on earnings, despite being hard for managers to observe.

Finally, one argument against sorting is that the duration and intensity of education seems to be a very expensive way for firms to learn about workers and for workers to signal their abilities to firms (particularly if the signal is based on the duration of schooling, rather than achievement during schooling). Of course, this begs the question of 'expensive compared to what?', in that testing to identify a trait such as perseverance may be very expensive if undertaken by individual firms (and by its nature takes years to identify). One option would be for firms to offer more probationary terms of employment, but then they would be 'volunteering' to pay the costs of screening, instead of the taxpayer funding education.

To complement this empirical evidence, human capital models have high explanatory power over frequency of job turnover, in that turnover declines with tenure as workers acquire firm-specific human capital and the costs of changing jobs rise. Although none of these arguments is fully persuasive, they tend to support the human capital model and, in the aggregate, appear to relegate sorting effects to Weiss's affective traits. Yet despite the evidence in favour of human capital models, analysis here is absent of how employers interpret educational qualities and what role information about workers plays in their job matching functions. Second and more importantly, the macroeconomic evidence should be used to test for the effects of education as human capital. Aggregate or general equilibrium effects are the critical test of whether or not education raises or simply redistributes economic returns. It is not possible for individual-level returns to more education to be used to identify the adverse effects on others' returns. This latter issue is considered in Chapter 9.

2.6   ISSUES AND CONCLUSIONS

This chapter has sketched out the human capital model, motivating investment in education over the life-cycle. This basic model has strong predictive power for the path of earnings, as well as allowing for individuals to augment human capital in response to exogenous productivity shocks or voluntary changes in labour market participation. However, the general model can only be extended subject to a number of conditions. Human capital may be an income-generating investment, but less is known about human capital yields across individuals or across pedagogies; the depreciation of human capital may also be significant. In addition, individual decisions to enrol in education programmes will be influenced by the relative scarcity of different types of labour; firms may be able to substitute between high and low skilled workers, reducing the returns to education. More generally, much of the analysis of the human capital model requires that the wage is equal to the marginal product, an assumption which requires formal substantiation.

Notwithstanding these (numerous) cavils, a plethora of empirical work – using a range of methods (although not typically using full, *ex post* investment streams) – has estimated rates of return across types of education, years of education and sectors. These rates have broadly been found to be above the opportunity cost of investment in other assets. Although these returns are possibly declining for new and future cohorts, the demand for education (in terms of participation rates) has risen sharply since 1990. At current rates of enrolment and reduced levels of public subsidy the marginal graduate – or the individual contemplating extra education at the margin – may even face a private rate of return which is below the next best opportunity. Conversely, the impulse of skill-biased technology change may serve to validate any increases in education levels.

To this caution should be added the issue of endogeneity: individuals choose their education, so inference from those who choose to accumulate human capital to those who did not is likely to be problematic. Various adjustments have been made in compensation, comparing individuals who are alike across key characteristics and these adjusted rates of return suggest that biases in the more straightforward measures are not significant. From a recent tranche of estimates, Ashenfelter et al. (1999) conclude that factors leading to under-estimation of individuals' Mincerian returns are as common as factors leading to over-estimation and neither endogeneity nor measurement errors are gross. As well, it is important to consider the likelihood of situations in which the costs exceed the benefits, however: over-education may occur, as individuals invest in too much or overly academic education; and education may serve to signal innate ability rather than augment skills.

On over-education, evidence differs across methods of calculation, although each methods shows non-trivial mismatch of education to work tasks. Moreover, these methods yield similar conclusions about the adverse effects of over-education on earnings and job satisfaction. Critical to an overall assessment of its impact, however, is how work tasks change in response to supplies of skills: firms may upgrade job tasks to fit with the greater availability of skills.

On screening and signalling, a substantial amount of evidence and testing has refuted arguments based on this alone. Education credentials may be useful in signalling how conscientious or diligent individuals are, for example, but the education itself is also useful in augmenting productivity. Although there is some signalling purpose to education, it is not typically regarded as the only or primary purpose.

In general, this overarching framework of the human capital model includes supply and demand elements and can be applied across topics in the economics of education. Hence, the form in which human capital can be accumulated will influence education provision in schools and universities, but it will also drive the demand for education. This demand for education is considered directly in the next chapter.

3.   The Theory of Enrolment Choice

3.1   INTRODUCTION

This chapter considers education as part of the micro-economic theory of consumer choice to enrol. Education may be thought of as serving both as a consumption good and an investment good: as part of an individual's utility, it may yield both direct benefits and a stream of future returns. The previous chapter indicated the benefits of human capital as an investment; here education as a commodity is further explored, elaborating how individuals choose to enrol on education programmes. If individuals cannot make reasonable or rational choices regarding their education, there may be a significant role for government and a lesser role for markets. But this presumption needs to be tested.

Set against the human capital benefits, it is commonly argued that education is not a good with a simple tractable demand function where information constraints are insubstantial: education may be risky and uncertain in both quality and future use, preventing individuals from making optimal investment/consumption decisions. These notions are taken up in Section 3.2. Notwithstanding, economists would argue that the demand for any good is affected by its price, by income levels and by the prices of other goods. As is argued in Section 3.3, the evidence shows these relationships to hold for education. Although this does not imply that education is a consumption good rather than an investment, it does imply that education demand can be rationalised. It may also permit more market trades in education, although there are wealth effects which may be considered inequitable. Finally in this chapter, ideas about choice are developed along three routes in Section 3.4. The allocation of education and who accesses education is important, because it allows for (one form of) adjudication on input-choice efficiency. Borrowing constraints are then discussed using Kodde and Ritzen's (1985) model; these are important because the life-cycle model of education emphasises the need for efficient capital markets. Lastly, education non-completion is modelled as a rational cost–benefit decision, with some evidence on what determines exits from education.

3.2   UNCERTAINTY AND RISK

3.2.1   Uncertain Individual Preferences

It is commonly believed that education is a 'difficult' good to express a demand for (Bell, 1999, 219). Winston (1999, 15) articulates this nihilistic position: 'People investing in human capital through a purchase of higher education don't know what they're buying – and won't and can't know what they have bought until it is far too late to do anything about it. Education is typically a one-shot investment expenditure, a unique rather than a repetitive purchase.' There are a number of possible uncertainties and risks around the decision to invest in education and these may either lead to sub-optimal demand for education or have implications for market structures. For the individual, three such uncertainties appear pertinent, although it is important not to overemphasise these: education need be neither a risky asset nor an illiquid one.

First, individuals may have imperfect information about their own abilities to absorb, understand and apply the education they receive. As Johnes (1993a, 13) puts it: 'To establish whether or not you have the ability to become a nuclear scientist, you must undergo the training involved. That involves an investment of time and money which is subject to risk. There is no way of perfectly predicting the outcome.' This applies to any good or investment yielding a stream of benefits over time, however, and as with other goods, agency markets may develop where education and careers advisers sell information to applicants. Also, for many types of education, the ability function is filtered by enrolment or application tests: some schools are selective and higher education institutions more so. Because of the particular role of students in the production of education, moreover, institutions have some incentive to take only students for whom the education will pay off (whereas vendors of most goods are indifferent to the consumer's actual need for the product). Finally, many students would, it might be said, be reasonably certain of their ability to be a nuclear scientist (or graduate from a music academy) and, after 12 years of compulsory schooling, may accurately choose their higher education at least.

A more general concern is that economic exchanges may not be suitable ways of determining amounts of education. Such exchanges work best if agents are assumed to be rational, that is, they have stable, well-behaved preferences and face low cost, non-volatile information flows (Blaug, 1992). This may not be the case for education: by definition, those choosing education are in some way ignorant of what precisely they are about to learn. Herrnstein (1997) has set out the basic tenets of economic theory of rationality where: an individual's choice set is assumed to be exogenous of the individual's preferences; all psychological effects are categorised into either tastes/preferences or information/knowledge; and the individual will always choose the optimal choice. There are several problems with these tenets.

If choices are distributed over a sequence (either in time or process) then a utility function may be difficult to specify. The optimal choice sequence could be determined by a number of steps, rather than through a constrained maximisation model. With no *a priori* identification of where individuals' decisions about education are separable, then it may not be possible to infer the optimal path of human capital accumulation (Machina, 1989). First, it may be hard to guess the incremental values of the next immediate course of study because utility is gained from immediate consumption and from repercussive effects on subsequent utilities. So, for example, two science courses might habituate one against arts courses or make it hard to signal for non-science jobs. Second, comparing the overall utility levels associated with full sequences is hard, for example, it may not be possible to compare the benefits of a science degree (perhaps leaving one constrained to be a scientist) with a social science degree (where one can apply for generalist occupations). Much higher education, as another example, is path-dependent and choices at school in large part drive university enrolments. Finally, informational cascades may arise, where individuals make decisions based on what others have done and so study the same subjects as everyone else. Sub-optimal subject choice may be the result. Such cascades form more quickly when there are information costs to investigating the signals emitted by providers (Bikhchandani et al., 1998); these costs may be high in the case of education provision (one needs to spend time at a school to determine its quality). Yet this last cavil should make the choice of schooling easier, because provision will be standardised. Moreover, it is not obvious whether the individual's or the cascade's information is better.

The second main difficulty in expressing demand for education is that it is a big or indivisible investment, possibly inducing capital constraints on the final amount of education.[9] Individuals' risk aversion may be increasing in the size of any proposed investment, influencing the form of the utility function and preventing optimal investment in full-time education. So education may be under-consumed because agents are risk averse about long term investments. However, if education increases the opportunity set, then it may lower uncertainty in the future: according to Behrman and Stacey (1997, 31), 'uncertainty may ... increase the expected returns because of the value of education in processing new information and facilitating adjustment to change'. Plus, insurance markets may assist in addressing the problems of uncertainty and risk. Nevertheless, there may be problems of moral hazard and adverse selection, as well as concerns over whether insurance needs are too lumpy or over the impossibly of insuring against innate birth differences. In this context, adverse selection has students remaining in education for too long; moral hazard may mean students choose easy courses rather than those with the highest return. As a counter-argument, education is available in various durations and the opportunity cost of children's time may be very low, suggesting against the adversities of the bigness and indivisibility of doses of education.

Figure 3.1 Wealth Effects and the Demand for Education

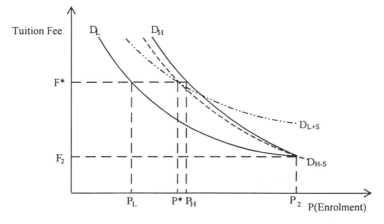

More plausibly, this risk aversion will influence the types of students who enrol, rather than the number. Figure 3.1 shows the demand curves for education of two groups – high-income D_H and low-income D_L but with equal ability distributions – which are downward sloping in the tuition fee. Because of differences in risk aversion, the low-income students' demand curve has a shallower slope: reductions in tuition fees have a relatively large effect on enrolment. At P_2 and tuition fee F_2, the probabilities of enrolment are equal. But this tuition fee does not cover costs, which are constrained at F^* (perhaps through political mandate to prevent funding of $2P_2F_2$). At this fee, the probability of enrolment by high-income students is higher than that by low-income students ($P_H > P_L$). One solution is to subsidise low-income students by S, shifting the demand curve out to D_{L+S} with D_H shifting in to reflect the burden of the subsidy to D_{H-S}. As all students have equal ability, this parity of access should be both more efficient and more equitable. The difficulty here is that setting S requires information on the slopes of the demand curves, the responsiveness to government subventions and knowledge of the distortionary effects of any taxation.

Continuing with reasons why student choices about education may be complicated, a third case is where future demand conditions cannot be known – many people suffer structural unemployment from having skills which are not in demand (although this might be because they have insufficient rather than inappropriate human capital). Because education may not be 'resold', its value in the market may decline rapidly if it is under-utilised (Groot, 1998). This zero resale value also means that there is no collateral for any loan and unsecured loans have high costs to ensuring repayments. However, supply conditions are reasonably well set; most governments publish their national quotas for higher education enrolments. More importantly, education may make individuals flexible rather than specifically skilled, reducing uncertainty and alleviating concerns about low resale value; and the zero-collateral argument is mainly pertinent to individuals with no outside assets. A more plausible, related argument would be that the demand for education may be sub-optimal because it is separated from its application in the labour market (Acemoglu, 1996). Individuals typically invest in irreversible, relationship-specific capital, such as a five-year degree in architecture, before complete employment contracts with firms are written. Faced with such capital, firms will have a stronger bargaining position and 'hold-up' the educated worker, whose education is depreciating. Recognising this, individuals will under-invest in education. In response, governments may calibrate enrolments so as to guarantee jobs for some qualifications, for example, jobs in medicine.

Generally, if property rights are not established and externalities exist (that is, if education has social benefits) then the demand by private individuals may be less than the social optimum. For many activities, there may be network effects, benefits arising from a group of people behaving in the same way. So the benefits of learning a new language will only be evident if there are lots of people who understand that language. This may compress educational choice into a narrower frame of only learning what other people learn or reduce education levels if there are difficulties to co-ordinating a common curriculum. Marginal social benefit is therefore likely to exceed marginal private benefit and marketing educational choices will produce sub-optimal outcomes. (These economies of standardisation and network effects need not imply public provision, however.)

As well as difficulties expressing a demand for education, there are also problems with its provision. From the supply side, there may be uncertainty about the quality of schooling. Education may only be assessed after purchase and is therefore an experience good, whereas most goods are more like inspection goods and can be assessed prior to purchase. But as with the first imperfection, agencies and intermediaries may sell information and education enterprises do provide prospectuses and open days (and their lower expenditure on advertising than firms in other service industries may reflect compulsory enrolment or absence of competition rather than the inability to convey quality). Moreover, this experience–inspection classification is not categorical: few goods' utility can be assessed solely on inspection. Perhaps if pupils cannot readily observe the quality of the education, a market in 'lemon' schools may develop: no good quality education is provided because it is competed out of the market by low quality, cheaper education.   This is plausible to the extent either that employers *ex post* cannot identify lemon schools and signal this to future cohorts or that 'plum' schools cannot substantiate their higher quality. Perhaps more of a problem arises from the previous students' testimony: an enrolling student may misinterpret graduating students' dissatisfaction as reflecting those students' low ability rather than the standards of provision.

3.2.2   Choosing Education Under Uncertainty

It is important to investigate the substantive significance of these barriers to investment in education directly.   On borrowing constraints, there is some evidence that the enrolment rate for education is sensitive to the availability of capital.   De Gregorio (1996) regresses secondary and tertiary enrolments on the ratio of total credit from the banking system to the non-financial private sector over GDP.   Across 20 OECD and 63 developing countries, there is some support for the contention that the higher the borrowing constraints, the lower the rate of human capital accumulation.

More evidence is available on the consequences of uncertainty and intractability on the demand for education.   Groot and Oosterbeek (1992) introduce uncertainty into the duration demand for schooling: post-education earnings are not known with certainty, yet job opportunities rise with schooling because one can accept a job below one's education level but not above it.   Using US and Netherlands data, they find uncertainty to depress the rate of return to education and compress differences across educational types.   Also for the US, increases in risk cause individuals to substitute away from human capital; for occupations where educational requirements are uncertain, workers may obtain compensating earnings premia (Robst and Cuson Graham, 1999).   Testing for uncertainty by looking at the highest and lowest possible earnings for a given occupation, broader spreads appear to raise the demand for education (Kodde, 1986, 465).   Finally, salaried workers are more encouraged to invest in time-shortening human capital than are hourly paid, less secure workers (Haber and Goldfarb, 1995).   In mitigation, the variance of earnings is lower for those with more education, reducing uncertainty (Dutta et al., 1999).

Although it should be conceded that individuals do not have perfect information either about their preferences or economic conditions, they have access to a lot of information and *a priori* it need not be assumed that this information set is prohibitively less than for other reasonably complex goods (for example, a computer or a car, goods equivalent in nominal value to a year of secondary education or a degree course, respectively).   As well, rather than perfect information, parents and pupils may merely have more information than the government; to reduce uncertainty significantly, therefore, governments may need to underwrite education costs substantially. And if government does have more information than parents, it might simply share it, rather than provide education. This discussion does not imply that, collectively, there is no scope for reducing the costs of gathering such information; indeed it suggests that inquiry about the distribution of information is key and should not be presumed.

Uncertainty, risk, capital constraints and externalities will, therefore, shape the demand for education but need not demolish the conceptual sense of a demand function. Some of the problems of separability of utility functions have been noted above, but even with substantial uncertainty, then a utility function may still be useful for expressing preferences (on expected utility, see Varian, 1999, 221). Henceforward, it is assumed that basic economic principles for modelling the demand for education are justifiable, a position which is supported by the substantial evidence that students do respond to market signals in ways which cohere with economic theory.

3.3   THE DEMAND FOR EDUCATION

3.3.1   The Demand Function

A demand function for education is presented in this section. Notwithstanding the emphasis of the previous chapter on education as an investment, it is also possible to consider the demand for education analogously to that for consumption goods. (The two conceptualisations appear ostensibly similar, and an adjudication between them is not made here.) The demand for education E can be formulated as a function of its price P_E, the prices of other goods P_X, current (parental) income levels Y (which may also be thought of as accumulated assets), forgone earnings during study w and the distribution of income (proxied by socio-economic status SES):

$$D_E = f(P_E, \ P_X, \ Y, \ w, \ SES) \tag{3.1}$$

This demand function is general, although it reflects a common approach of utilising a single equation framework and typically a Cobb–Douglas function (with the perhaps implausible assumption that the utility of education is separable from that of other goods).[10] The price (income) elasticity of demand for education can be derived straightforwardly with differentiation of the log of this demand function with respect to price (income).

Exposition of the demand function for education is obviously useful for admissions tutors (although supply constraints may prevent their utilisation), with the elasticity of demand capturing how participation rates respond to the setting of tuition fees. Estimates of the excess demand for education are also pertinent, particularly for deriving user fees in developing countries (Thobani, 1984; Birdsall and Orivel, 1996), but also for modelling the rapid expansion of higher education in Western economies in the 1990s (complementing studies of student motivation, Stanley and Reynolds, 1994; Pitcher and Purcell, 1998). However, there are likely to be few substitutes for education: a lot of education – schooling in particular – is allocated by fiat and many education providers use a standard technology, perhaps making substitution and price elasticity of demand moot concepts.

Instead, the income elasticity of demand for education may be useful for assessing the effects on education participation by socio-economic status and parental income. Education may be considered as a normal consumption good, with demand increasing with (parental) income. Yet it need not be, if it has negative consumption value and there are other higher-yielding investments. This income effect, compounding the (more significant) credit constraints for borrowing, may have adverse effects on equity and efficiency if education is subsidised and students from high-income families crowd out more able students from low-income families. One test of this is that, if students are fully credit-constrained, then a rise in family income should have the same effect as an equivalent nominal value fall in the price of education. To advance these ideas, evidence on demand responsiveness can be considered.

3.3.2   Estimates of Demand Responsiveness

In looking at demand responses, the freedom of choice of enrolees needs to be taken into account. Most education enrolments are, in fact, in state institutions and so constraints on choices may be substantial. In the UK, private schooling is not extensive: 7% of school children attend independent schools (0.6 million pupils). There are few private general universities, although the private training agency industry is growing. This reflects the recent past history of government funding and provision of education in the UK, a history which is not universally similar: James (1987), surveying 50 countries in the early 1980s, illustrated the significantly higher proportion of education provided by the private sector in developing countries and variations across Western economies (Ambler, 1994, offers updated figures). Generally, public sector education is more prevalent in economies with low cultural or religious diversity – reducing the need for differentiation in demand – and in economies where there is less scope for non-profit entrepreneurship – dampening supply effects.

In countries where education is mainly non-marketised, though, demand parameters are obscured and only occasional examples of unrestricted demand choices are available. One case was the responsiveness of overseas students' demand to the elimination of their subsidies for higher education study within the UK in the 1980s, with Woodhall (1991) reporting higher elasticities for less advanced courses.   More generally, demand for education has risen significantly over the last two decades. Enrolment is extending across a range of programmes including tertiary education, with the age participation index for higher education rising sharply over the period since 1985 (for international evidence, see OECD, 1997). These time trends in education may allow demand to be estimated (although there may be insufficient variation in fees to identify price effects). Moreover, international evidence on the responsiveness of demand for education to prices and incomes is substantial, with most evidence available from the US on the responsiveness of student enrolments to higher education tuition fees.

Leslie and Brinkman (1987, 1988) find that enrolment rates vary: negatively with prices (especially tuition charges); positively with the amounts spent on student aid (discounts on the price); and positively with the tuition prices of competitor providers. Citing 25 empirical studies, they find a broadly consistent effect on enrolment from changing price (that is, the price elasticity of demand for education is non-trivial). At 1982–83 prices, the mean price response is about 0.7%; for every $100 increase in annual tuition price, participation for 18–24 year olds drops by 0.75% (this should be set against the relevant mean price, including tuition and living expenses, of $3420). Further, higher tuition rates reduce per-student credit hours, with higher elasticities for freshmen entrants; and private and public providers are reasonable substitutes, as private college tuition prices appear responsive to competitor public college prices (Chressanthis, 1986; Harford and Marcus, 1986).

Heller's (1997) updated survey broadly corroborates these findings: increases in tuition fees again lead to falls in enrolment, with reasonably strong price elasticities. Cameron and Heckman (1999, 81) estimate this elasticity with respect to tuition prices to be approximately –0.3. Decreases in aid also lead to declines in enrolment, with grants having a particularly strong effect on enrolments. As Heller (1997, 650) notes, many of these studies were undertaken during a period when tuition fees were much lower (as a proportion of costs) than those in effect in the late 1990s. Price elasticities are likely to vary with differences in the costs paid per enrolee and if demand for higher education is more sensitive at higher tuition fee levels, as is likely, then current elasticities are likely to be even higher.

Demand parameters can also be estimated from recent expansions of student numbers in many Western countries. Higher education in Belgium, for example, has few access constraints and tuition fees are negligible, making unfettered changes in demand possible. Such changes have been significant: between 1953 and 1991, the age participation rate rose from less than 5% to over 45%. Duchesne and Nonneman (1998) use this expansion to examine the responsiveness of the demand for education to current earnings. Although incomes have risen, suggesting more people can afford higher education, such higher incomes also represent the opportunity costs of study and so should reduce enrolment (recognising that the opportunity costs of forgone earnings should be calculated for the individual's potential earnings, not their actual earnings). Their evidence suggests that higher forgone earnings have a negative impact on enrolment, indicating that the substitution effect of price dominates the anticipated positive income effect, with an elasticity of demand of −0.4. (Similar logic can be applied to the link between enrolment and unemployment: enrolees may either be 'waiting out' a recession or may perceive lower returns to schooling.) Fredriksson (1997) models enrolment at universities in Sweden, finding this to be most sensitive (near contemporaneously) to the university wage premium; and that unemployment raises the demand for higher education, as does greater subsidy. As well, decreases in transportation costs and housing or mobility costs from introducing more regional universities have had a positive impact on demand (Leppel, 1993).

On the demand for schooling, there is some US evidence that the market is segmented: Bezmen and Depken (1998) find private school applicants to be much less price and income sensitive than state school applicants (for distance effects on the demand for schooling, see Moll, 1998, 269). Local house prices may also reflect willingness to pay for education, particularly if schools can enrol only from their local community. Looking at 39 US school districts, Black (1999, 578) finds residents' willingness to pay increases by 2.1% for a 5% increase in elementary school scores. Both quality and quantity appear to be sensitive to the standard demand-side variables of equation (3.1).

One important finding is that related to family background, where education appears to be particularly price-sensitive, with the most price-sensitive consumers likely to be in the low-cost, least-selective institutions and to have the lowest incomes. Heller (1997) finds a wealth effect on participation, with lower income students more sensitive to changes in tuition; Leslie and Brinkman (1987, 195) contend that sociological variables – parents' socio-economic status or education – usually dominate economic ones. Duchesne and Nonneman (1998) find that income has the strongest influence on demand for higher education, suggestive of imperfect capital markets driving enrolments. Although there are no evident differences in rates of return by socio-economic status for the US, there do appear to be so for UK graduates (Altonji and Dunn, 1996a; Dearden, 1999): for Australia, the introduction of greater higher education contributions by students since 1989 does not appear to have reduced entry for the economically disadvantaged (Chapman, 1997). For schooling choices, Kodde (1985) uses evidence from Dutch school-leavers, finding parental income to have a positive effect on the demand for education. As well, forgone earnings appear to have a different income effect to tuition fees: direct costs of education appear to have a more significant impact on the demand for education than forgone earnings.

The lack of price sensitivity for more able students suggests grants may be serving almost as simple net transfers – perhaps this is evinced by increased university enrolments in the UK during declines in grant awards. (Whether or not these grants are regressive, however, depends on which groups are funding them through the tax system.) McPherson and Schapiro (1991) have examined the influence of student aid on enrolments, noting the absence of a long term trend between enrolment and US federal student aid policies, and following studies which indicated that greater financial aid had not increased access for families with incomes below the median (Hansen, 1983). Increases in net cost do reduce enrolment for low-income groups (McPherson and Schapiro, 1991, 313): for these students, a $100 net-cost increase (in 1990 prices) results in enrolment declining by about 2.2%. More generally, Cameron and Heckman's (1999) evidence suggests average income elasticities cluster close to 1; similarly, Duchesne and Nonneman (1998) estimate the income elasticity at 0.84. Again, though, such income effects need to be explained in terms of the derived demand for education. If education is a normal good, a fall in demand with a rise in price is a simple demand effect and not necessarily evidence of borrowing constraints. Moreover, on the pure credit constraint hypothesis, where a fall in tuition fees should have the same effect as a rise in income, Cameron and Heckman (1999, 113) find income effects to be much smaller than tuition price effects.

These demand estimates are broad and alternative approaches to studying the demand for education are examined in the next section. In passing, several areas appear uncharted. Such studies typically only model first-year enrolments. Different costs – tuition, living costs or forgone earnings – may have differential sensitivity: tuition fees are the most visible and the least escapable whereas other costs may not be observable until after enrolment. The transfer of such information into pricing behaviour is unknown: only the elasticity of demand has been considered here and not the cross price demand for different institutional types or modes of study. Tuition effects may be viewed from an institutions' revenue perspective – elasticities of less than one (as appear common) suggest that revenues should increase from an increase in tuition fees. Yet few education systems allow for the use of such 'precisely' calibrated enrolment functions. Few investigations examine the price effect for a given quality of education, for example, how much enrolment would increase for a given increase in academic outcomes (with the exception of Black, 1999). This would generate a much clearer estimate of willingness to pay. Instead, simple enrolment numbers are charted.

Finally, it is worth repeating that the evidence presented above does not allow for a distinction between education as an investment good against education as a consumption good. Parameters which may be regarded as having 'price effects' could also be construed as effects on the rate of return to a human capital investment.

3.4   ALLOCATIONS OF EDUCATION

3.4.1   Cognitive Partitioning

The evidence on strong income effects for education may suggest that more education is bought by wealthier households, which may be a source of inequity. But such income effects need not be considered inequitable if they are analogous to income effects on other goods. It is necessary to distinguish between government expenditures on education which are regressive with income against standard consumption of education; the former does allow wealthier households to buy more education, but at an increasing price. The arbitration position depends on how much more education is 'bought' by the wealthier and its impact on the distribution of aggregate education expenditure. But in order to assess this the scale of parental inputs or the relative benefits of private over state schooling would need to be ascertained. Nevertheless it is possible to leave aside issues of equity, because there will also be inefficiencies from constraints of access to education for the more able. Such inefficiency depends on a number of criteria: the allocation of innate or developed ability (which may be difficult to measure); the relative efficacy of educating the less able over the more able; and the relative efficiency with which such education is delivered. In economic terms, if ability is randomly allocated, if parental inputs do not offset differences in ability or embody differences in tastes, and if society finds it most efficient to educate its most able students, then the wealth effect is also an inefficiency. Education is not being allocated to where it will have the greatest effect, that is, society is not being partitioned cognitively.

Notwithstanding scepticism about measures of ability, it is possible to operationalise these concepts. For UK schools, 98% of those with the highest schooling scores remained in post-compulsory education at 16 (DfEE, 1998b). For the US, Herrnstein and Murray (1994, 29, 143) chart cognitive partitioning from 1950, with estimates that by 1990 four-fifths of all students in the top quartile of ability continued on to college after high school and that, at least to high school, high ability students do obtain education: all of the upper quarter of the distribution of high ability students graduated from high school. Remembering that so far only efficiency effects are being considered, what needs to be distinguished here is the education systems' capability (a) to attract the more able students into college as against its capability (b) to identify and reward the enrolees according to their ability levels. It is the on-entry attraction effect which is being considered here. (The on-exit assessment effect relates to rates of return to education by exam scores).

Figure 3.2 Efficiency Effects from Enrolment Criteria

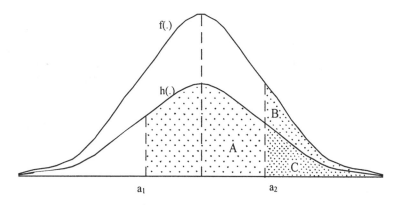

A more formal approach to assessing the efficiency of selection criteria for education programmes has been developed by Jimenez and Tan (1987). Figure 3.2 shows how selection criteria can be tested for efficiency. The function f(.) describes the population distribution of ability and function h(.) the distribution of ability of the top quintile of wealth. These are drawn so ability and wealth are independent. With a selection cut-off at a_1, only wealthy students enrol and buy education. These students are denoted as the shaded area A + C under h(.) in Figure 3.2. If the selection criterion is determined by ability, the enrolment cut-off is higher at a_2 denoted as B + C. The ratios of the marked areas (A/B) indicate the inefficiency of the a_1 cut-off.

With such inequities, it may be possible for the government to offer redress through targeted financial aid. However, even if enrolment is sensitive to price, there are problems in giving targeted financial aid. Student aid may be effectively used – Stampen and Cabrera (1988) present US evidence that aid is reasonably effective in preventing attrition – but should not be presumed to be so. First, it is typically only indirectly aimed at low income students when efficiency mandates it should be aimed at the most able. Second, its volume may be insufficient to influence behaviour.

Finally, financial aid does not seem to be viewed simply as a discount to the 'sticker price' of college, but may also convey information about the government's expectations of the returns to higher education and perhaps about the quality of the education. If quality is hard to observe, governments may not find it easy to offer a discount on such education.

Table 3.1   Highest Qualification at Age 33 by Father's Occupation

	Ability Test Level at Age 11			
	Low	Middle	High	*n*
Father: professional				
Up to A-level, GCE/GCSE	60.0	49.5	35.0	*140*
Above A-level, below degree level	24.0	29.0	9.7	*55*
Degree and postgraduate degree	16.0	21.5	55.3	*149*
	100.0	100.0	100.0	
Father: managerial				
Up to A-level, GCE/GCSE	85.2	66.2	47.7	*527*
Above A-level, below degree level	12.3	20.4	17.4	*158*
Degree and postgraduate degree	2.5	13.4	35.0	*208*
	100.0	100.0	100.0	
Father: other				
Up to A-level, GCE/GCSE	93.2	82.8	63.7	*3984*
Above A-level, below degree level	5.7	11.9	15.1	*542*
Degree and postgraduate degree	1.1	5.3	21.2	*449*
	100.0	100.0	100.0	

Source: Egerton (1997, 269)
Data: National Child Development Survey

Turning to the evidence, Table 3.1, reproduced from Egerton (1997) and using data on those born in the UK in 1958, shows ability and education levels, stratified by their fathers' occupations. The evidence suggests strong parental occupational effects in the sorting of education by ability level. Children of professionals, particularly, but also of managers, have a much higher level of educational attainment than the average for the population (skewed to degree-level education). More striking are the proportions of low/mid ability professional children reaching the highest level of qualifications compared to the proportions of mid/high ability children from the other backgrounds (16%/21.5% compared to 5.3%/21.2%). The likelihood of studying for a degree is greater for low/mid ability professional children than it is for mid/high ability children from other backgrounds.

Using the same data, Dearden (1999) finds the returns to education also decrease as father's education increases (although other family background variables are less significant). These occupational differences may reflect imperfections within the education screening mechanism and Egerton's data represent a benchmark against which to evaluate the efficiency of the sorting of the education system.

3.4.2   Rationing Using the Interest Rate

The above discussion has highlighted the importance of capital constraints on the demand for education. Participation in education is likely to be influenced by the availability of borrowing and this may adversely affect both efficiency (sub-optimal amounts of education undertaken) and equity (as wealth effects determine who receives education). Regarding efficiency, Kodde and Ritzen's (1985) model of intertemporal consumption can be used to explicate this through the structure of the capital market. In this model, the demand for education is cast within a two period utility maximisation framework.

Utility $U(c_1, c_2)$ is a function of consumption c in either of two periods. The individual is assumed to have an endowment wealth of W_i across the two periods; during each period the individual can work for T hours at a wage w_i ($i = 1,2$). The individual may borrow in the capital market and funds invested in education in the first period influence the wage in the second period. These are the sources of income. The optimal rate of return depends on circumstances in the capital market, that is, whether the interest rate is fixed, rises with the amount borrowed or is capped at a threshold. Each of these circumstances may be explored.

Assuming a constant interest rate, maximisation of utility is subject to two constraints, one for each time period, reflecting the fact that consumption must equal income:

$$p_1c_1 + (w_1 + p_E).E = W_1 + w_1T + B \qquad (3.2)$$

$$p_2c_2 + B.(1 + r) = W_2 + w_2(E)T \qquad (3.3)$$

The first terms on the left-hand side of equations (3.2) and (3.3) represent consumption in the respective periods: the prices of goods p_i for consumption c_i. The second term on the left-hand side of (3.2) represents the amount of education E times its full price p_E plus the forgone earnings (opportunity cost) w_1. In the second period, the wage $w_2(E)$ is a function of the amount of education undertaken in the first period. Of interest, however, is the borrowing B which must be paid back in the second period at interest rate r. This is the discount rate between the two periods. The relevant first order conditions for maximising utility are:

$$(\partial U/\partial c_1)/(\partial U/\partial c_2) = (1 + r)p_1/p_2 \qquad (3.4)$$

$$(w_1 + p_E) = T.(\partial w_2/\partial E)/(1 + r) \qquad (3.5)$$

Equation (3.4) says that the ratios of the marginal consumption utilities over the two periods should be equated to the discounted price ratios over the two periods. Equation (3.5) says that the full price of education $w_1 + p_E$ should be equated to the marginal discounted second period earnings, enhanced by greater education.

The partial derivatives of the model yield further implications (Kodde and Ritzen, 1985; Kodde, 1986). First, either a higher interest rate or a higher wage rate in the first period will reduce education and reduce borrowing ($\partial E/\partial r < 0$, $\partial E/\partial w_1 < 0$, $\partial B/\partial r < 0$, $\partial B/\partial w_1 < 0$). Hence those enrolees who face higher interest rates – perhaps because they face less developed financial markets – will demand less education. Second, although there are conventional education price effects – a higher price of education reduces the amount of education – this may not reduce the amount borrowed for education ($\partial E/\partial p_E < 0$, $\partial B/\partial p_E > 0$ or <0). Third, wealth effects are expected to be neutral. Higher wealth (in either period) will increase consumption but have no effect on the demand for education ($\partial E/\partial W_i = 0$); higher wealth in the first period will reduce borrowing and higher wealth in the second period increases borrowing ($\partial B/\partial W_1 < 0$, $\partial B/\partial W_2 > 0$). This is because it is the income-augmenting educational rate of transformation between periods which determines how much education is undertaken; and this education effect is invariant to wealth. (Although greater wealth may be positively correlated either with a greater effect of E on w_2 or with more generous interest rates, perhaps through intra-family borrowing.)

An alternative credit market may operate, however, where the interest rate is increasing in the amount borrowed. With this regime, maximisation of utility is subject to the constraints:

$$p_1c_1 + (w + p_E).E = W_1 + w_1T + B \qquad (3.2)$$

$$p_2c_2 + B.(1 + r(B)) = W_2 + w_2(E)T \qquad (3.6)$$

The first period constraint is unchanged, so equation (3.2) is repeated; equation (3.6) is a revised version of equation (3.3) and now includes a borrowing term to reflect the increased interest rate as borrowing rises, r(B).

The first order conditions for a maximum are:

$$(\partial U/\partial c_1)/(\partial U/\partial c_2) = (1 + r(B) + B.\partial r/\partial B)p_1/p_2 \qquad (3.7)$$

$$(w_1 + p_E) = (\partial w_2/\partial E).T/(1 + r(B) + B.\partial r/\partial B) \qquad (3.8)$$

Equation (3.7) establishes that the marginal rate of substitution between the two periods should be equal to the discounted price ratio, reflecting initial borrowing costs and an increased interest rate because of the higher borrowing. Equation (3.8) says that the full price of education should be equalised to the marginal discounted second period earnings. However, the right-hand side of (3.8) now includes the rate of return to education as the critical discount rate rather than the interest rate, yielding several new implications.

First, there are now wealth effects on the demand for education. Higher initial period wealth does encourage more education although either higher wealth or a higher wage in the second period reduces the demand for education ($\partial E/\partial W_1 > 0$, $\partial E/\partial W_2 < 0$, $\partial E/\partial w_2 < 0$). Second, a higher wage rate or higher wealth in the second period now increases borrowing ($\partial B/\partial w_2 > 0$, $\partial B/\partial W_2 > 0$). These two conditions obtain because the role of education in augmenting second period earnings is weakened. Third, a higher wage in the first period now has an ambiguous effect on education ($\partial E/\partial w_1 > 0$ or < 0); there may be an income effect on education, allowing greater purchase of education with first period wages.

A third variant of credit conditions assumes that there are credit constraints on borrowing for individuals up to an amount B_X (and individuals would want to borrow above this amount). Utility is now maximised subject to:

$$p_1c_1 + (w + p_E).E = W_1 + w_1T + B_X \qquad (3.9)$$

$$p_2c_2 + B_X.(1 + r_X) = W_2 + w_2(E)T \qquad (3.10)$$

Equation (3.9) asserts that the individual cannot borrow more than B_X and the second period constraint (3.10) therefore includes the repayment of that borrowing at an interest rate of r_X. The first order conditions for a maximum are:

$$(\partial U/\partial c_1)/(\partial U/\partial c_2) = (1 + r_X)p_1/p_2 \qquad (3.11)$$

$$(w_1 + p_E) = (\partial w_2/\partial E).T/(1 + r_X) \qquad (3.12)$$

Equation (3.11) repeats the condition that the marginal rate of substitution should equal the discounted price ratio.   Equation (3.12) establishes that the full price of education should be equal to the marginal, education-augmented discounted earnings.   For both conditions, it is the threshold interest rate, and not the rate of return to education, which serves as the discount rate.

The implications of this model also differ from those of the initial model. First, the rate of return is likely to exceed the borrowing rate: individuals would like to borrow until the rate of interest equals the rate of return on education, but they are unable to.   Hence the optimal amount of education in this capital market is likely to be less than that in the first case where borrowing is available at the constant interest rate.   Second, an increase in the interest rate may actually increase the demand for education because it lowers second period income and consumption, which has to be compensated for ($\partial E/\partial r_X > 0$, $\partial c_2/\partial r_X < 0$).   This (counter-intuitive) result reflects the fact that, when education capital markets are constrained, the interest rate and the returns to education are not coterminous ways of linking the two periods.   Education, as a way of augmenting second period consumption, allows consumption paths to be smoothed.   Finally, increasing initial wealth increases the demand for education –acting as a way of lowering interest costs – but increasing wealth in the second period reduces the demand for education ($\partial E/\partial W_1 > 0$, $\partial E/\partial W_2 < 0$).

This two-period model illustrates the intertemporal trade-offs made when individuals can invest in education, allowing consumption to be optimal across both periods.   Kodde and Ritzen's model can be used to explain why the rate of return to education is high in developing countries – where capital markets may not allow unconstrained borrowing for education – and why the rate of return to education is not the same as the rate of interest. With imperfect capital markets, the demand for education need not be equated to net present values using the interest rate, although the demand for education remains positively related to its net present value.   An increase in wages raises the opportunity costs of schooling but, if the wage offer dispersion is increased, the future rewards to education will also be raised.

Further, constraints in the capital market may mean that greater intergenerational wealth and assets (as distinct from income) become important.   Those with initial wealth need not engage in the capital market to borrow for education.   Not only does this influence the demand for education (because the capital market is not perfect), it also creates a spread between the borrowing and lending rates which are used to discount the earnings effects of education.   Individuals may discount the future differently, depending on divergence between the borrowing and the lending rates, which allows those with high ability, but also high wealth, to invest more in education.   It is these factors which drive the empirical results described above.

3.4.3   Non-completion Models

Most individuals terminate their full-time education before the age of 30, notwithstanding notions of 'lifelong learning'. Many stop at the end of a discrete dose of education, but a large proportion drop out of school, college or university. This imposes both individual and education provider costs and may reflect error or student misperceptions at point of enrolment. Pertinent to the discussion in this chapter, knowledge about what influences non-completion may allow for the formulation of a demand function for education (and may assist in institutional management). The initial assumption is that enrolment and dropping out are rational decisions: they reflect the relative opportunities at different points in time as more information is obtained about the costs of dropping out. Manski's (1989) model of dropping out, which assumes utility maximisation across different activities, is useful here.

Manski (1989) denotes U_w as the expected utility from working, U_c the expected utility from completing a post-compulsory school examination and U_d the expected utility from dropping out. Each of these will vary across students, but the most realistic assumption is that $U_c > U_w > U_d$ (as those who drop out could have worked from the beginning). If P is the probability of completion, then the student will enrol if:

$$PU_c + (1 - P)U_d > U_w \tag{3.13}$$

Rearranging terms, the enrolment criterion is therefore set in terms of the probability of completion. A student enrols when:

$$P > (U_w - U_d)/(U_c - U_d) \tag{3.14}$$

The level at which the left-hand side and right-hand side of equation (3.14) are equated can be denoted as π, that is, the threshold completion probability at which enrolment is worthwhile. It is this threshold probability which is of analytical interest and the probability can then be aggregated across a cohort of students, whose P values will differ. With Q denoted as the fraction of the student population who enrol across a distribution denoted by F, then Q is the fraction of the population for whom P exceeds π. Then Q_c denotes the completion level and Q_d is the drop-out level. Finally, r_d is the drop-out rate. These variables can be represented:

$$Q_c = \int_{\pi}^{1} P dF, \quad Q_d = \int_{\pi}^{1} (1 - P) dF \tag{3.15}$$

$$r_d = Q_d/Q \tag{3.16}$$

This model can now be used to examine the consequences of a change in the threshold completion probability which induces enrolment (π) and in the distribution of drop-out probabilities (F). This π variable depends on changes in the expected utilities from the three options. So a rise in π may occur whenever enrolment becomes less attractive compared to working. This may happen if: the relative earnings of the educated fall; if the school system's standards are such that dropping out conveys strongly adverse signals in the labour market; or if student support is reduced.

If the threshold completion probability at which enrolment becomes worthwhile does rise then the likely consequences are falls in enrolment levels, completion levels, drop-out levels and drop-out rates. Raising π shifts the composition of enrolment toward those students with the highest completion probabilities (r_d falls), reduces the numbers enrolling (Q falls) and so the numbers completing and the numbers dropping out (Q_c and Q_d fall). The logic here is that students who now choose to work rather than enrol are those with the lowest completion probabilities. This has implications for student aid policies: if student aid is reduced, then π rises but the drop-out level Q_d and the drop-out rate r_d fall. These look like improvements in the efficiency of education provision: yet reducing aid has also reduced the completion level.

A second change may be to the distribution of completion probabilities, F. This may happen if there are improvements in teaching quality or greater state investments in the education system. If each P value (the completion probability of each member of the population) rises: the enrolment level and completion level rise but the drop-out level and the drop-out rate may either rise or fall. A policy change which raises completion probabilities does lower drop-out among students who would have enrolled initially. But the change also induces new students to enrol, of which some will not complete. The aggregate effect on drop-out levels depends on whether (a) the number of induced enrolees who then drop-out is greater than (b) the reduction in drop-out among the initial, pre-change enrolees.

Manski (1989) extends this model to incorporate the endogenous effort choices of students. From the perspective of the student, enrolment does not guarantee completion but will depend also on the effort the student makes in class. An enrolee will choose to complete if the effort needed to graduate Z is less than the difference between the utility from completion versus that from dropping out:

$$Z < R = U_c - U_d \qquad (3.17)$$

Here R is the threshold beyond which effort to complete is not worthwhile. The student may be assumed to know the U_c, U_d and U_w parameters but does not know effort Z before enrolment, which can be assumed to be drawn from some probability distribution G. Hence the expected utility of enrolment is: the sum of utility U_c (should effort needed to graduate Z be lower than the threshold level R) and utility U_d (should effort needed exceed the threshold), minus the effort incurred up to the threshold:

$$U_c\text{Prob}(Z < R) + U_d\text{Prob}(Z > R) - \int_0^R ZdG \qquad (3.18)$$

Hence the student chooses to enrol if this expected utility is greater than U_w, the utility from working. Enrolment is thus determined by the student's effort expectations in G and the relationship between expected effort and required effort.

This condition applies to the individual student and so is efficient at the micro-economic level; but it is possible for social and private interests to diverge such that this condition is not socially efficient. This inefficiency arises because society also has a preference over the optimal number of drop-outs. Manski (1989) assumes society values completion more than the students do privately, such that the social value of completing is $U_c + M$ with students having to put in more effort (and with the social values of dropping out and working still U_d and U_w). Hence society prefers that the student enrol if:

$$(U_c + M)\text{Prob}(Z < R+M) + U_d\text{Prob}(Z > R + M) - \int_0^{R+M} ZdG > \\ U_w \qquad (3.19)$$

Thus the social optimum would have more students enrolling who would previously have worked. Also, society would like an enrolled student to complete if $Z < R + M$. Hence society would like some students who drop out to complete school, so Q_c rises relative to Q_d. However, society's preferences may not translate into a lower rate of drop-out if it has also induced more students (with relatively high drop-out probabilities) into the enrolment cohort.

Overall, the drop-out rate depends on the distributions of effort levels, the completion probabilities and the value of outside options. The aim is not therefore to simply minimise the drop-out level or rate, but to raise the completion probability P, the quality of education programmes or students' effort tolerance R. No immediate and clear inference about education quality can be inferred from drop-out rates because the enrolments levels and completion levels are determined together. (In turn, this suggests that single equation estimation of drop-out may be over-identified.) Observed drop-out parameters will represent a compromise between schools and parents demanding a positive drop-out rate – as a sign that the education discriminates between students and as a way of inducing effort – and students 'supplying' a drop-out rate through non-completion, non-attendance and/or misperceptions about necessary effort levels (Koshal et al., 1995). Fundamentally, the decision to drop out will be a rational one, with students equating the returns from further participation to the opportunity costs and returns from other activities.

Evidence on factors affecting non-completion can be considered in the light of this model. For the US, Bickel and Lange (1995, 363) identify three aspects: characteristics of students; family background or socio-economic status – which might be proxies for community inputs; and the institutional context, such as a school's policies. Although the first two aspects are exogenous to the school, the unresponsiveness of the institution may still be significant. For schooling in the UK, institutional type is significant: grammar schools have lower non-completion rates than comprehensives; independent schools have lower drop-out rates than state schools. As evidence that reductions in teaching quality or institutional organisation cannot be inferred from rising drop-out rates, the rate does appear to vary negatively with respect to the unemployment rate or wage levels (for New York, see Rees and Mocan, 1997).

For higher education, DesJardins et al. (1999) present a discrete time hazards model of dropping out (in their application and that of Chuang, 1997, drop-outs often re-enrol, complicating the concept of non-retention further). Their evidence – separating the effects of prior characteristics and outside options – confirms prior ability as a strong determinant of drop-out, particularly in the early years of participation. As well, employment on campus has a positive effect on retention, suggesting the importance of the wage effect and borrowing constraints. For UK higher education, Johnes (1997) finds that the strongest effect operates via on-entry qualifications, but there are also subject effects on drop-out: medicine, agricultural studies, education and languages have low rates; Architecture typically has relatively high drop-out rates. Johnes (1997, 358) also calculates the marginal effects on drop-out from a change in student quality: a one point decrease in the average on-entry qualifications would raise non-completion in UK higher education by 9–28% (1990 cohort). The costs to the education system of this completion failure are considered in Chapter 5.

3.5   ISSUES AND CONCLUSIONS

This chapter has looked at the difficulties of specifying a demand function for education, reflecting a general concern that such demand cannot be readily formalised. Some difficulties with such a formalisation may be identified, the strongest of which is the existence of poorly functioning capital markets. Either insufficient or sub-optimal equilibrium quantities of education are likely to be the outcome. Relatedly, competitive checks on any prolonged disequilibria which might emerge in education markets may be absent or muted. Notwithstanding these problems – and there is not overwhelming evidence on their substantive significance – it is very difficult to investigate a set of behaviours where individuals are assumed to be irrational and where there are significant costs to being so. Moreover, the depth of these difficulties may be overstated and they need not lead to government intervention, either if individuals have more information than the government or if rectifying the inefficiencies and shortfalls induces other new costs.

In addition, the evidence on the demand for education plausibly conforms to economic principles: own price, relative price and income effects are evident for most education. As well as price and income parameters, the demand for education will be influenced by determinants of the rate of return. In both this and the previous chapter evidence has been catalogued on how future earnings drive the demand for education. This suggests that education is an investment good, although most of the evidence presented here is compatible with education as either a consumption or an investment good. The presence of income effects, for example, may indicate that education is a normal consumption good, although it may alternatively reflect differential access to the capital market. Hence increased demand for education may be considered as a consequence of either (expected) increases in the returns to education, reductions in the opportunities in the youth labour market or a change in preferences for formal schooling (over other forms of education, such as apprenticeships). The standard economic stimuli and barriers have predictable effects on demand, although cross-subsidies remain to be investigated, as does students' sensitivity to direct rather than indirect costs (especially if capital constraints are important).

Three extensions to models of consumer choice have been explored above. First, there is strong evidence of wealth effects in education, perhaps beyond those anticipated for an endeavour which has been cast primarily as an investment good. In general, an education system which generates human capital based largely on the income of a student's parents is unlikely to be efficient. But it needs to be established that family income effects are not a proxy for other impetuses, such as tastes for education, motivation or unobserved ability. Cameron and Heckman (1998, 1999) contend that, at least for the US, income effects have been substantively negligible across most types of provision for several past decades. Notwithstanding, this general concern serves to emphasise the importance of the allocation of students within the education system and the conditions under which students make enrolment choices. In terms of policy, student aid may be calibrated with respect to enrolments to serve both efficiency and equity goals, although there are obvious problems in identifying – pre-enrolment – those whose life-cycle income will be the highest. A second extrapolation has been to look at the effect of the interest rate and terms of borrowing on the demand for education, exploring the differences between unconstrained capital markets, rising interest rates and constrained borrowing. Finally, dropping out of education reflects a particular expression of demand and the propensity to quit has been modelled; evidence about drop-outs is supportive of drop-out as rational calculus, albeit dependent on the (potentially unobservable) technology and efficiency of the education provider. It is this technology which is discussed in the next chapter.

4.　The Theory of the Enterprise

4.1　INTRODUCTION

Schools, colleges and universities are educational enterprises using resources to achieve learning outcomes, analogously to how firms produce outputs. Economic principles may be used to assess their efficiency at doing this. Hoenack (1994), for example, situates the economics of education firmly in the study of organisational behaviour, stressing the advantages of decentralisation in defraying information costs and in introducing incentives to improve technologies and to motivate personnel. Such study may therefore lead to a better understanding of efficiency and cost-effectiveness in education provision. Such inquiry might be considered particularly important, given the substantial amounts of time and money dedicated to the provision of schooling and education.

Improvement in the cost-effectiveness of educational organisations is of course useful, but a necessary first step is to model the education production function. This is the focus of this chapter: articulating and applying the theory of education enterprises, drawing on basic economic principles of the theory of the firm (Varian, 1999). The outcomes and processes of these enterprises – which differ in several important ways from those of firms – are modelled first. Section 4.2 clarifies the definitions of efficiency and describes the 'technology' of education enterprises, including methods to describe the production of education. Particular to education is the assessment of learners' achievements; the form of this assessment – which can be set endogenously – will also affect the operation of education enterprises and the behaviour of their inputs. Following this, Section 4.3 presents analysis of cost functions, which may be thought of as embodying the technology of education; this section also describes the revenue sources for education providers, where students both pay for education and receive a wage. Section 4.4 offers a summary, prefacing the evidence on production functions which is given in Chapter 5.

4.2   PRODUCTION FUNCTION MODELS

4.2.1   The Educational Enterprise

Education production function models describe how education institutions generate a vector of outcomes from a flow of inputs. This 'education production function' is of course a stylisation, suggesting that the technologies needed to educate students are analogous with the technologies used to manufacture goods. This may not be appropriate: although what is 'got out' from a school will be related to what is 'put in', there may not be a straightforward way of capturing the relationship between the two, particularly if there are substantial, endogenous home and student effort inputs, along with general equilibrium effects. Hence more ephemeral 'outcomes' are thought of, rather than 'outputs': outcomes may be academic attainment or wages but they could be any or many of the individual or aggregate benefits of education. The first task is therefore to model such enterprises' objective functions and processes.

At their most basic, production function studies compare differently sized lumps of resource against homogeneous units of outcome, with less focus on how these outcomes are created: aspects such as learning technologies or styles of management are abstracted out. One crucial distinction is therefore between the efficiency of production and the amount of resources. Well resourced efficient colleges should produce better outcomes than poorly resourced inefficient colleges; but there is no obvious way of ranking the absolute outcomes of poorly resourced efficient colleges against well resourced inefficient ones. In modelling the production function as the relationship between inputs and outcomes, therefore, differences in efficiency levels need to be looked at within the context of overall resource levels.

Figure 4.1 An Efficiency Matrix for Four College Types

	High per-student resource input	Low per-student resource input
Output efficient (high value-added)	*A*	*C*
Output inefficient (low value-added)	*B*	*D*

Two dimensions of efficiency as noted in Chapter 1 are pertinent here. First, input-choice efficiency refers to the selection of all inputs so that the social marginal costs equal the social marginal benefits. Second, output-choice efficiency is associated with choosing the right amount of production of each education programme, again so that the social marginal cost equals the social marginal benefit (of outcomes). At this stage, it is not necessary to prescribe what these outcomes are (examination scores, earnings, well-being, and so on)

A simple exposition of output-choice efficiency may help here, assuming four types of college as in Figure 4.1. College type A is efficient and is well-resourced; it should have the highest absolute outcomes. College type D is inefficient and poorly resourced; it should have the lowest possible absolute outcomes.   College type B is inefficient but well-resourced, whereas type C is efficient but poorly resourced; *a priori*, the absolute outcomes of B and C cannot be ranked. In value-added terms, however, types A and C should score the same and better than types B and D. Typically, the grouped type AB is compared against CD, with differences in efficiency assumed away. The simple test is whether or not AB do achieve higher outcomes than CD and, given uniform efficiency, this should be expected. However, if this expectation is not met (as is discussed in the next chapter), then the distinction between high and low unit of resource is irrelevant and 'money [input resource] does not matter'. Yet this also implies that not all college types are efficient. In fact, the 'money does not matter' result necessarily implies that types CD are more efficient than types AB.

A number of inferences may follow. College types AB may be presumed to simply 'waste' the extra resource input they receive and types CD are not really 'efficient', but that need not be true and needs to be established (perhaps longitudinal or historical evidence may be cited, as by Hanushek, 1998). Resources given to A and B may be scaled back, although there may be political and transitional adjustment costs involved in so doing. Resources may be transferred, preferably to college types C – assuming these can be identified – or at least to college types CD; but it would need to be established that they would be able to replicate their efficiency with more resources (that is, there are no diseconomies of scale). One possible inference is that, if the college system is committed to equality of value-added, then the allocation of unit resource is in fact not far from optimal: transfers to D from A, who deploy their inputs better, ensures that all students receive the same additional education. The most fruitful inquiry in the face of evidence that 'money does not matter', however, would be to look at how and why the low unit resource colleges are efficient.

4.2.2   Production Functions

From an individuals' perspective, education is demanded as one element of a general utility function and so will be incorporated depending on how readily it can raise utility levels, compared to other elements. Drawing on industrial organisation analysis, the underlying production of education may be written more formally in terms of:

$$A_t = h(R_{t-1}, F_{t-1}, P_{t-1}, A_{t-1}, Z_{t-1}) \tag{4.1}$$

Here, A_t is student achievement by time t; R_{t-1} is the school resource input; F_{t-1} is family and household input during the previous period; and P_{t-1} is peer input. Prior student achievement A_{t-1} should also be included as an embodiment of prior ability or the initial context for learning, so that achievement at time t is related to resources devoted toward that achievement. Finally, a student's effort Z_{t-1} should be included; this variable, which may be determined endogenously with the other elements of the production function, is critical to the efficiency of education providers. The function can then be modelled under the implicit assumption that individuals are maximising A as their outcome. This maximisation may be considered as subject to a number of constraints: R may be assumed to be fixed independently through government disbursements; for family inputs, the time price of F cannot exceed expenditure on other goods plus any income from borrowing and is likely to be jointly determined with R; P_{t-1} and A_{t-1} may possibly be thought of as exogenous; Z is likely to be a function of previous achievement and cognitive ability and it too may be measured using time prices. It is expected that the partial derivatives for the outcome against each of the inputs would be positive. Less clear is how the partial derivatives (measured in nominal terms) rank against each other (for example, whether $\partial A/\partial F > \partial A/\partial P$ or vice versa).

For education enterprises, the maximand is less straightforward: it may be either the sum of the individual students' A values; a uniform value of A across n students; or a threshold value of A per student. More generally, education providers may be considered as multi-product enterprises: universities produce both student and research outputs; schools may produce both socialised and human capital augmented students. (These multi-product effects are considered below.) Conventionally, and for simplicity, the single maximand is assumed to be an aggregation of students' outcomes. The education provider therefore has to allocate students and resources across schools (and classes within schools) to achieve this maximand, conditional on the ability distribution of the students:

$$\text{maximise } \int_0^{B'} \sum_{j=1}^{J} n_j A_j(B) dB \tag{4.2}$$

$$\text{subject to TC} = \sum_{j=1}^{J} R_j n_j$$

Hence a school would maximise achievement A_j of n_j students, conditional on ability B up to a threshold of B', across $j = 1 \ldots J$ classes (Arnott and Rowse, 1987). This maximand of equation (4.2) is subject to a budget constraint, which is here designated simplistically as total costs TC equal to the amount of resource R (given via an exogenous funding formula) multiplied by the numbers of students. Given this optimal level of achievement, it is then assumed that such achievement unambiguously or monotonically translates into further outcomes of direct utility, such as higher earnings or improved health.

Such a production function is typically modelled using Cobb–Douglas or Constant Elasticity of Substitution functions (Hanushek et al., 1996; Figlio, 1999, uses a translog functional form). However some of these inputs, for example, family and student effort, do not have market prices which can be attached to them, at least from the perspective of the school (although social planners may be able to impute prices). Furthermore, the above discussion and Figlio's (1999) modelling suggest that it is unlikely either that inputs are additive, i.e., there is no differential effectiveness, or that the function is homothetic, i.e., that the marginal rate of substitution between the inputs depends on the proportions of the inputs, not the scale of production. Using the individual's production function equation, additivity implies that all the interaction terms have zero coefficients:

$$A_t = m_1(S_{t-1}) + m_2(F_{t-1}) + m_3(P_{t-1}) + m_4(A_{t-1}) + m_5(Z_{t-1}) \tag{4.3}$$

A homothetic production function would require that, for equation (4.4), $m(.)$ is monotonic and that $h(.)$ is homogeneous of degree 1:

$$A_t = m(h(S_{t-1}, F_{t-1}, P_{t-1}, A_{t-1}, Z_{t-1})) \tag{4.4}$$

Public and private involvement in education is likely to undermine each of these assumptions. School resource is likely to be partly related to family inputs, if only through local taxation and median voter preferences; peer inputs are likely to be linked to resource amounts; and parental and student effort is likely to be endogenous to teacher effort. In general, assumptions about pedagogies, modes of instruction and school compositions, that is, the education technology, should be factored in. More critically, schools aim to produce both high outcome scores but also high absolute numbers of students, so there is likely to be a trade-off between these two outcomes (which is not fully captured in the above optimisation).

Figure 4.2 Output Functions for Education Enterprises

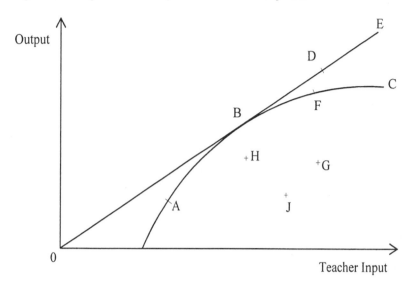

Another method for measuring efficiency from the perspective of the enterprise is to use approaches which relate production to a notional frontier and do not impose a standard technological form across institutions. Figure 4.2 shows a simple measure of efficiency in relating one input (teachers) to output, holding all other inputs fixed. Mapping the performances of seven providers (A, B, F, C, H, G, J), a production function relates the outcomes to changes in this common input, allowing a distinction between technical and scale efficiency. The contour ABFC marks the technically efficient providers and B is also scale efficient (tangential to OBE), whereas A appears too small; provider F is efficient in one domain, but it also appears to be too large. Of interest here is the shape of ABFC and the proportions of schools on it. Inefficient providers are identified as G, H and J, all of which provide significantly lower outcomes than are subtended on the efficiency contour.

A similar approach to measuring efficiency using linear programming is data envelopment analysis. In this analysis, schools and colleges are thought of as decision-making units producing s outputs using m inputs. The kth unit produces A_{rk} outputs r = 1, ..., s with G_{ik} inputs i = 1, ..., m. This kth unit is aiming to maximise its weighted output set, where weights for the inputs v_{ik} and weights for the outputs u_{rk} have to be selected. These weights must be chosen such that the ratio of weighted output to weighted input is equal to or less than 1; the weighted sum of inputs should equal unity; and the weight attached to each input and to each output must be non-negative (Johnes, 1999). For each of the decision-making units, therefore, the linear programme should be solved to maximise the weighted sum of the outputs. For the kth unit, this maximisation problem is given as:

$$\text{maximise } h_k = \sum_{r=1}^{s} u_{rk} A_{rk} \qquad (4.5)$$

Scores of h_k equal to 1 represent technical efficiency. As each provider unit is evaluated in terms of outputs endogenously chosen, the mode of efficiency is not prescribed. In effect, providers can be identified as efficient, given the outcomes they have set for themselves. This approach may be particularly useful if the technology is not well-defined or if there are multiple outputs which schools would be aiming for as part of their missions (for a discussion, see Johnes and Johnes, 1995ab). For example, universities are differentiated by their teaching versus research mix; schools may be differentiated by their pastoral provision and their examination scores; school district boards or education authorities will have a range of types of provision to optimise. These missions will drive input choices and the composition of outputs; data envelopment analysis measures the institutions' respective technical efficiencies.

4.2.3   The Economics of Standards

In the above models, achievement is assumed to be an exogenous, 'natural' dose of human capital which the student obtains. The school simply has to work out the most efficient way to generate and deliver this dosage. More realistically, schools and universities set standards which students aim to attain and so in part determine what is meant by achievement. More importantly, such standards determine effort levels. How these standards are set – either through formative or summative assessment, externally or internally – and at what level these standards are set, will affect the efficiency of the education system.

It is likely that students who are assessed, that is, measured against specified learning criteria, will face a greater incentive to study. The returns from low effort or from simple attendance will have fallen: employers will now be able to observe that low effort as manifest in gradations of examination scores and set wages accordingly. This assessment effect may also be stronger to the extent that it is imposed as an external, cross-sector standard. Such a standard may both convey more reliable signalling information and reduce the incentive for zero-sum within-class effects, where effort is competed downwards. International evidence may support this general argument: regressing as a dependent variable the median maths and science test scores across 39 countries (controlling for per capita GDP), Bishop (1997, 262) finds countries which have curriculum-based external exit exams obtain substantively higher achievement levels.

Examinations may also clarify the goals of an education programme, boosting internal efficiency. At the school level, Bishop (1997, 263) provides evidence from Canadian schools on improvements to internal efficiency where there are external exams, as embodied in school administrator and teacher behaviour. Summative assessment through end-of-course examinations may be lower cost and reduce sorting costs for firms, but repeated, formative assessment may give students more information about their learning achievement (generating more endogenous feedback effects). This greater information set may improve student choices and effort levels over their entire schooling, reducing drop-out and mal-investment (over-education). At the individual student level, Betts (1998a) evaluates the incentives in the Chicago Summer Bridge Program. This Program gives students the opportunity during summer to retake tests they had failed in the spring; the incentive is that those who pass after summer school do not have to repeat the grade the next year. This may be thought of as formative assessment regarding a student's ability to progress through school. Betts (1998a, 108) produces a cost–benefit analysis of this Program, estimating it to be 2.2–7.4 times as cost-effective as regular schooling, with positive incentive effects.

As well as the mode of assessment, there will be external efficiency effects from the rigour of the standard, and the influence of standards on students' subsequent earnings has been modelled by Costrell (1994, 1997) and Betts (1998b). In Costrell's model, there is a binary pass–fail credential and the standard for this credential is set by the government's exam board to maximise social welfare. Students choose whether or not to make the effort to meet that standard. To society, the marginal benefit of a more rigorous standard is the induced extra productivity from those who put in the effort to meet it; the marginal cost is the reduced productivity of those who do not meet the new standard (because it is too rigorous).

Costrell's model is represented in Figure 4.3A and B. The function $U^i(L, Y)$ is the utility function of individual i which depends on leisure L and earnings Y. The education production function is $A^i(L_i)$ and L_0 is the optimal amount of leisure, compatible with an achievement/effort of A_0 and income of Y_0. Leisure is available if the student does not study, but earnings are correspondingly reduced. In Figure 4.3A, the individual will supply effort into education up to the tangency between the utility function and the education production function for generating earnings. Under this model, there is no demarcated educational standard and firms perfectly observe student quality on a continuum. Hence income and student quality are strongly positively correlated (perhaps more so than is empirically observed in actual labour markets). Individuals can choose the achievement level which maximises utility. For this individual, utility is maximised at an effort level of A'; this translates into an income level of Y_i.

Figure 4.3A   Perfect Information Curriculum Standards

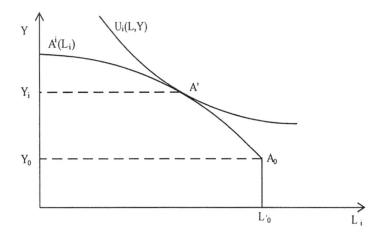

Figure 4.3B   Binary Curriculum Standards

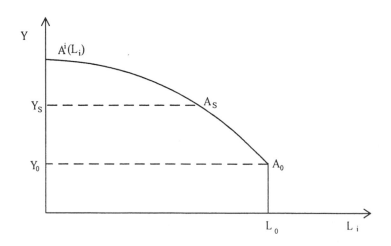

However, if the education system is one with a uniform outcome qualification, which students may pass or fail, then students will have an incentive just to graduate. If A_S is the exogenously set achievement level needed to graduate, then only two effort levels will result: those to reach A_S and A_0 as in Figure 4.3B. There is no incentive to work harder than A_S or within the range A_S–A_0. As the standard increases, the numbers of students meeting the standard falls and the numbers resorting to the minimum effort level rises. Across the effort distribution, therefore, there will be students who would have supplied less effort than A_S and earned lower incomes and there would also have been students who would have supplied more effort and earned higher incomes. The standard serves to direct student effort levels toward two groups: with a distribution function $F(A_i)$, $F(A_S)$ is the group of students making no effort and earning Y_0 and $[1 - F(A_S)]$ is the group exerting sufficient effort to meet the standard.

For the policy-maker, only students' incomes are of interest, not their leisure, and the objective function is:

$$V(A_S) = [1 - F(A_S)]h(A_S) + F(A_S)h(A_0) \qquad (4.6)$$

Here h() is the earnings for each student conditional on the (two) effort levels. The first order conditions for an optimal standard A* are derived from:

$$\partial V/\partial A^* = [1 - F(A^*)]\partial h/\partial A^* - f(A^*)[h(A^*) - h(A_0)] \qquad (4.7)$$

Here f(A) is the density function for F(A). The first term on the right-hand side of equation (4.7) is the marginal social benefit of a rise in the standard. It represents the extra effort students exert to meet the standard and so, in becoming more productive, generating higher incomes. The second term is the marginal social cost of the students on the margin who fail to meet the standard and so experience a fall in earnings (firms now have very limited information about the quality of these workers). The government or the exam board aims to set a standard so that these marginal costs equal the marginal earnings premia ($\partial V/\partial A^* = 0$).

Costrell's model allows for exposition of a range of scenarios facing such social planners. For example, students may increase their preferences for leisure, so a given standard looks harder to meet. This preference shift reduces the benefits of raising the standard, since the number of graduates at the original optimum has declined. But it may also reduce the costs, depending on how many students are now on the margin. A rise in preferences for leisure therefore has an ambiguous effect on standards. As a second example, if there is an adverse shock to the production function such as a decline in the quality of teachers, this is equivalent to shifting inward of the function $A^i(L_i)$ represented in Figure 4.3B. This will lower standards in most cases because it is unlikely that the shock will have influenced those who put in no effort. This group is likely to rise and so represent a larger part of the benefits of a lower standard. It is possible to apply the model in the context of changing education credentials over the previous decade. Assuming (perhaps speculatively) 'grade inflation', the lower standards will reduce the effort of those who would have met a higher standard. But such 'inflation' should reduce the spread of earnings: those who would have met a higher standard now possess the same labour market credential (and similar human capital) as a larger group who could only meet the lower standard. In contrast, the lowered standard now conveys labour market information about a larger group of students who have been motivated to study by the likelihood that they would now meet that standard.

There are two concerns faced by students deciding whether or not to meet a given standard. One is their uncertainty about their ability to meet the standard if they attempt to. The other is their uncertainty about what standards firms will demand or be willing to accept. If median ability is below mean ability, the student cohort may therefore press for standards to be lower, preferably in ways unobservable to firms. Costrell (1994) represents this effect as typifying a decentralised education system with competition between the different standard-setting boards such that each board has no interest in setting high standards. Grade inflation may be the result. Firms interpret a given diploma as signalling the average quality worker; this gives education enterprises the incentive to award the diploma to students of lesser quality, because the full cost of diluting the standard (firms lower the wages paid to diploma-holders) is borne by all diploma-holders from all schools. Analogous effects may occur if there is greater than one region setting standards. Consequently, with many exams boards across regions and educated workers moving between districts, the wage earned by those meeting the standard is:

$$Y = (1 - \theta)A_S + \theta A_X \qquad (4.8)$$

Here A_S is the home standard and A_X is the standard set in other districts, with the parameter θ embodying the imperfect reputations of extra-district standards (as opposed to home standards). The objective function for an individual standard-setting board now must include this reputation effect:

$$V(A_S; A_X, \theta) = [1 - F(A_S; A_X, \theta)]h[(1 - \theta)A_S + \theta A_X] + F(A_S; A_X, \theta)h(A_0) \qquad (4.9)$$

If θ rises, then the benefits of the home board setting a higher standard are reduced, being spread across graduates from other districts. Home students will also be more likely to decide that the effort needed to meet the standard is not worth it. Hence, with more standards within a single labour market and with greater mobility of workers across exam board catchments, the earnings effect of a given standard will be lowered. Thus, it is less likely that an optimal standard will emerge where there are many atomistic exam boards; instead a single national standard is likely to be more efficient. This national standard need not be government-run: Liebowitz and Margolis (1990, 1994) give economy-wide evidence, albeit not specifically on education, that efficient standards can emerge within market frameworks. The greater the labour market, however, the lower the likelihood that a binary standard (with one national exam board) will convey sufficient information for sorting workers.

Finally, Costrell (1994) argues that such standard setting may be an improvement on a system which gives perfect information about students' performances. Under a perfect information system, it is likely both that students at the minimum ability level would be willing to make at least some effort and that students near the top would make lots of effort. However, many students may reluctantly meet an imposed standard, even though under a perfect information system they would probably supply less effort. The relative efficacy of the systems depends on the distribution of abilities and the returns to student effort. It may be that the optimal standard induces more effort, such as to outweigh the losses in efficiency in sorting workers. Politically, though, moves to a perfect information system may be less contentious because setting the standard in effect defines the winners and losers from the education system (Costrell, 1997). However, it is unlikely that binary credentials will either be sufficiently discriminating of capability to perform work tasks or be sufficiently motivating to students of heterogeneous abilities.

Of key interest is how the value function of the social planner influences standards, worker productivity and so income levels. If standards are set high, then this will raise wages for those who meet the standard. If this higher standard leaves the wages of those who fail to meet the grade unchanged, then it will increase inequality. So although a low standard would be more equal and hence would be preferred by egalitarian planners, it would reduce aggregate income. This is an egalitarianism–efficiency trade-off. Yet Betts's (1998b) model suggests instead that higher standards might emerge if the goal is in fact to reduce inequality. Because workers differ in abilities, raised standards will increase the earnings not only of the most able but also of the least able. The earnings of the able group will be higher because they have supplied more effort and met the standard. The earnings of those who do not meet the standard should also increase because firms realise that their average quality has risen, now including some individuals who would have passed if the standard had been lower. This justifies higher wage offers.   This argument suggests that the setting of standards should not focus only on the marginal student, whose performance is close to the standard, but also on students who are clearly above or below that standard.

4.3   COST AND REVENUE FUNCTIONS

4.3.1   Cost Functions

The cost function represents one embodiment of the technology facing an education enterprise.   Such functions are useful for identifying where expansion is possible and whether education is a natural monopoly, that is, with a continuously downward sloping average cost curve at current demand levels.   Alternatively, if marginal cost is less than average cost (equal to marginal and average revenues), then efficiency may be improved through expansion of student numbers.   As well, cost function analysis reveals whether universities cross-subsidise research at the expense of teaching, or whether schools cross-subsidise over or under school-leaving age pupils. (Such cross-subsidy may be hard to identify: it would occur if a provider could enter and offer education to one of the age groups at a 'profit'; yet provider entry in education markets is often regulated.)

A simple version of the cost function is the sum of variable costs VC dependent on student numbers Q – rather than achievement or the quality of performance – plus fixed costs FC:

$$TC = VC(Q) + FC \qquad (4.10)$$

Such a function excludes parental and peer inputs as these are external to the education provider.   More problematically, such cost functions assume that provision is homogeneous, without adjusting for differences in the quality of outcomes.

A number of stylised facts have been amassed about the costs of education (Tsang, 1988).   First, one of the main determinants of per-pupil cost is likely to be the staff–student ratio.   This ratio serves as a proxy for the education technology, albeit a process measure rather than a measure of performance.   This staff–student ratio may also be used as a measure of resources, although this is only valid if other expenditures are not adjusted. So the average class size for schooling in the OECD in the 1990s is approximately 10–20, being slightly higher in primary schools and lower in secondary schools (DfEE/OFSTED, 1998; Bishop, 1996a), but lower again in tertiary and higher education institutions (around 10–15).   This in part explains the greater per-student costs in higher education over secondary and primary education (although greater use of physical capital is also salient).

Second, per-student costs will depend on the characteristics of what is taught, both the curriculum and the pedagogy. Subject differences are evident – in UK universities science and medicine courses are approximately 8 times more costly than humanities (HEFCE, 1995) and vocational courses are typically more expensive than academic equivalent ones. Costs are typically lower for the more able, although this is usually confounded by the greater investment in their education and by the fact that more selective institutions tend to be more efficient. Further, the mode of delivery affects the shape of the cost curve: distance-learning has high fixed costs and is therefore most sensitive to per-pupil enrolment; out-of-hours education typically has high pupil–teacher ratios and is therefore lower cost.

Third, capacity and utilisation rates will influence the cost function – evidence on higher costs in rural schools, particularly in developing countries, and on drop-out rates may be cited here. Both in the UK and the US, per-student expenditure is higher in inner-city areas, principally because of declining student rolls and part-historical funding (Barrow, 1991; Hoxby, 1996b). Relatedly, fixed costs may be relatively high if the education provider has to generate its own curriculum and assessment materials: Varian and Shapiro (1999) argue that information material is generally 'expensive to produce, but cheap to reproduce'; this suggests that the marginal cost and average cost of generating instruction materials (and setting curricula) are downward sloping for a large scale beyond the production of the initial units.

More generally, the unitised production of education (in classes) suggests that step-costs may be important. To illustrate, Winkler's (1984, 142–143) cost function is depicted in Figure 4.4. With capital facilities costs of R, the average recurrent cost function ARC yields a downward sloping curve towards average variable costs. The sawtooth cost function is the marginal cost MC function from expanding enrolment. Generally, these are all downward sloping in enrolment, but at certain step enrolment levels (E_a, E_b) new facilities have to be provided. Up to those steps, marginal cost is falling. At points E_1 and E_2, therefore, 'profits' are made equal to the difference between tuition charges and marginal cost plus capital charges. As enrolment continues to expand, average variable cost AVC diverges from marginal cost.

Conventionally, the average cost curve should initially fall, because of declining fixed costs, but then rise because of increasing average variable costs. Most investigations do show a U-shaped cost curve: Tsang (1988, 209) cites a range of studies; Koshal and Koshal (1995, 777) graph U-shaped cost curves in higher education in the US. This evidence suggests that diseconomies of scale are reached at some point, although these diseconomies may be forestalled by resource reallocation, better utilisation or the introduction of new technologies (that is, long run cost curves will be lower per unit of output).

Figure 4.4   Cost Functions in Education

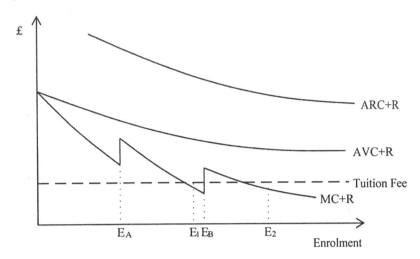

However, as student numbers increase, marginal cost rather than average cost is critical because the former must be equated to marginal revenue to determine whether expansion is efficient.   Assuming student numbers increase by 500, four options would need to be evaluated: [$MC_{500 \text{ in } A}$], that is, the cost of adding 500 students to school A; [$MC_{500 \text{ in } B}$], the cost of adding 500 students to school B; [MC_{500}], the cost of creating a school for 500 students; and, finally, the marginal cost of mixing the students across the schools.   The optimal solution of course depends on the shapes of the respective cost functions, assuming homogeneous outcomes from provision (Verry, 1987).

Expansion may be considered in terms of either synergies of education production across its multi-products or school capacities.   Alternatively, there may be gains from specialisation, as in single-sex schools, specialist colleges or age-banded schools.   The synergy effect may be exemplified in a university where costs are a function of teaching T and research R (for a given teaching–research student ratio):

$$TC = \alpha_0 + \alpha_1 T + \alpha_2 R - \alpha_3 T^{0.5} R^{0.5} \tag{4.11}$$

$$\partial TC/\partial T = MC_T = \alpha_1 - 0.5\alpha_3 (R/T)^{0.5} \tag{4.12}$$

$$\partial TC/\partial R = MC_R = \alpha_2 - 0.5\alpha_3 (T/R)^{0.5} \tag{4.13}$$

Here the marginal cost of teaching, given in equation (4.12), is a positive amount α_1 minus an amount which depends on the ratio of research to teaching (Verry, 1987).

Regarding capacity effects, Bradley and Taylor's (1998b) description of the school cost function illustrates their importance:

$$C_i = C(CUR, CAP, Z_i) \qquad (4.14)$$

Here CUR represents the capacity utilisation rate and CAP the actual pupil capacity (along with other possible factors counted by Z), analogous to the step function in Figure 4.4. A school's CUR is an indicator of changes in student numbers in the short run, while CAP measures the influence of school size on unit costs. Hence, for a given level of pupil capacity, more pupils (greater CUR) mean lower unit costs, since fixed costs are being spread over more pupils. For any given capacity utilisation, schools with a larger pupil capacity (greater CAP) will have lower unit costs because of economies of scale. Looking across 3000 UK secondary schools, Bradley and Taylor find a negative non-linear relationship between unit costs and (a) school size and (b) each school's capacity utilisation rate, with more than 50% of all unfilled school places in schools with under 80% of the average pupil capacity. Although this evidence suggests small schools with low utilisation rates are the main target for school closures, the CAP rates are likely to be strongly influenced by demographic changes. The basic cost function shows that short run flexibility arises from enrolling extra students (rather than adjusting the capital–labour mix).

4.3.2   Revenue Sources with Customer-input Technology

Revenues for education enterprises may take a number of forms. In a market, revenues might be expected simply to be per-student tuition fee prices. But if education is state-funded, revenues are fixed subsidies or transfers calculated either historically or per-student or some combination thereof (different modes of funding are discussed in Chapter 8). However, these government subventions do not completely determine the revenue functions of education providers. More importantly, they do not capture the optimisation goal of schools as represented in equation (4.2), where education enterprises must generate achievement. This is because a key input to education may not be accurately priced through government subsidies. This input is student ability and a number of models of education provision have been developed which explicitly acknowledge the key role of this input. The models for higher education are considered first, followed by Epple and Romano's (1998) model of peer effects in public and private schooling.

Economic models, particularly those stressing competitive pricing and allocative efficiency, must take account of the particular fact that the customers, that is, students, are also inputs into the education process. Education enterprises use what Rothschild and White (1995) have labelled 'customer–input' technologies. Hence, from the perspective of the institution, output-linked pricing is not straightforward; education resembles a joint venture between students and teachers more than it resembles a simple traded service or good. In terms of equations (4.1) and (4.2), the production function for education, it is student effort which is critical to maximising achievement or human capital. With such joint-venture technologies, Rothschild and White (1995) model the aim of an enterprise such as a university as the allocation of the (fixed) number of students Q_n in a way which maximises human capital across students and institutional types:

$$\text{maximise } \sum_{t=1}^{T}\sum_{n=1}^{N} H_n^t - \sum_{t=1}^{T} R^t \qquad (4.15)$$

$$\text{subject to } R^t = G^t(s_1^t, \ldots s_N^t; H_1^t, \ldots H_N^t), t = 1, \ldots T$$

$$\sum_{t=1}^{T} s_n^t = Q_n, n = 1, \ldots N$$

Here R^t is the amount of general resources used for a given technology t, where technologies differentiate universities; the number of students of type n attending university t is given by s_n^t ; and H_n^t is the aggregate amount of human capital of type n produced by university t. The general resources depend on student inputs and human capital and the production function G^t is likely to be positively enhanced by H^t. There are two pertinent first order conditions for a maximum output (for derivation, see Rothschild and White, 1995). First, the optimal allocation of students occurs where the marginal rate of substitution of students of type n against the general human capital input is equivalent at all universities that such students attend. Second, when produced at a given university, each type of human capital should be utilised up to the point where its marginal cost is equal to marginal product (which is measured here in nominal money terms). Arnott and Rowse (1987) develop a similar set of conditions for schooling: both human capital and students are inputs; standard efficiency conditions mandate that they should be allocated across education providers – and classes within providers – where they augment outcomes to the greatest extent.

Modelling the generation of human capital from the perspective of the university, if prices across students and technologies are p_n^t then profits will be:

$$\pi^t = \sum_{n=1}^{N} p_n^t s_n^t - R^t \qquad (4.16)$$

Under standard competitive market assumptions and constant returns to scale, Rothschild and White (1995, 579) establish that profit-seeking universities will generate an optimal outcome:

$$p_n^t = \hat{H}_n^t \Big/ \hat{s}_n^t - \hat{w}_n \qquad (4.17)$$

Each student pays p_n^t, receives human capital of $\hat{H}_n^t / \hat{s}_n^t$ and $\hat{w}_n$ is the net gain (with obvious analogies to the rate of return to education). If students can choose universities and have no exogenously driven preferences across technologies, these prices should reflect zero profit for the university (hence satisfying standard efficiency conditions). Universities must choose the amounts of human capital to minimise the function G^t such that its total is equal to the optimal amount, that is, the amount where the marginal product of human capital equals its marginal cost.

Because human capital cannot be traded directly, education is offered where one of the inputs – the student – pays to be included in the production of human capital. Universities are in effect putting a positive price on student inputs into the production process. More desirable students are simply those who are better as inputs at generating the output of human capital. Hence they should get a better wage or larger financial scholarship, even though they may still make net tuition payments to their university. This model shows how universities differ across technologies, may admit different mixes of students, give different levels of human capital and charge different prices. Even within a given university, students of different types may be charged different prices and may receive different amounts of human capital. The net gains of individual students depend on their marginal productivities in generating human capital and their marginal costs to the institution they attend.

Although plausible as a model for the allocation and pricing of student inputs, this technology may not be fully applied across many universities. On pricing, universities do seem to offer uniform prices for degrees which seem very different in marginal cost (for example, the uniform pricing across broad subject groups such as sciences). This may in part be explained in terms of courses being priced as an open menu (students may choose any course) in the US and by government mandate for European countries such as the UK. Nevertheless, there is a positive correlation between the cost of a course and student entry grades, suggesting that more able students are contributing more as inputs and require greater capital outlays. Market clearing prices might also be difficult to set if universities want a large pool of applicants from which they can select. The first round of pricing may therefore involve 'underpricing' to get a selection of possible undergraduates; net fees are then offered in subsequent pricing rounds. Nevertheless, if there is heterogeneity across students and across optimal technologies, such models have important implications for higher education systems where provision and funding are standardised.[11] Such standardised providers may fail to appropriately price human capital, leading to divergence from the optimal investment path.

Winston (1999) has extended the optimisation constraint for education providers facing a customer-input technology and so illustrated how education providers obtain revenues. Most education providers are not profit-maximisers: they declare zero dividends and are not taken over in capital markets, which is likely to affect the value of their physical assets. The purpose of non-profit, government-run systems is that 'the non-distribution constraint serves to soften the incentive that a for-profit supplier has to take advantage of the partially informed buyer [student]' (Winston, 1999, 15). This 'softening' has its problems and cannot be pushed too far: market pressures may mean teachers, seeing high salaries in private sector occupations, push for higher wages with knock-on effects on the quality of the education; and there may still be substantial non-pecuniary rents within the enterprise to bargain over. Perhaps workers in education institutions care about the outcomes of the goods they make, whereas for-profit firms care only about the profits they make. The maximand is 'pursuit of excellence' or 'prestige', rather than profit, because workers share the 'ideological' objectives of the non-profit firm. (One may be sceptical that workers in for-profit firms do not care about the standard of their product; the difference may be one of degree rather than kind.)

Nevertheless, such non-profit enterprises face a non-distribution constraint and so although they can earn 'profits', that is, revenues can exceed expenditures, there is no one to whom the profits can then be allocated. Revenues cannot, therefore, exceed costs for a long time, although the enterprise may redistribute incomes within the non-profit agency into activities which enhance the privileges of its workers (in this respect this model is similar to 'prestige-maximisation' models of higher education). Examples of this might be graduate student teaching at universities or smaller group sizes in schools.

For the education provider, Winston (1999) renders the optimisation constraint as:

$$pr + dr = c + re + d \qquad (4.18)$$

Priced revenue plus donative revenue (pr, dr) equals costs plus retained earnings and dividends (c, re, d). For a non-profit organisation, d is zero; but for a profit-maximising organisation donative revenue dr is zero. Non-profit schools and universities obtain such donative revenues from governments, firms, alumni, parent–teacher associations and charitable organisations (as well as priced revenues from commercial activities). These revenues accrue because funders and donors share the aims of the enterprise and so non-profit enterprises may seek to publicise and encourage adoption of these aims. In receipt of donative revenue, universities can then subsidise their actual customers (students). Taking alumni donations as an example, these can either be considered as a simple subsidy between generations or as a 'deferred payment' for tuition (an intertemporal subsidy); in the latter case, the institution is bearing some of the risk of the human capital investment during the period of study which it recoups when students begin earning (Harbaugh, 1998).

To recap, although the student as customer pays its higher education institution a tuition fee, the student as input is paid a wage – the difference is the net tuition fee and this ultimately determines enrolment. Hence there are market-clearing prices for outcomes such as degrees, varying across education enterprises, and market-clearing prices for student inputs, varying across students' ability. These variations force universities to invest heavily in identifying student quality and make enrolment decisions a critical element in education provision. As more resource-rich institutions can offer greater subsidies (higher wages), this causes the private individual students' returns to education to diverge from the amount which the higher education institution can appropriate – unless donative revenues come only from these students later on as alumni – and this divergence may rise with prior ability. High achieving universities enrol good inputs and so do not recoup much rent from these individuals. A positive feedback effect then arises as students choose universities with other good students, further boosting donative revenues. Such a process defines the particular characteristics of such enterprises, distinguishing between universities and so influencing hierarchies and relative performances. The effects are likely to vary across country, depending on the heterogeneity of incomes, abilities and sources of funding. For example, where the student cohort is relatively homogeneous, as in the UK, education providers are less likely to offer scholarships. And in the UK higher education sector, most revenues for education are obtained from the state, although alternative streams of revenue are growing in significance.[12] Given its importance in influencing incomes, the pricing of human capital appears to be a critical variable against which to assess the efficiency of education systems.

So student types and institutional technologies are codetermined: resource-rich higher education institutions can use lower grade faculty to teach undergraduate programmes, for example, exploiting the excellent peer group effects among the students.   Also, because higher education institutions differ in terms of their student quality input, they allocate resources in different ways, ones which economise on scarce student quality. For example, high quality students of similar ages tend to be put together in residential areas or in small classes; and it may be more efficient for students to choose their own peer groups for studying (within tutorial systems).   For colleges which cannot easily augment demand, increased reliance on distance-learning, and enrolment of non-traditional students may be more appropriate.   Differences in donative wealth may – Winston (1999) contends – swamp differences in technical efficiency, muting competitive pressures except over the long term; Tight's (1996) description of 16 groupings for UK higher education institutions, which finds reasonably stable groupings over time, may be interpreted in this light.   The positional rankings of the institutions can therefore remain very stable.   Consequently, competitive pressures may be dampened and creative destruction less of a feature in education markets.   Finally, this model also suggests that full allocation of resources based on student ability (as perhaps may be obtained through the market) may polarise the allocation of education resources still further.   Together, these arguments suggest that an important equity–efficiency trade-off has to be resolved.

A similar approach to modelling student input has been applied to schooling, by Epple and Romano (1998).   In their model, two factors are important: school students differ in ability; and the demand for education also depends on parental (household) income.   The schooling sector is composed of public sector (state) providers and private schools, where these schools are distinguished by the mean ability of their student enrolments. Critically, state schools put a uniform (zero) price on peer effects.   In neglecting to 'price' this mean ability effect and in establishing the number of schools which simply minimise unit costs, state schools are likely to be input-choice inefficient.   In contrast, private schools cultivate a market in peer inputs such that low-ability, high-income students cross-subsidise low-income, high-ability students.   For private schools, a profit function is necessary as such schools seek to maximise revenue over costs:

$$\text{maximise } \pi = p_i(b, y)\alpha_i(b, y) - VC(Q_i) - FC \qquad (4.19)$$

Here $p_i(b, y)$ is the amount of tuition payable to enter school i, where b is an individual student's ability and y is the household income; $\alpha_i(b, y)$ is the proportion of students of ability type b and household income y that enter school i; $VC(Q_i)$ is variable costs for Q students and FC are the fixed costs. Private providers will set optimal tuition fees $p_i(b, y, \theta_i)^*$, where θ_i is the mean ability of the school, and offer schooling provision if resulting profits are non-zero. State schools are financed through taxation and charge tuition $p_0(b, y)$, that is, with no mean ability parameter.

Enrolment patterns across the proportions $\alpha_i(b, y)$ can be derived, where students enrol in a private school up to the point where the marginal revenue equals marginal cost. The marginal revenue is the tuition fee, but marginal cost depends not only on the rate of change of variable cost but also on the externality effects generated through the student peer group. This externality will be a function of the difference between mean school ability θ and individual student ability b. Critically, the admission of a student j with below mean ability is costly. Such an admission imposes externalities on other students and so forces the school to reduce the tuition fee to all its students. These pricing effects can be represented thus:

$$\text{if } b_j < \theta_i, \ \partial p_i / \partial b_j < 0 \tag{4.20}$$

$$\text{if } b_j > \theta_i, \ \partial p_i / \partial b_j > 0 \tag{4.21}$$

Epple and Romano's (1998) model yields several important results and predictions. First, the mix between state and private schooling can be evaluated. Compared to state schooling, an entirely private schooling system is likely to yield an optimal allocation of students. But it need not yield an optimal number of schools because private schools make entry decisions which will have adverse cost implications for other schools (in taking away their brightest students). A mixed schooling system, however, may have sub-optimal numbers of schools and sub-optimal allocations of students, because the array of provision demand cannot be sufficiently discriminating with respect to the distributions of student ability and household income. Second, a hierarchy of schools is likely to emerge where mean ability is lowest in state schools and such mean ability is increasing in private schools. This hierarchy arises because high-income households are willing to pay for private schooling and it is efficient for them to cross-subsidise higher ability students and so attract them out of the state schools. Third, within each private school there should be a negative correlation between household income and student ability. Tuition prices should be declining in ability levels, reflecting the greater contribution to the school's profit function. Finally, a voucher system, which encourages students to transfer to schools which value them the most, should lower the real price of private schooling. In turn, this may raise the demand and so reduce the amount of state schooling ultimately to zero.

Finally, these models do generate powerful predictions about efficiency but they do require the assumption that it is appropriate for student quality to be a tradeable input. This assumption may or may not be acceptable to those with a more egalitarian approach to education systems.

4.4   ISSUES AND CONCLUSIONS

In this chapter, the basic production function for education has been described, both from the perspective of the individual and the education provider. This function should include a number of inputs which are not priced and particular attention should be paid to the roles of students – especially their effort levels – in the production of education.

As well as looking at atomistic production of education (by individuals or schools), the economics of standards has also been developed. This reflects the fact that schools both offer provision which meets certain thresholds of learning and set those thresholds of learning. Costrell's (1994) models of standards indicate the importance of the trade-off between absolute numbers of students completing their education and the academic levels these students reach. Such models are useful in that they highlight the multi-product nature of schools and the need to identify the marginal rate of transformation between academic performance and graduate numbers. However, no automatic conclusion emerges as to how to set an optimal standard.

Returning to the notion of technologies, cost functions for education have been considered. These represent a useful shorthand for education technologies, emphasising the teacher–pupil ratio and the capacities of education providers. The synergies between the costs for research and teaching may be explored, along with size effects.

In looking at the roles of students, Rothschild and White's (1995) model has been drawn on, specifically the use of students themselves as generators of human capital. This yields several efficiency conditions: at the optimum, resource expenditure on education should have the same effect whichever class it is invested in and the net value of students across ability levels should be equivalent across classes or across schools. Consequently, customer-input technology predicts that universities will search hard for good quality inputs and implement a pricing mechanism and a technology of education which reward such quality. With differing levels of donative resources, universities can then offer subsidies and generate strong positive feedback. This model leads on to the description of education providers as partly paying students for education and charging them a net tuition fee. The model also allows the market for education to be described and hierarchies of education providers to be stylised. Relatedly, Epple and Romano's (1998) model incorporates peer-input pricing within the school sector.

More generally, such production function models are useful to the extent that they shed light on the technical and allocative efficiency of education providers. One direct test of such internal efficiency would be if institutions with more input resources produced improved educational outcomes, that is, if there are positive resource effects.

Applied to any Western economy, the hypothesis of positive resource effects on education outcomes is important for a number of reasons. First, education is a large proportion of government spending, with the possibility of a spiral of rising costs and no guarantees of improvements in performance. Second, the distribution of resources varies across education institutions; such institutions differ widely in quality yet little concrete is known about the role of resource deployment or the potential consequences of any resource redistribution. Third, the distribution of funding for education may influence equity, with substantial social consequences. Finally, with significant changes in the amount of resource going to education, rates of return to specific educational resources need to be assessed. Based on these imperatives, empirical work is necessary on how education is produced so that spending on education inputs can be directed to the resource areas which yield the highest return. Crucially, however, these areas need to be identified. So far, simple models of how education is produced have been discussed, along with probable cost and revenue functions. With these models in mind, therefore, the evidence on the production function for education is surveyed in the next chapter.

5. Evidence on Education Enterprises

5.1 RESOURCE EFFECTS

This chapter draws on the model of the education production function to consider the evidence on how education enterprises perform. From the preceding discussions of efficiency and the education production function, a plausible assumption is that more resources would raise achievement, that is, there would be substantial evidence of 'positive resource effects' ($\partial A/\partial R >$ 0 across all student groups). This chapter considers whether or not this is the case, which then leads on to a discussion of how resources might be allocated within education systems and how education providers might be organised.

Section 5.2 explores three ways in which resource effects have been examined: in terms of academic achievement, earnings and other process and performance measures. A substantial investigation has been made into this in the economics literature and the results here are not comforting. This bulwark of evidence, marshalled principally by Hanushek (1986, 1995) for US schooling, and spanning a range of outcomes, suggests that resources 'do not matter' much to absolute outcomes and so internal efficiency. Since this evidence is controversial (and seems contrary to parental behaviour in their choices of schools), the discussion here begins with what has been reported. Subsequent sections examine the validity of that evidence and the inferences which can be drawn from it. Explanations may be sought either in methodological or empirical critiques and these are described in Section 5.3. Particularly, customer-input technology would predict reasonable variation in the performances of education providers, as they target different market segments. An additional area of work is on scale effects in education, that is, whether schools are the most efficient size and whether provision is optimally combined or could be expanded. Here the multi-product nature of education enterprises is emphasised and more consistent evidence is available. The calculation and estimates of optimal school size and economies of scale and scope are considered in Section 5.4, along with the costs of non-completion by students. In the final section, an overview is given, looking back across the theory and evidence of internal efficiency from this and the previous chapter, and looking forward to the following chapter, where input-choice efficiency is considered.

5.2 EVIDENCE ON RESOURCE EFFECTS

5.2.1 Resources and Academic Achievement

For the resources to academic achievement link in schools, Hanushek's (1986, 1162) comprehensive survey noted 'no strong or systematic relationship between school expenditures and student performance'. In a more recent review, Hanushek et al. (1996, 106) summarise the evidence as yielding 'no consistent or systematic relationship between achievement and either pupil–teacher ratios, teacher salaries, years of teacher schooling, years of teacher experience or per-student expenditure'. One recent example is that of Lamdin (1995), who uses data from 107 Baltimore schools and finds no positive resource effect for either reading or maths scores.

Table 5.1 Effects of Teacher–Pupil Ratio and Expenditure Per-pupil on Student Performance

| | Statistical significance of the effect on student performance (%) | | | |
	+	-	Insig.	N
Effect of teacher–pupil ratio				
Local	13	14	73	266
State	64	0	36	11
Effect of per-pupil expenditures				
Local	17	7	76	135
State	64	4	32	28

Source: Hanushek et al. (1996, 118)

More comprehensively, Table 5.1 reproduces a summary of 277 separate estimates of the significance of school teacher–pupil ratios and per-pupil expenditures on student performance from Hanushek et al. (1996). Notably at the local school level, less than one-fifth of studies yielded a statistically significant positive relationship between student performance and either teacher–pupil ratios or per-pupil expenditures; most were insignificant. Some US writers have found a positive link between resources and academic outcomes (Hedges et al., 1994; Verstegen and King, 1998). Yet the counter-intuitive supposition – that resource-rich schools do not produce better education – is only infrequently rejected.

Other evidence suggests schools may use resource amounts in ways which compress or offset differences in technologies. Bigger classes may adversely affect outcomes, but only when account is taken of class size policies of schools (Akerhielm, 1995). Schools may set class sizes optimally, given their knowledge of how the pupils will interact. Plausibly, more experimental evidence, which controls for such endogeneity, yields positive resource effects. Angrist and Lavy (1999) use imposed upper limits on class size in Israeli schools to test for the effects of class size on school performance; they find effect sizes of 0.18 standard deviations with larger classes generating inferior outcomes. Krueger (1999) reports on the positive effects of lower class size from the randomised experiment of the Tennessee STAR project. He finds both immediate effects as pupils enter a small class and cumulative effects for each year that they remain in such classes. For the UK and using detailed longitudinal data, Dolton and Vignoles (1998) produce the expected link with lower pupil–teacher ratios related to better academic outcomes.

However, class size differences may not reflect different resource amounts, but instead different factor usage. A lower pupil–teacher ratio may be correlated with poorer physical resources across a school. So class size is only a proxy for total resource levels. Even for the positive findings, moreover, reducing class size appears to be a very expensive way of raising outcomes. Looking at the educational and resource significance of the statistical significance of the Tennessee STAR project, Prais (1996) equates the difference in outcome for the pupils in smaller classes to three extra days of teaching. These gains could, it may be argued, be much more cost-effectively obtained through alternative education technologies.

A more general concern is the difficulties in using academic scores as outcome measures. The first is a general concern that the measures of learning utilised are sufficiently accurate or valid. In reference to the UK system, for example, further education colleges offer a variety of programmes from A-levels to GNVQs, as well as enrichment services which may be valued separately. Universities also offer an educational experience which extends beyond examinations and these cannot easily be concatenated into a single outcome measure. Value-added academic scores should be used, to take account of family background and intake characteristics, and these are not uncontentiously modelled (for schools, see Goldstein and Spiegelhalter, 1996). If schools are differentially effective (by gender, for example), point estimates of outcomes at a school level may be invalid (particularly for judgements about equity). Also, academic scores may not increase proportionately with performance but may be expressed in relation to the whole cohort's performance (for example, some credentials are awarded to a fixed percentage of all enrolments), obscuring any improvements over time. Time-series comparisons may be further impaired by legislative or curricula changes to the awards conferred for a given academic performance. Finally, because many educational institutions receive more funding if they have higher academic outcomes, a positive relationship between resources and educational standards might evolve automatically, albeit with a lag.

5.2.2   Resources and Individual Earnings

An alternative outcome measure to academic achievement may be the future earnings of students. This outcome may be superior to academic scores, as it has greater implications for individuals' well-being over the longer term (Betts, 1996c) and is logically in keeping with the rate of return approach in Chapter 2. If education contributes to economic growth, then higher earnings from greater investments in education and human capital may also be a policy target. Importantly for vocational or post-compulsory education, many programmes are fee-paying: the participants may therefore expect the education to translate directly into higher earnings.

For the resources to earnings link, and holding family background constant, positive US findings have emerged from Card and Krueger (1992); Griffin and Ganderton (1996); and, in summary, Verstegen and King (1998). Comparing siblings, Altonji and Dunn (1996b) find positive effects from education quality (through increased teacher pay) on students' wages. In Card and Krueger's (1992) large scale mapping of resource effects from cohorts across 1930–60, decreasing the pupil–teacher ratio adds about 1% to the rate of return (earnings premia). Subsequently, Card and Krueger (1996, 133) estimate a 10% increase in school spending to be associated with a 1–2% increase in earnings annually.

Again, though, there is counter-evidence, particularly over the cost-effectiveness of greater investments in education quality. Figlio (1999) uses a translog production function to estimate the effects of differences in resources on earnings (finding no resource effect with the standard Cobb–Douglas functional form). Various resource measures are tested, with no effect either from greater instructional hours per year or from higher percentages of teachers with MA degrees. Although pupil–teacher ratios and teacher starting salaries are found to have a statistically significant effect on earnings, the effects of extra resources are again not substantively large. Similarly, for Grogger (1996), school expenditure has only a small effect on earnings; Betts (1995, 1996c) finds neither the teacher–pupil ratio, nor relative teacher salaries nor teacher educational attainment to have a positive effect on earnings, as well as no significant relationship for cohorts after the 1960s. For the UK, Dolton and Vignoles (1998) give similarly null results: additional resources either at the level of the classroom, school or education authority do not lead to higher earnings. Certainly the link between earnings and increased per-pupil expenditures cannot be presumed to be positive; incremental investments may not therefore pass a cost–benefit test.

Furthermore, even if there is a positive link between more resources in the intensive margin and outcomes, the specific components of expenditure which substantiate this link have not been found, allowing specific investment areas to be identified. A number of alternative ways of testing this link have been developed; two examples for post-compulsory education are given below.

As noted in discussions of the human capital model, few rate of return studies postulate a relationship to particular resources deployed at education enterprises, but there is some indirect evidence. For higher education institutions, James et al. (1989, 249) tested for the effects of college quality on earnings, concluding that 'measured college effects are small, explaining 1–2% of the variance in earnings' and that, notably, the log of general per-student expenditure is not significant and sometimes has a negative sign. There is evidence of a positive relationship between earnings and college characteristics, such as tuition costs; the size and quality; individual student performance, as measured by on-entry SAT scores (Pascarella et al., 1992; Smart, 1988; Datcher Loury and Garman, 1995). Also, Eide and Showalter (1998) show that attendance at better colleges is associated with progression to higher degrees. Perhaps the consistent finding of a subject of study influence on salary (Dolton et al., 1990; Hecker, 1998; James et al., 1989) is in part a resource effect, although the differing curriculum content across subjects may generate different skills (Grogger and Eide, 1995, 300).

Belfield and Fielding (2000) investigate the production function relationship between educational resources and labour market outcomes, testing for a significant positive relationship with data on 8097 graduates (class of 1990) from 27 UK institutions. Despite a nationally determined higher education sector in the UK, there is reasonable inter-institutional variation in the amounts of resource allocated across students and simple per-year expenditures are positively correlated with earnings. In order to identify more precisely whether such correlations reflect actual resource effects, however, a per-individual effect and a per-institution effect need to be identified. From this breakdown, the proportion of the per-institution effect attributable to differences in resource levels (rather than differences in mission, say) can be isolated. This approach recognises that individuals are clustered within institutions which may themselves have particular fixed effects and that most of the variation in earnings will be attributable to the students' characteristics (as evinced in data on intra-class correlation coefficients in schools across ten countries, Ross and Levacic, 1999, 103). Belfield and Fielding (2000) find the variation between individuals, explaining 10–13% of the total variation in earnings, is much greater than the variation between institutions, that is, there is much greater difference across individuals than is caused by particular institutions. However, the results support the broadly neutral conclusion regarding the effect of resources on outcomes. There is limited statistical evidence that increased resources explain much of the per-institution effect on earnings, and any effect appears to be substantively small.

A second example is Kang and Bishop's (1989) use of the US High School and Beyond survey. Here, the investigation is of the types of courses that students should take – academic, vocational or general courses – rather than the amount of resource applied to each student. This reflects the fact that the curricula and amounts of resource are likely to be interdependent. Basic tabulations show vocational courses – which are likely to be the higher cost courses – positively related to labour market outcomes, with the earnings effect of academic courses having an inverse U-shape. Using the production function model, Kang and Bishop (1989, 137) regress labour market earnings and employment on the numbers of vocational and academic courses taken, controlling *inter alia* for grades and socio-economic status. The key tests are for the interactions between academic and vocational education and whether or not there are diminishing returns to particular compositions of course uptake.

The marginal return from an additional course is the partial derivative of earnings with respect to course enrolment:

$$\partial Y/\partial ACAD = \alpha + \beta \Sigma ACAD + \delta \Sigma VOC \qquad (5.1)$$

Here ACAD and VOC represent academic and vocational courses taken and Y is earnings. If β is negative, there are decreasing returns to academic courses. If δ is positive, vocational and academic courses are complements (the marginal effect of academic course uptake increases if vocational course uptake is increased); if δ is negative, they are substitutes. Generally, Kang and Bishop find complementarity between the two types of course, although the marginal returns are greatest for vocational courses. Hence students should mix their courses between vocational and academic; and the share of vocational courses taken (approximately one quarter of the total number taken) is sub-optimal in that fewer academic courses should be taken. Kang and Bishop's (1989) evidence has since been updated by Mane (1999), who again finds vocational courses to have a positive impact, and greater than that of academic courses. Such evidence, indicating the differential impact of curricula, may also be (indirectly) supportive of resource effects in education provision.

5.2.3   Resources and Performance

A third outcome to consider is an evaluation of an education provider's performance, such as that from student satisfaction scores or inspection evidence. (Another related measure of performance is Black's, 1999, usage of implicit evaluations from higher property prices near good schools in the US.) More commonly, student satisfaction scores may capture many of the unobservable, expected life-cycle gains from learning.   However, expectations of students are very diverse (and adjusting for these may be complex); students only experience one education provision, are unlikely to know what educational resources they ought to be receiving and will find it difficult to make an appropriate comparative judgement. Often satisfaction questionnaires are issued during education programmes, rather than at the end or after the education has been applied in the workplace. Finally, if education assessments sort more able students from less able ones, the positive satisfaction of students who pass may be counterbalanced by the dissatisfaction of those who fail. Student assessments therefore appear to be only cautiously valid proxies for the efficiency or cost-effectiveness of education provision.

Alternatively, the performance of the institution as measured by government inspection scores may be an outcome.   In the UK, the substantial commitment to school inspections yields information about educational outcomes, which can then be related to resource levels.   This inspection information may therefore embody all the goals of a school, that is, its objective function. Looking specifically at school inspections, but without adjusting for value-added, Levacic and Glover (1998) find unit costs are not a significant influence on inspection grades (only a free schools meals parameter, representing socio-economic effects, is influential). Belfield and Thomas (2000) consider further education college inspection scores as outcome variables, finding strong evidence for economies of size – colleges with better grades are those with higher total levels of expenditure – but little evidence for higher per-student expenditures translating into superior inspection grades. Again, evidence of positive unit resource effects is not clear.

Finally, most of the above evidence has been derived using regression analysis. Instead, evidence from data envelopment analysis may be used to explore differences in efficiency across education providers. This method has been applied across the education sectors, but the evidence here relates to schooling (for higher education, see Johnes and Johnes, 1995a; Johnes,

1999). For the UK, Bradley et al. (1998) estimate how efficient secondary schools are, assuming they are optimising exam performance along with attendance rates (or the inverse, truancy rates). Their evidence of 2254 schools suggest that a number of different ways to be efficient. There is reasonable flux in the most efficient schools over a four-year period and efficiency is not strongly related to overall performance – as per Figure 4.1, schools with poor inputs can be identified as efficient. Also, Noulas and Ketkar (1998) measure efficiency levels for US school districts in New Jersey. They find that average efficiency is 0.81, meaning the current proportion of students can pass to their current performance if approximately 80% of the current inputs are used. This figure is generally consistent: estimates of inefficiency as the ratio of actual costs to predicted costs yields figures of 10–20% of average cost (for secondary schools in the UK, Spain and Norway, see Jesson et al., 1987; Mancebon and Bandres, 1999; and Bonesrønning and Rattsø, 1994).

Plausibly, in that it supports arguments about the importance of complementary home and school inputs, schools in the neediest districts have the lowest average efficiency score and those in the wealthiest districts the highest. Abstracting out such socio-economic characteristics, Noulas and Ketkar (1998) find overall average inefficiency falls by about one-sixth, but the neediest schools still appear less efficient than the wealthier, even as their efficiency is improved by about one-third. Such evidence is important as a way of identifying differential resource use within the system, as well as how much opportunity there is for improvements in efficiency.

5.3 SPECIFICATION OF RESOURCE MODELS

5.3.1 Methodological and Data Issues

Regardless of its substantial evidence base, the preponderance of null-resource effect findings remains surprising. One response is to examine the methodologies used, as there are a number of reasons why the lack of correlation between outcomes and resources may be spurious.

First, the method of research may be incorrect: outcomes cannot be stylised as a function of inputs. At the conceptual level, this seems unlikely; rather, it may be that the form of the relationship is incorrectly modelled or is insufficiently matched to how education enterprises operate. This is possible, given the complexities of customer-input technologies and of separating endogenous from context effects, although it is untested. Second, academic scores may be spuriously variable or the assessment bands may vary insufficiently. Yet these scores are one of the main optimands of schools which might be expected to be aimed for, and certainly are important to pupils and parents. Third, differences in efficiency are critical: institutions with fewer resources may be more efficient, obscuring the fundamental resource effect. However, it seems unlikely that resource effects will be reversed or fully offset by differences in efficiency.

Perhaps these ambiguous results regarding resource effects are not surprising, because all other things are not equal and behaviour in practice ameliorates or counterweights resource differences. First, schools often compensate less able students with more resources, so lower ability pupils may be placed in smaller classes, distorting the effect of class size on education achievement. Yet although the compensatory schemes for disadvantaged pupils do exist, Burtless (1996, 11) argues that the targeting of resources on these groups is not nearly enough to eliminate wide spending differentials across US school districts. Relatedly, school pupils can often choose classes – if good teachers attract more students, then larger class size may represent an offset against higher teacher quality. Second, education is often endogenous as better students may study for longer, with returns diminishing to the mean.   This path-dependence needs to be acknowledged, but may be difficult to model.[13]   Third, and in contrast to the previous concern, better schools may be chosen by higher ability students or those in wealthier families, although this should make the relationship easier to discern if home inputs for these groups are higher too. Yet customer-input technologies and peer-input pricing (as discussed in Chapter 4) may complicate this simple relationship, in that resourcing may be driven by ability rather than income.

A set of other circumstances may be added to these three. One problem may be that school children often move from one institution to another and this may be in response to school quality. For example, Schultz (1999, 84) describes how greater investment in target Kenyan schools pushed up their enrolments, leading academic performance to actually decline in the target schools. Another hindrance is that regional funding for education, coupled with regionally segmented labour markets, may obscure the resource effect (Heckman et al., 1996). As well, credentials awarded at different education levels may induce sheepskin effects depending on the relative supply and demand for different education levels (Heywood, 1994). These sheepskin effects may not be much affected by greater intensive resources because they depend on ranks rather than absolute amounts.   Finally, some individuals may have vocational education beyond schooling which is serving as a substitute for low academic performance.

These concerns may be less troublesome to research on post-compulsory education, however.   Universities, for example, may offer fewer compensatory allocations to poorer students (in delivery of education) and the pedagogy of lecture delivery and independent study may favour more able students.   University education is typically of prescribed length, militating against attenuated returns caused by the more able enrolling for longer. Mobility between higher education institutions is low: graduates from a particular institution are highly likely to have fully studied there. Graduates may be mobile across regions and a nationally clearing market for higher education – as exists in the UK – should reduce labour market segmentation. If graduates all receive a degree with ostensibly uniform signalling quality, sheepskin effects from different levels of credentials may be reduced. Finally, by examining the relationship at the most advanced level of education – the level closest to labour market participation – then concerns over offsetting amounts of vocational training may be lessened. Generally, because of selectivity into university, a lot of the unobserved characteristics of students should have been accounted for. Moreover, the institutional autonomy of higher education institutions and colleges is also favourable to such research on efficiency: universities have reasonable latitude in determining their own mission, more so than state schools; and in the UK further education colleges are incorporated and so can undertake differential resource allocation and employ alternative managerial strategies. Hence, at the conceptual level, resource effects should be more easily identifiable in this sector than for schooling, which is longer and compulsory.

Nevertheless, endogeneity is a key problem in these studies. If one wants to be a high earning lawyer, one needs to obtain a resource-intensive education beforehand; Card and Krueger (1996, 112), for example, find much stronger effects on earnings of additional school spending and a lower pupil–teacher ratio when occupational effects are removed. All current work variables may be sensitive to this issue as these status variables are contextual outcomes, not inputs. Another problem may be multi-collinearity between college choice and family background (James et al., 1989). Although this is likely to bias the resource effect upward, ordinary least squares modelling assumes that the marginal impact of resources is equivalent, when measured against other characteristics (for example, for all family backgrounds). But depending on how education is accumulated, the impact may be through changing either the slope of the earnings function (Card and Krueger, 1992) or the intercept (Heckman et al., 1996; cf. Behrman and Birdsall, 1983). Moreover, educational courses may not have simple additive effects: a two-hour course may not be twice as good as a one-hour course. The presumptions of additive impact imply that (a) the marginal pay-off to courses in a particular field is not subject to diminishing returns and (b) the marginal pay-off to courses in one field do not influence those in another field. Neither of these assumptions need be valid, as Kang and Bishop's (1989) evidence cited above suggests.

As well as methodological issues, data inadequacies may impair education production function analysis. Table 5.1 indicates that production function estimates may be sensitive to the level of aggregation up to the institutional, regional or state level; with the last much more likely to yield significant resource effects.   Betts (1996a) discovers this bias: inputs measured from the bottom up are much less likely to yield statistically significant effects.   There are also more specific problems, as well as possible measurement error.   First, resource measures may be inaccurately measured: a common proxy is average per-pupil funding at the state level; and educational resources are often proxied using only one year's schooling. Second, information on the students themselves, such as their background and home environment, may be limited.   Third, there may be no obvious interval either at which the gains from education will have taken effect or over how long they endure (Betts, 1995, 1996c; Grogger, 1996).   Many aspects of school quality may be revealed by experience on the job, so if earnings over time are not charted the effect of school quality on earnings may be understated.   Fifth, institutional attributes may be missing, such as measures of the quality of the instruction (to the extent that these are not reflected in resources).   Finally, variance in the use of capital and the rates of depreciation of assets of public sector education establishments may obscure the actual resources used.[14]

5.3.2   Mapping the Production Process

Although numerous concerns over production function modelling have been noted, the insignificant evidence of resource effects may be valid for several reasons.   Straightforwardly, there may be diminishing returns to the education production, particularly if education – with a high proportion of labour input – is subject to the relative price effect of labour-intensive services.   Particularly in Western education provision, input pricing may not generate sufficient variation: teacher salaries, for instance, are compressed into scales which may not reflect differences in productivity.   Furthermore, school quality may have converged, perhaps with greater mandates towards equity and funding equalisation, and perhaps with limited entrepreneurship, so that there is only limited observable difference.

Contra-positively, Case and Deaton (1999) examine apartheid South African Black education to test for positive effects of lower class size on pupil's performance.   In that education system, with very limited school choice and large discrepancies in funding, strong and significant effects of lower pupil–teacher ratios on enrolment, achievement and test scores emerge.   However, these discrepancies in funding are far greater than those in most education sectors: resource effects are indeed likely to be evident if one class is four times the size of another, as in this South African example and in some developing countries (where positive resource effects are more frequently found, as in Hanushek, 1995).   But class sizes in Western schools are clustered within a much narrower band and involve much smaller absolute student numbers.[15] Cutting class sizes by a factor of four is rarely a viable policy option.

Looking over time, public funding for education may be offsetting deterioration or diminution in other inputs, such as family inputs into education. Education systems may also have evolved whereby schools are spending up to the same rate of return, with resource effects being indicative of how hard some groups are to educate. In this case, the null resource effect may effectively be revealing the equality of resource allocation in public education: if outcomes are to be equalised or harmonised then this might imply null resource effects precisely to offset differences in efficiency. On the output side, perhaps the effect of education quality is on other aspects of labour market behaviour – such as employment probability or job satisfaction – rather than earnings, or perhaps non-pecuniary benefits are increasing.

Hanushek (1998) suggests that additional resources can make a difference, but schools or school systems may not be able to use them effectively enough to produce improved student outcomes. In turn, this suggests that resource redistribution from, say, human to physical inputs is not easy to justify or substantiate. Schools may differ dramatically in quality and are likely to, but this is not easy to see in terms of intermediate outputs, variations in expenditure, class sizes or organisational structures. Even if measurable teacher characteristics have little impact on student performance, for example, unobserved characteristics still seem to matter a lot. One reason why it may be hard to enhance educational effectiveness, particularly through the application of economic models, is that it is not easy to stimulate efficiency. The very problem faced in identifying outcomes may also dampen efficiency within education providers. Yet it does seem clear from Chapter 2 that education boosts earnings. Burtless (1996, 4) notes the contrary nature of the two possible conclusions: added school resources do have an effect in the labour market yielding high rates of return, but not so within the school. In other words, schools seem to be good at optimising something which are they are not directly teaching, assessing or indeed observing.

Lastly, these production function studies typically involve building input-driven models of the process of education, but there are alternatives. One approach is to describe the industrial structure, conduct and performance of education institutions. For example, changes in UK education provision have resulted from the desegregation of higher education institutions in 1992 and from local management of schools in 1988; decentralisation has been an important international trend (Bullock and Thomas, 1997); and in the US, school districts are increasingly consolidated (Hoxby, 1999). It might be expected that better performing institutions would be revealed through competition; and to the extent that such competition is lacking, so might be the drive for efficiency. These concerns are considered in Chapter 7.

A second alternative is to study what characteristics make institutions effective, linking the economics of education to school effectiveness research (Thomas and Martin, 1996). Coe and Fitz-Gibbon (1998) have surveyed the school effectiveness literature for the UK, however, and their conclusions are also rather negative. First, school effectiveness research uses a narrow range of outcomes (and assumes these are universally applicable). Second, there are problems of using value-added and modelling the education process. Third, there is little evidence of a causal connection between schools' performance and factors within these schools.

A final alternative is to use case study evidence and modelling on how education institutions respond to new circumstances. Johnes (1999) portrays universities as conglomerates of faculties within a central administration: maximising competing objectives, such universities can be analysed through principal–agent models. Case study evidence has illustrated some mutability in resource usage as revenues change: in UK further education with declining per unit resourcing, for example, there is evidence of changes to a lower labour-intensive pedagogy and reduction in the durations of courses.

5.4   SCALE EFFECTS

5.4.1   Economies of Scale and Scope

Rather than focusing on the efficiency of education providers, a more modest investigation may be made of the size effects of education enterprises. In particular, the high fixed costs and relatively low variable costs of education programmes suggest there may be substantial economies of scale, particularly if enrolments can be expanded to capacity. Moreover, as schools and colleges typically operate in command economies rather than markets and in part are funded historically, there may be a co-ordination failure in attaining optimal capacity.

Yet as education providers might be classed as multi-product enterprises, that is, in producing academically and socially able pupils, then economies of scope are also pertinent. As illustration, for a university generating two outcomes of teaching and research from two inputs of faculty and library facilities, a number of combinations are open: (a) more faculty may be needed, holding library facilities fixed (and vice versa); (b) both faculty and facilities may need expanding, to reduce average cost; and/or (c) each output of teaching or research may need expanding, to lower unit cost.

Ray economies of scale occur where the composition of output remains stable, but its size is allowed to vary, that is, a university provides the same mix of research and teaching but more (of each) in total (Dundar and Lewis, 1995). Formally, ray economies of scale S_N are given as:

$$S_N = \frac{C(y_N)}{\sum_{i=1}^{n} y_i C_i(y)} \qquad (5.2)$$

In the above equation, $C(y_N)$ is the vector of costs for all outputs and $C_i(y) = \partial C(y_N)/\partial y_i$ is the marginal cost of producing output i. Ray economies of scale exist if S_N is greater than or equal to one. If so, it would be more efficient, assuming other factors remain constant, to expand all outputs together. Within this overall provision, product specific economies of scale may occur. These measure how costs change as both outputs and the composition of provision changes (for example, more teaching inputs, disproportionately fewer research inputs). A two step calculation is needed. First, the cost of producing all outputs except the ith one is calculated:

$$IC(y_i) = C(y_N) - C(y_{N-i}) \qquad (5.3)$$

The average incremental costs from the marginal product of the ith output are:

$$AIC(y_i) = [C(y_N) - C(y_{N-i})]/y_i \qquad (5.4)$$

From equations (5.3) and (5.4), product specific economies of scale are designated:

$$S_i(y) = AIC(y_i)/C_i(y) \qquad (5.5)$$

Product specific economies of scale exist if S_i is greater than one and diseconomies if S_i is less than one.

Considering production from the output side, economies of scope may also exist, where there are cost complementarities. These would be the cost savings from producing at least two outputs (for example, universities are both teaching colleges and research institutions). Global economies of scope occur if costs are lower from producing more than one output. With $C(y_i)$ as the cost of separately producing each outcome i = 1,...k, global economies of scope are defined as:

$$GE = [C(y_1) + C(y_2) + \ldots + C(y_k) - C(y_N)]/C(y_N) \qquad (5.6)$$

If GE is greater than or equal to zero, then there is a cost advantage from joint production. Product specific economies of scope are estimated in relation to one output:

$$SC_i = [C(y_i) + C(y_{N-i}) - C(y)]/C(y) \tag{5.7}$$

SC_i represents the proportionate increase in costs resulting from producing all outputs except the ith. There are cost advantages from producing output i jointly with other outputs if SC_i is greater than or equal to zero.

These parameters can be illustrated using the simple example of a university providing undergraduate courses U, postgraduate courses G and research R in quantities Q_i. Ray economies may be represented as:

$$S_N = TC(Q_U, Q_G, Q_R)/[Q_U MC_U + Q_G MC_G + Q_R MC_R] \tag{5.8}$$

For the university again, average incremental cost and product specific economies of scale for undergraduate provision are:

$$AIC_U = [TC(Q_U, Q_G, Q_R) - TC(0, Q_G, Q_R)]/Q_U \tag{5.9}$$

$$S_U = AIC_U/MC_U \tag{5.10}$$

Finally, global economies of scope and product specific economies for undergraduate provision are:

$$GE = \frac{[TC(Q_U, 0, 0) + TC(0, Q_G, 0) + TC(0, 0, Q_R) - TC(Q_U, Q_G, Q_R)]}{TC(Q_U, Q_G, Q_R)} \tag{5.11}$$

$$SC_U = \frac{[TC(Q_U, 0, 0) + TC(0, Q_G, Q_R) - TC(Q_U, Q_G, Q_R)]}{TC(Q_U, Q_G, Q_R)} \tag{5.12}$$

As well as the indirect evidence on school capacities and rolls considered above, direct evidence of economies of scale and scope has been generated, both for the US and UK. Dundar and Lewis (1995) use four output measures across departments – annual credit hours across undergraduate, Masters and PhD programmes and the number of publications – and generate AIC and MC estimates for engineering, physical science and social science courses at 119 US universities. Their evidence on scale and scope economies for social science and physical science departments are presented in Table 5.2.

These figures show strong economies across the two departments, both for single outputs and multiple outputs. The top half of the table shows that, particularly for social sciences, more output could be produced at lower unit cost in the established proportions. As well, each of the individual outputs could be expanded, as product specific economies of scale are all positive. The bottom half of the table shows unit costs are lower with the simultaneous production of multiple outputs (GE > 0). For social sciences, Dundar and Lewis (1995) report cost complementarities between joint supply of undergraduate and masters programmes; joint supply of producing undergraduate and postgraduate students; and joint supply of undergraduates and research. Marginal costs appear highest for extra publications. There is however only mixed evidence of graduate education and research being comparable for physical sciences, suggesting cost complementarity is likely to be subject specific. In particular, each output should be efficiently produced in combination with other outputs: economies of scope are evident for institutions which combine undergraduate and graduate programmes and, perhaps more importantly for policy, for institutions which combine research with teaching (see also Koshal and Koshal, 1999).

Table 5.2 Economies of Scale and Scope in US Higher Education

| | University subject | |
	Social Sciences	Physical Sciences
Scale economies		
Ray economies S_N	3.917	1.689
Product economies S_i		
Undergraduates	2.345	1.056
Masters	1.119	1.025
PhDs	2.949	1.789
Research	1.217	1.348
Scope economies		
Global economies GE	0.125	1.348
Product economies SC_i		
Undergraduates	0.899	0.404
Masters	0.620	0.451
PhDs	0.726	0.485
Research	0.531	0.396
n	*119*	*98*

Source: Dundar and Lewis (1995, 137, 138)

Other international evidence provides further support that there is scope for expansion either to lower unit cost or to alter the output mix. Evidence of scale effects for higher education have been found using different output measures (Smart, 1988; Hoare, 1995); although Kyvik (1995) finds no evidence of a positive relationship between university department size and research performance. UK evidence yields a slightly different picture.

Table 5.3   Economies of Scale and Scope in UK Higher Education

	University Type		
	'Typical'	Arts based	Science based
Scale economies			
Ray economies S_N	1.07	1.13	1.00
Product economies S_i			
Undergraduates: Arts	1.32	1.30	1.35
Undergraduates: Science	0.93	0.95	0.90
Postgraduates	1.81	1.81	1.82
Research	1.44	1.43	1.45
Scope economies			
Global economies GE	–0.08	–0.04	–0.10
n	*99*	*99*	*99*

Source: Johnes (1997, 731)

For the UK, Johnes (1997) has estimated economies of scale and scope for 99 universities and his evidence is given in Table 5.3. These figures show some opportunities for ray economies of scale and for product economies of scale, except for undergraduate science provision ($S_{US} < 1$). Unlike for the US data, however, global economies of scope do not appear to exist (GE < 0), prompting scepticism that there are significant synergies for UK higher education provision. From these estimates, Johnes (1997, 732) reconfigures university provision, either by reapportioning existing provision or by altering the numbers of universities. Reapportionment of existing provision would reduce costs by 7.5%, mainly by concentration of research institutions; alteration of the size of the sector may reduce costs by as much as 39%, with much greater specialisation of provision into undergraduate and research institutions. This result, contrasting with that for the US, may reflect the different absolute sizes of UK universities.

5.4.2   Optimal School Size

The above evidence on higher education also coheres with the broad evidence that there are capacity effects in school provision (Dolton and Bee, 1985; FAS, 1999, 50; for Norway, Bonesrønning and Rattsø, 1994). Smet and Nonneman (1998) use a translog cost function to estimate economies of scale and scope for Flemish schools. Ray economies are, they find, greater than 1 for all school types, even at 300% of present school operations. There are also global economies of scope, as highly specialised schools have more than double the costs of generalist schools. For the US, short run economies of scale at both primary and secondary level may be evident, but not economies of scope, with diseconomies of transport services and of capital utilisation (Callan and Santerre, 1990). Similarly, probable scale economies in primary and secondary schools in Bolivia and Paraguay exist, although full complementarity in combining primary with secondary education is not established (Jimenez, 1986). Yet the evidence on scale is not conclusive: evidence that curriculum comprehensiveness does vary with school size may only pertain at quite small school sizes, that is, an enrolment of fewer than 300 pupils (Monk, 1987).

An alternative to comparing unit costs (assuming homogeneous quality of outcomes) is to look at the sizes of education enterprises and the quality of their outcomes. Bigger schools may be able to offer a better standard of provision and this may be reflected in their students' grades (and perhaps in other proxy measures such as student retention rates). Table 5.4, presented in Bradley and Taylor (1998a), shows how school examination performance in the UK increases as the size of the school increases, up to a size of around 1200 (for ages 11–16) or 1500 (for ages 11–18). Without adjusting for prior attainment and other confounding factors, the examination performances of the largest 11–18 schools are 60% better than those of the smallest (see also Johnes, 1993a, 96). Given such a disparity, this evidence about size effects is robust to the inclusion of proxies for academic ability (via admissions policies and special educational needs enrolments) and for family background (via the percentage of pupils with free schools meals entitlement), as well as some teacher input differences and contextual factors (gender composition, independence of the school from local control). But Luyten's (1994) literature summary and evidence also suggest that capacity effects may not be significant across all countries: no statistically significant relation between school size and achievement, independent of student background, is evident for secondary education in the US, Sweden and the Netherlands.

A number of explanations for these size effects may be offered. First, there may be economies of size to curriculum operations: larger schools can offer a wider range of courses, increasing the likelihood of students' choices being satisfied; if there is more than one teaching group, better allocation of students to teaching groups may be possible. Furthermore, there may be economies of size to factor inputs: lecturers may be able to specialise in their chosen field of study; physical capital, such as libraries and sports facilities, may be better utilised in large schools (some inputs may be indivisible and there may be higher returns to specialisation). There may be economies of size to assessment of students: creating assessment materials – for examination and course work – may require high initial fixed effort.

Table 5.4 Exam Results by Sizes of Secondary Schools in England

	% of students with ≥ 5 GCSE grades A*- C			
Size of school (pupils)	**11–16 schools**	***n***	**11–18 schools**	***n***
0–399	31.8	*82*	29.4	*17*
400–599	29.5	*321*	30.5	*95*
600–799	35.4	*409*	36.6	*271*
800–999	38.5	*341*	41.7	*359*
1000–1199	41.4	*171*	45.5	*397*
1200–1399	45.4	*47*	44.8	*236*
1400–1599	39.4	*25[a]*	48.8	*127*
1600+	-	-	49.2	*73*
All schools	35.7	*1396*	42.3	*1575*

Notes: [a] Includes three schools with over 1600 pupils. 1996 data.
Source: Bradley and Taylor (1998a)

    For most enterprises, constant returns to scale may be possible because tasks may simply be replicated; this might be possible in education, given there are natural subdivisions into classes. However, replication of tasks may not be possible if inputs are indivisible; or if institutions try to scale up by non-integer amounts (for example, scaling up by ten pupils if classes normally have 30 pupils); or when some inputs, such as good teachers, cannot be replicated. If the pedagogy is fixed, perhaps through political mandate, in terms of pupil–teacher ratios, for example, then this may constrain the opportunities of schools to exploit economies of scale. And although many studies have found significant economies of scale, larger education institutions may have more principal–agent communication problems between lecturers, administrators and students. These problems may include: anonymity for students; diseconomies in providing information to all students; alienation of students and staff; heterogeneity across learning needs; difficulties in establishing student comprehension; loss of direction in student groups; and variation across assessment (Habeshaw et al., 1992). Also, it should be recognised that the cost functions represented here are calculated from the perspective of the education provider: larger schools may impose greater commuting and monitoring costs on parents and students.

Alternatively, the causality may be the opposite way around: schools may be large in size because they are higher performing. Bradley and Taylor (1998a, 316), examining changes in school size and changes in exam performance, find a statistically significant positive relationship between exam performance and the change in school size as pupils switch to better performing schools. But the effect is substantively small: an increase in school size by 100 pupils (that is, at least a 10% increase) is associated with examination scores which improve by only 0.7%; this is to be compared with the actual increase in examination performance over the period of 6.6%. Generally it seems that, although they have plausible tendencies, school size changes cannot explain much of the improvement in UK examination scores in the 1990s.

Nevertheless, if minimum efficient scale is reached at school sizes bigger than the current size, then there may be cost savings from increasing school sizes or from combining education provision. These can be estimated by comparing the optimal size of a school with the mean actual size. Bradley and Taylor (1998a) find the average school size is around 60–70% of its optimal size. Similarly, Duncombe et al. (1995) have analysed cost savings from consolidation of school districts looking at total per-pupil expenditure in 1990 in New York state. School districts with fewer than 500 students have an average daily attendance cost which is 37% greater than those school districts with more than 10 000 students. Although education does not appear to be suited to a highly concentrated command structure, significant savings are possible from increasing institutions' sizes.

5.4.3   The Costs of Non-completion

A final pass at scrutinising the efficiency of education providers is to look at non-completion. Such completion failure or drop-out is an important source of ineffectiveness – the *ex post* (academic) achievements of drop-outs may be low and dropping out has obvious implications for students' careers. Moreover, the scale of drop-out may be large: the drop-out rate for higher education in the UK is 19%, even though this is one of the lowest rates in the OECD (DfEE, 1998a, 105). Looking at UK schooling, according to the Audit Commission/OFSTED (1993, 1): 'between 30% and 40% of students starting on a course do not succeed [to achieve the qualifications] they set out to gain', with an estimated absolute cost to the UK taxpayer of £500 million (1993 prices). This cost is only an approximation and should not be considered as a net cost, however, for a number of reasons.

First, such costing estimates need to take account of when the students failed to complete. A student who drops out in the first few weeks will not have absorbed the same resource as the student who drops out within a few weeks of the examination. Second, an optimal drop-out rate is non-zero: the possibility of drop-out may be a motivation to students as well as an important signal to employers (as in the model of standards in Section 4.2.3 above). Models either of education standards or of the option to drop out suggest that a non-trivial, positive drop-out rate may be optimal for society and workforce productivity. Third, considering general equilibrium effects, absolute estimates need not imply anything about the opportunity costs of educating or supporting students who do not complete their courses: some of these students may have changed to alternative activities or educational institutions. Fourth, one possible definition, lack of success in examinations, may include students who reduce the number of credentials, or receive some lower credentials or return in a subsequent year to complete. Finally, there may be interaction effects between the policy, management or size of the institution and the number of drop-outs: smaller institutions, for example, may offer provision which is more expensive, but they may also have differential drop-out rates. The costs of drop-out will be sensitive to each of these factors. Overall, because years prior to dropping out generate observably positive effects on earnings, drop-out is only a source of inefficiency compared to the opportunity cost or alternative returns to individuals.

With data on 6764 enrolments in nine further education colleges, Fielding et al. (1999) compare non-retention rates across A-level subjects. They find drop-out rates which vary from 6.1% to 43.5% and average just under 20%, with considerable variation in the period at which individuals drop-out and a sizeable number failing only to attend the examination. Using a highly disaggregated estimation of costs, these rates can be apportioned to each teaching group and the attrition costs calculated. Teaching group costs per enrolment can be weighted according to the length of time spent on the course, so as to match more closely the actual resource instruction costs of each enrolment. The percentage of resource instruction costs which are expended on drop-outs can be estimated and these vary between 2% and 30%. As well as showing that a large amount is indeed expended on drop-outs, these percentages are significantly different from estimates based on absolute numbers. Of particular concern in most colleges is the large expenditure of resources on candidates who, whilst completing the course and by convention incurring the same resource outlay as examinees, did not enter for the examination.

On this evidence the costs of drop-out appear to be significant, particularly as only the providers' costs and not the individuals' costs have been counted. An estimate of the benefits of a positive drop-out rate need to be calculated, however, and this will not be straightforward. It may be legitimate to assume that there are no benefits from a positive drop-out rate if students are compelled to repeat school years which they initially failed or if drop-out students are subsequently educated through other education providers. Indeed, repetition rates in developing countries, for example, are particularly high; Harbison and Hanushek (1992) describe how substantial cost savings can be made from reducing repetition rates in Brazil. Breneman (1998) also calculates high costs of remediation education in the US, redressing students' initially poor achievements at school. Such drop-out effects are likely to impose significant burdens on other education or public service providers, especially if there is no contracted obligation between first-attended schools as to the quality of education provided and so no incentive for reduced drop-out rates across the education system.

5.5   ISSUES AND CONCLUSIONS

In this chapter, the evidence on internal efficiency has been investigated using production function studies. Production function evidence may shed light on internal efficiency; on how effective schools generate learning and on specific changes to patterns of investment, such as the reduction in per-student educational expenditures over the decade of the 1990s for the UK. Similarly for the US, Hanushek (1998) charts expenditure over the longer term, where, although increasing enrolments have contributed to some of the changes in expenditure on education, the largest part of the changes has been through increases in total instructional salary changes. In turn this increase reflects a decline in the pupil–teacher ratio, in an attempt to move to an efficient production function, and rising wages for teachers.

From a raft of studies on resource effects and charting student performance over time and in cross-section, Hanushek (1986, 1995, 1997, 1998) argues that US schooling outcomes have not improved: educational outcomes do not appear to have been observably enhanced by increasing resources (and allocating those increased resources primarily to teacher inputs). Betts's (1996a, 148) conclusion is stark: 'schools differ substantially in quality but that standard measures of school resources do not capture these differences.' Behrman's (1996, 354) is similar: 'general school effects are much larger than the effects of specifically identifiable inputs.' A positive link between resources and outcomes is important because of the scale of education expenditure, of its role in redistribution and because of changes in spending over time. The policy implication is clear: given pre-defined policy goals, money for education should be allocated to investments which yield the highest return. Yet the lack of evidence on whether increased investment – either in the aggregate or on particular items – has demonstrably positive effects must call this policy rule into question. These efficiency studies suggest the scope for improving outcomes with extra resources may be either complex or limited.

Yet one main finding from this chapter is that the specification for such investigations is critical. It is essential to have a secure prior foundation about what represents a resource effect as against a curriculum effect, an on-entry ability effect or a motivation-to-study effect. When looking at input–output relationships, all other things need to be assumed unchanged and each outcome measure is susceptible to criticism. Academic scores may vary because of grade inflation or deflation, that is, differences (either across time or across examining boards) in standards of grading. Earnings may differ because of economic effects such as changing returns to physical investment or a higher demand for those who have studied particular subjects. Inspection grades may vary with legislation or changes to the motive for inspection; student satisfaction may rise if the economy changes to favour the more highly skilled (or indeed if courses become easier). Although a number of explanations for the evidence have been offered here, a significant unknown is not resource levels but variation in family inputs and peer inputs, recognising the mutuality of student, school and home inputs.

Two inferences may be made, none the less. First, there is plausible evidence that education providers are sub-optimal in size either when looking at unit costs or at outcomes. (Referring back to Figure 4.2, most schools appear to be operating in the area bounded by AHB.) This inference is reasonably robust across countries and across sectors, although particular context effects may dominate. This evidence has yet to conclusively establish why size has an effect: perhaps the teachers are better; perhaps the subject mix is better; perhaps there are specialisation effects; perhaps there is competitive pressure between pupils. This sub-optimal composition of institutions may be reformed through consolidation, although if education is provided through a command economy, it is not obvious how this would be obtained. Second, the compelling evidence in Chapter 2 on positive rates of return may be juxtaposed with the more ambiguous findings in this chapter. The returns to the extensive margin of education are obvious and substantial; the returns to the intensive margin decidedly less so. On efficiency grounds, keeping students in school appears more strongly justifiable than giving those in school more resources. Burtless (1996, 11) makes this point empirically: 'the internal rate of return on investing in smaller class size, even using favourable assumptions... is only 2.35% [see Betts, 1996a] … In contrast … the internal rate of return on an extra year of school attainment is in the range of 5 to 12%. Borrowing money to finance extra schooling is much more attractive in this case.' This mandate does assume unchanged parameters (for example, earnings premia for the educated) when provision is expanded, but it seems strongly plausible when the two sets of evidence are contrasted.

To conclude, following Hoenack (1994), it is important to map the production possibility frontier for education. Only with this frontier defined does it become possible to analyse how to use particular factors as inputs into the education process, or how to structure incentives so that schools remain on the frontier. Having looked at the technological constraints facing the enterprises across the two previous chapters, the two subsequent chapters consider other constraints – how inputs can be used to ensure input (allocative) efficiency and on how markets shape education provision.

6. Factor Inputs

6.1 CONCEPTS

Chapters 4 and 5 considered the theory of the enterprise and presented an array of evidence on resource usage and external (output) efficiency. This chapter considers efficiency from the input side: how particular inputs can be combined in appropriate proportions. A single quantum of resources can be used in a diversity of ways and input-choice efficiency is defined as where factors are employed to the condition that the ratios of marginal product to factor prices are equalised. Building on the production function of education enterprises, factor inputs for education include: the students (both their effort and ability); the students' peers; contributions from within the household; physical resources, both within the provider institution and the community; teacher and other staff resources within the provider enterprise; and managerial inputs. The deployment of and returns to each of these factors is important.

Of these factors teacher input has received by far the most analytical interest. The demand for teachers, their supply and attempts to equilibrate the two are discussed in Section 6.2, along with the critical question of whether 'teachers matter'. The remaining inputs are then considered in Section 6.3, but in much less detail. This reflects the lack of market prices for these inputs and so the lesser research enquiry devoted to these other factors, although this should not belie their potential importance to education provision. The efficiency criterion requires each factor to be considered both individually and as a complement and substitute for other factors. These issues of factor substitutability and complementarity are considered in Section 6.4.

The technology of education (pedagogy) presented here is a simplified one: students are educated by teachers using few other inputs beyond their labour time. This is not universally true – schools and colleges are not the only education providers and increasingly new input combinations are being utilised. Evidence on these is thin, though, and so the treatment here is 'stereotypical' to this schooling pedagogy.

6.2   TEACHER INPUTS

6.2.1   The Demand for Teachers

Education enterprises are distinguished by their reliance on labour inputs. The UK public sector employs around 380 000 school teachers, 70 000 and 60 000 further and higher education lecturers (DfEE/OFSTED, 1998). Together, these represent around 2% of the UK workforce (although given the relatively high skills of teachers and lecturers, the reservation pool of workers is much smaller). Table 6.1 shows how instruction by teachers is a key component of the technology of education, giving the proportions of expenditure across inputs in schools in England. Around two-thirds of all expenditure is on teaching staff, with comparatively little spent on other inputs (in part because capital funding may come from other sources). In grant-maintained schools, for example, 70% of costs were spent on staff; 11% on premises; 17% on supplies and services; and 1% on depreciation (FAS, 1999). These proportions very by sector: in further and higher education, staff costs are about 10 percentage points less (HESA, 1996ab). But the proportions are broadly similar across countries. For the US, Brewer (1996) estimates that, of all payroll expenditure, 62% is spent directly on teachers and 27% on para-professionals (with 12% on administrative staff). International evidence presents a similar picture: data on 24 OECD countries shows resources spent on staff costs to range between 63% and 90% (DfEE/OFSTED, 1998); for developing countries, see Tsang (1988).

Table 6.1   Distribution of Expenditure of State Schools in England, 1996–97

	Pre-primary and primary schools	**Secondary schools**
Teaching staff	66	71
Premises	12	12
Books/equipment	4	5
Other staff	14	4
Other	4	8
	100%	*100%*

Source: DfEE/OFSTED (1998)

Figure 6.1 shows this again using data from 2191 UK enterprises across all sectors of industry and makes clearer how atypical educational enterprises are.   Whereas almost 60% of firms in the education sector expend more than three-quarters of their operating costs on labour, less than 10% of private firms do this.   From the perspective of managers of an educational enterprise, teachers are therefore a significant input to education and this in part justifies the substantial investigation into the economics of teacher inputs.

Figure 6.1 Proportion of Operating Costs Paid to Labour

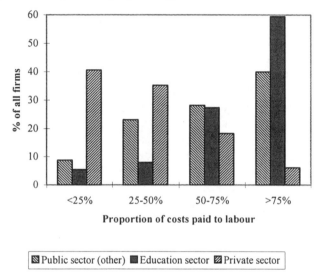

Source: Workplace Employee Relations Survey (1998)

Teacher inputs are indirectly controlled by the government in that UK university teacher training college enrolments are decided by fiat.   Wage negotiations are bargained over collectively and at a central level (in the UK, the private sector employs less than 10% of all teachers), although each school's governing body does have charge of hiring individual teachers.   As a monopsonistic purchaser of labour services, government seeks to ensure a sufficient and quality workforce for education provision.   This demand for teachers derives therefore from the demand for education, given the production function.   The UK government also has control over resource allocation and outcomes for education, in that it can control the production function to take account of relative shortage or excess supply of teachers in the market.   Thus, the demand for teachers is highly regulated from 'outside' the educational enterprise: the scope either for market signals to operate or for a school's management to shape its own demand for teachers is therefore constrained. As evident from the theory of the enterprise, command of the inputs into education and prescription as to the technology of education will drive much of the outcomes. This government control means that discussion easily departs from the application of economic principles: factor demands will still be downward sloping with input price to be equated to the marginal revenue product. However, this output price is not readily observed in state schooling.

Salary setting, for example, is often on spine points, applicable across many educational enterprises. In the UK, salaries were set by the Burnham Committee until 1987, with the School Teachers' Review Body set up in 1991. The use of a unified salary schedule (where pay is driven by teacher credentials and teaching experience and not related to the subject of instruction) may result in adverse selection in the market for teachers. Without flexibility in pay setting to reflect differential scarcities of teacher types, market signals will be muted and the result is likely to be a sub-optimal composition of teachers. As Southwick and Gill (1997) indicate, a unified salary schedule implies that less able people with Math–Science backgrounds will choose to be teachers compared with those from other subject backgrounds; the former are rewarded relatively more in alternative occupations. The quality of the Math–Science teachers will fall, relative to the quality of other teachers, implying lower relative output of those teachers. Southwick and Gill establish this with evidence on lower achievement scores of students in Math–Science compared to verbal tests. Moreover, because this effect is hard for consumers to detect and for voters to bargain over specifically, it may persist over the longer term.

Another constraint on the optimal deployment of teachers may arise from accreditation barriers to entry, following Polachek and Siebert's model (1993, 326–28) for the medical profession. Teachers are appointed by district education authorities and/or school governing bodies; most of these teachers must have teacher training diplomas. This accreditation barrier may raise the quality of teaching and so boost demand; Edwards et al. (1996) do find accreditation raises the demand for the services of pre-school centres. But accreditation may also act as a restrictive practice – in that earnings are forgone whilst obtaining a diploma – and so constrain supply. The test of whether the benefits outweigh the costs rests on whether the equilibrium volume of provision rises or falls. Lowenberg and Tinnin (1992), for example, have looked at the effects of mandated education credentials for child-care directors across the US; such mandates reduce the amount of nursery care rather than raise it. Such accreditation constraints may therefore reflect an imposed barrier to entry.

But it is important not to overstate government influence in setting wages and working conditions. Government has some influence over teacher salaries, in that it determines demand and may impose some access constraints on supply. However, it can only control public sector teachers' earnings and not those of other graduate jobs: its influence over factor prices is in no sense complete.

6.2.2   The Supply of Teachers

Fundamentally, the supply of teachers will be conditional on the wage offer, relative to other opportunities. Table 6.2 gives international evidence on teacher compensation. These figures suggest that full teacher pay is higher than average worker pay, to broadly the same extent across most countries (although see Barro and Lee, 1996, 222). However, teachers are typically from the more highly educated strata of the labour market and so it may be more appropriate to compare their earnings with other highly educated workers. Dolton (1996, 195) describes the relative earnings of teachers over the period 1956–88 for the UK: except for a period in the 1960s, pay of teachers has been less than the average pay for non-manual earnings. It has also been an unstable percentage of non-manual earnings, reflecting fluctuations in relative factor supplies and demands. (This variation appears to follow a worldwide trend, as given in Barro and Lee, 1996.) Similarly for the US, Lankford and Wyckoff (1997, 379) chart beginning salaries relative to the starting salaries of college graduates in other fields over the period 1972–94: the salary ratios are all less than 1 and vary significantly over the 20-year period. Looking across time, however, there has not been a substantial decline in relative teacher pay.

Moreover, these earnings figures do not, of course, represent 'full earnings'; lifetime teacher pay may be higher because of greater job security or better working conditions. Teacher remuneration may be expected to differ from remuneration in the private sector for several reasons.

First, teacher salaries may be naturally compressed. Given reasonable labour mobility, standardised prior training (education diplomas) and a uniform education production function, salary levels might be expected to be similar across regions. Teacher mobility is likely to compress salary differentials (and so may represent the benchmark against which the mobility of other workers may be compared, Bempah et al., 1994).

Second, because of the complementarity between teaching and family formation, with compatibility of the working day with childcare and ease with which people can return to teaching, it could be anticipated that gender inequalities in salaries might also be low. Verdugo and Schneider (1994, 258) test this by regressing earnings on the concentration of female workers in that occupation; they find a male earnings premium of up to 13%, with cost to being a female teacher of 5% in annual salary. Toutkoushian (1998) estimates that the unexplained male–female faculty wage gap is around 7–

10% (but that this difference is lower amongst younger faculty, a finding compatible either with the intermittency theory or with greater convergence in salaries over time). These estimates of the gender gap appear only slightly lower than cross-economy estimates.

Table 6.2   Teacher Salary to Average Worker Earnings Ratios

	Ratio of secondary school teacher salary to average worker earnings
Sweden	1.14–1.32
Denmark	1.16–1.83
Italy	1.31–1.35
United States	1.33
Spain	1.40–1.72
Australia	1.60
United Kingdom	1.63
Canada	1.68
Japan	1.71–1.73
Germany	1.82–1.98

Source: Bishop (1996a, 115)

Third, job security is higher in the public sector, as is the incidence of training. Non-pecuniary benefits may be higher than in other occupations: less information is available on the compensating differentials to working in teaching, although the pupil–teacher ratio may be a useful proxy for quality of work. In order to supplement salaries, and because teaching is a profession with low job monitoring, teachers and higher education faculty may undertake extra work, particularly in less-developed countries and in internationally open labour markets. Little research has been done on the consequent boost to earnings, although US evidence on moonlighting teachers suggests that teacher salary has little influence on extra work and that teacher effort is not impaired in terms of either instruction-related activities outside school or homework assigned (Ballou, 1995, 12).

Notwithstanding differences in terms of employment between public and private sector jobs, the supply of teachers will still be influenced by their relative pay. The problem for an education manager, however, is to pay teachers according to their productivity or to their reservation wage. Although pay is relatively easy to observe, neither productivity nor reservation wages are. Teachers work relatively autonomously and their performance is teamed with students, who may be imperfect judges of their productivity. But it is not necessary for such productivity to be observed by an outside agency: if employment terms for teachers fall relative to those for other jobs, then *ceteris paribus* the supply will diminish or effort levels will deteriorate. Only if transfer earnings are substantially below the current wage or there are significant switching costs will such effects be cushioned in the short term. Generally, this diminution or deterioration is independent of whether or not researchers or policy-makers can observe it. Plausibly, though, there is evidence that the supply of new teachers, the re-entry of teachers and their exit to outside jobs is sensitive to the salaries offered. Dolton and van der Klaauw (1995, 1996) find this for the UK, although Hanushek and Pace (1995) find that entry to teacher training programmes is not much influenced by teacher salaries for the US. Theobald and Gritz (1996, 19) have studied teacher mobility and exit decisions, establishing quits to be substantially reduced by the raising of teacher salaries, with the elasticity of supply of male teachers being particularly high. The overall test as to whether pay reductions are efficient depends on whether the fall in effort is less than proportionate to the fall in the wage bill.

6.2.3   Equilibration of Supply and Demand

Inflows to and outflows from of the teaching profession can be represented using basic supply and demand functions to establish the equilibrium amount of teaching resource. Figure 6.2 gives Dolton's (1996) basic, reduced form model of supply and demand, with a market adjustment equation. In such models, the government's role is incorporated directly: not only is the government the main demander of teachers, but it is also a supplier through the higher education system (and publicly sponsored teacher training colleges). The supply of teachers S_T is upward-sloping in the relative teacher wage W. Demand is mandated through the demography of student numbers and parental preferences for a particular pupil–teacher ratio at T^*. This would result in teacher pay of W^*. For the government, the relevant budget constraint is the numbers of teachers times the wage; this locus is given by D_{GT}. This constraint prevents (in the short run) the payment of wages W^*, and instead results in a teacher shortfall of T^*-T_M. The discrepancies between the actual and the optimal position arise because of incompatible commitments over spending and the mode of provision. In the medium and long term, this excess of demand over supply should prompt movement of the relative wage.

Given these supply and demand functions, market equilibration can be modelled. Zarkin (1985) has modelled occupational choice for US teachers, making explicit reference to future as well as starting salaries and rationally incorporating stocks and flows, along the lines of the adjustment effects in

Figure 6.2. School teachers' occupational choices are ideally suited to such modelling because the demand for teachers can be reasonably well predicted from demographic changes (as changes in education preferences are highly constrained), with the numbers receiving secondary school certification responsive to future cohort sizes. Including both aggregate and individual teacher level information in their excess demand function, for example, Bee and Dolton (1995) find a significant positive association between the rate of adjustment of teachers' earnings and the level of excess demand. Again, this is supportive of standard economic stimuli influencing the behaviour of teachers.

Figure 6.2 Teacher Supply with Government Intervention

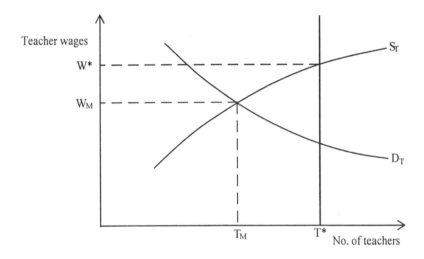

This evidence does not however imply that workforce planning would be straightforward. For the UK, Dolton (1996) is critical of past attempts to establish an equilibrium of teacher supply and demand, describing significant change over the years, with '(almost) continuous disequilibrium' (for Brazil, see Harbison and Hanushek, 1992). After a long period of shortage of teachers up to the 1970s, a period of surplus then changed to shortage again in the 1980s, with substantial flow changes in teacher numbers. For example, Dolton and van der Klaauw (1996, 239) chart how the annual numbers of new teachers entering the profession in the UK fell from around 27 000 in 1975 to around 7000 by 1986, creating a significantly different stock of teacher skills. There is additional evidence for this thesis in the matching of high quality teachers to well-paying jobs: Ballou's (1996) model, looking at the demand for US teachers, finds no positive impact of teaching college quality (and hence teacher quality) on the likelihood of being offered a teaching post.

Teachers are also highly mobile labour and – where there are rigid national salaries yet differential regional costs of living – there may be significant mismatches in supply across the country, as well as problems of ensuring the supply of particular types of teachers (if the constraint in Figure 6.2 is applied generally across the profession). These allocation difficulties can be compensated for by older teachers being retained, by substitution away from physical inputs and by re-entry into the market by past teachers. Also, merit pay and flexible career ladders may ameliorate shortages of particular types of teacher. However, in the context of temporary teacher arrangements, of changes in the pupil–teacher ratio and of the substitution in of untrained teachers, changes in supply and demand may be difficult to predict. These arguments are likely to apply particularly to higher education, as academic salaries are typically set in internationally competitive markets and international mobility is high.

Yet despite high within-occupational mobility, teaching and higher education may have low between-occupational mobility: Ehrenberg et al. (1991) find faculty retention rates to be stable over time, for several reasons. First, changing average real earnings levels will influence faculty job search behaviour only if these changes are relative to other institutions (because these are where most faculty move to). Second, there are few non-academic options for faculty so their labour mobility is constrained (although this is increasingly less the case). Third, departments may be able to lock staff in over teaching years so that job changing is costly and so that such costs rise as outside options become more attractive, offsetting any changes in faculty mobility. Finally, part-time faculty may be used to stabilise the market. As well as the external efficiency referred to above, this may also impact on input-choice efficiency through obstacles to the hiring of teachers.

In summary, then, terms and conditions for education staff may be changed to ensure a sufficient supply of teacher inputs to equilibrate with demand, and markets appear effective in doing this. However, terms and conditions also need to be set to ensure that effort levels are maximised. The latter concern, that of optimal teacher deployment, is taken up next.

6.2.4   The Effects of Teachers

As well as getting sufficient numbers of teachers, education enterprises also need to get the complement of staff so as to maximise factor productivity. To ensure the optimal allocation of teachers, productivity needs to be identified and embodied in pay decisions. The intention is then to use teaching inputs efficiently, that is, where their productivity is an optimal complement to other factors. This may be particularly important for education, because consumers of education (pupils and their parents) may not have a very direct mechanism for expressing their desire for better teachers (particularly if education is state-controlled). In part this is because education is compulsory but it may also be because identifying the 'optimal wage' is difficult: teachers share students and students bargain with the school, not with individual teachers. It may also be difficult because teacher pay will not be flexible enough to reflect individual productivity. Of course these factors may apply in other industries, but two important influences on the optimal staffing allocation, which may be particularly pertinent in education, are identified here.

One salient factor influencing the optimal allocation of teacher inputs is unionisation, as teachers are commonly members of unions and professional associations. Dolton and Robson (1996) describe trade union concentration within the teaching profession, charting the rapid growth in UK membership (as a percentage of all employed teachers) since 1970. They note that teachers do not lapse membership when out of the labour market and so hysteresis and insider–outsider dynamics may therefore be muted amongst them. Teacher union influence may therefore be resistant to long run (Western economy) trends of declining unionisation (and teacher union power may vary counter-cyclically with employment growth). As well, because the government is a monopsony, trade unions may have an important role in redressing the bargaining power which the government has in setting employment terms in the teaching profession and determining the production function.

Teacher unions may influence the preferences of government about how much to spend on education, both on the union members and on other inputs. The most evident and direct effect is likely to be on teacher earnings. For the US, average teacher salaries appear to be 9.5% higher in districts where there is collective bargaining; unions may also increase professors' salaries by 6–13% and increase the returns to seniority (Duplantis et al., 1995; Lillydahl and Singell, 1993). They may also compress salaries: the salary premium to unionisation for US faculty is approximately 4% but with significant positive and negative variation (Ashraf, 1992). These figures are comparable to, but slightly lower than, effects of unions on other occupations' earnings.

The important question is whether or not such bargaining represents a distortion from efficiency; Hoxby (1996a) has investigated this. Teachers should be maximising the same objective function as the pupils or parents, that is, the outcomes of educational achievement. More likely, as with other worker groups, teachers may optimise a different function where activities which differentially affect them are given greater weight than those which influence student performance. So teachers would prefer investment in direct teacher resources, rather than on general school resources, such as libraries or computers. If there is little competition to state schooling and low between-occupational mobility, for example, teachers and governments may collude to reduce productivity and so generate 'wealth transfers' to educators (West, 1970; Lott, 1987a). However, teachers and their unions may have some inside information about student needs which parents do not have, such as students' relative aptitude or the most effective pedagogies, and this information can be incorporated into provision.

Thus, teacher unions may be described either as rent-seeking, that is, where teachers do not have the same objective function as parents, or efficiency-enhancing, that is, where teachers do have the same objective function but they also have greater information. There are a number of channels through which either union effect could be mediated: through school inputs, school budgets, productivities of inputs and through teacher effort. Duplantis et al. (1995), for example, find the average US school district expenditure to be around 16% higher because of greater unionisation. However, because of increased budgets under either type of union (efficiency-enhancing or rent-seeking) and because it is not easy to distinguish between inputs benefiting teachers and inputs which only teachers know will benefit students, it is the productivity of school inputs which separates rent-seeking from efficiency-enhancing unions. For the US, Hoxby's (1996a) findings – that trade unions typically increase inputs but also seem to worsen performance – are in line with Peltzman's (1996) evidence that unions lower scores for non-college students and Eberts and Stone's (1995) summary: union workers earn more, teach smaller classes and spend less time instructing students. In standardising education provision, US unions appear to raise the costs of a given quantity and quality of education.

A second pertinent factor arises because it may be hard to structure incentives to improve teacher performance. An efficient payments system is one where the person who makes the effort decision is the residual claimant to the extra output or profit. Identifying this residual claimant is not easy in not-for-profit enterprises. Managers typically improve productivity through merit pay schemes or through incentives, but casual evidence suggests that teaching is not extensively or intensively monitored by management. Thus, if monitoring is low level and outcomes are hard to measure, this increases the need to structure incentives in an appropriate manner and to devise efficient payment systems for teachers.[16] If incentives matter, and there are intuitive reasons why they would be expected to (along with evidence that they do), then enterprises should offer incentive pay schemes. One way would be to calibrate teacher pay: teaching staff effort could be influenced through changes in the relative pay of junior staff compared to senior staff; through greater performance-related pay; through changes in part-time to full-time teacher pay; or through targeted pay to teachers in particular subjects.   Collective, national bargaining over teaching contracts may restrict these options, however.

Such incentive schemes impose risks on workers (which they may be averse to) and are effective only to the extent that there is a clear link between pay and performance. However, for professional occupations such as teaching it is not likely that all (or even the most salient) aspects of the job can be specified in a formula or contract, so incentive schemes may be hard to devise (although for higher education research, salaries may be highly determinate because research hierarchies are reasonably well-formed). Simple formulae may be used, such as paying teachers by the pass rates of their students, but the efficacy of this depends on whether or not this simple measure captures a teacher's role in the school's production function. If it does not, teachers will behave dysfunctionally (counter-productively) by, in this case, teaching to the test. Relying on subjective evaluations of performance may allow for an overall assessment which is more finely nuanced and so may get closer to the productive contribution of the teacher to the institution.   But these evaluations also have their disadvantages: workers can behave dysfunctionally in subjective as well as objective ways, by producing only the outcomes which their managers will observe, for example. Principals or governing bodies themselves may also be unable to implement subjective evaluations: they may either be too lenient, unwilling to give bad ratings to workers, or they may compress evaluations, not distinguishing the gap between good and bad workers (Prendergast, 1999). For these reasons, incentive schemes in education are hard to devise and to implement.   Furthermore, because of the education production function, institutions may find that one of the two common incentive schemes – working in teams – is not practicable either. Promotion may therefore be the main incentive.

In addition to promotion and/or calibrated salaries, higher education institutions use an idiosyncratic mode of employment: tenure. A number of models have been used to explain this mode (although it has become less common during the previous two decades).   One such is Carmichael's (1988), predicated on the assumption that new faculty members are selected by incumbents and they might never be willing to hire someone who is better than they are.   Hence tenure for incumbents ensures that they will make an optimal decision on new hires.   Tenure effects can also be considered in contracting theory: agents such as university faculty cannot easily contract because they do not know the outcomes of their employment. Tenure is a way around such ill contracting, arising where future abilities are uncertain and staff are highly autonomous in contributing to the enterprise's output.   This autonomy may be a valid assumption for research work by higher education faculty, but less so for teaching if students are co-taught.

These factors – unionisation and incentives – are important to the extent that the allocation of teachers matters to educational achievement. On this, there is some economic evidence. Ehrenberg and Brewer (1994, 1995) find teachers' verbal ability does matter in improving student outcomes, albeit with data from the 1960s (although they also point out that teacher scores have fallen since then). Hanushek (1992, 107), in a model of family composition, estimates the effect of teachers on student achievement and finds 'estimated differences in annual achievement growth between having a good and having a bad teacher can be more than one grade-level equivalent in test performance'. If a student has a sequence of poor teachers, this could significantly compound performance differences.

Other economic investigations of teacher deployment have not been generous. Ballou (1996) describes the hiring processes for teachers in the US, finding these to be not particularly effective in hiring more able teachers and so impairing input efficiency and reducing the efficacy of teacher training programmes. Lankford and Wyckoff (1997, 372) describe the incompatibility of payment schemes for teachers with 'recruiting and retaining the most able college graduates' and find 'the vast majority of teaching districts are likely to have inefficiently allocated a disproportionately large share of resource to veteran teachers for whom job tenure is only marginally affected' (for similar international evidence, see Bressoux, 1996).

Other tests using international evidence of the optimal use of particular inputs have been offered by Pritchett and Filmer (1999). They argue that the production function for education relies too heavily on teacher inputs in that the cost-effectiveness of achievement gain is much lower for teacher inputs than it is for alternative inputs. (This argument need not be refuted by a comparison of teacher salaries with those of other professional workers: overspending on teachers may apply to the teacher budget rather than to individual teachers.) Pritchett and Filmer use three methods to justify this conclusion. First, they use cost-effectiveness ratios: physical inputs have the highest cost-effectiveness ratios. Second, they cite production function studies: teacher variables have the lowest confirmation ratios on improving the output of students. Third, they use parental evaluations, which downgrade teacher performance. Each of these expositions suggests that teacher input may be over-used compared to other factors. (This evidence need not be discrepant with the conclusion that teachers matter – teachers may matter, but either less than other inputs or in ways which do not obviously relate to their earnings.) Together this information on the potentially sub-optimal use of teacher inputs is powerful. However, the general issue regarding the appropriate mix of factors to produc education is taken up more formally in the section on factor complementarity. Before this, the other inputs into education are considered.

6.3   OTHER INPUTS

6.3.1   Student Inputs

Students occupy a critical place in the analysis of education provision: they are both an input and an output, but in aggregate they are also a much larger composite of effort than the teacher input (even allowing for the lower opportunity cost of children). Clearly, education is not simply imposed on students, differences in student effort will impact on the efficiency of education providers and the quality of the student input may in fact be a defining characteristic of many education providers, particularly if other inputs are constrained. This has been discussed in Chapter 4, reflecting the role of students in driving both education revenues and technologies. Moreover, students are an input which may be unusually intractable (that is, have a low elasticity of substitution): schools have only limited opportunities to 'fire' students (expel them) and in the aggregate this is of course not possible up to the school leaving age.   This problem of controlling and deploying student inputs is clearly important: much of this student resource input has been lumped together as 'developed ability', analogous to a factor endowment and so less amenable to economic interpretation. In developing models of student effort, two aspects should be considered.   In evaluating the cost-effectiveness of educational programmes, recognition should be made for the prior attainment of students, that is, their quality as inputs. This is a technical, modelling problem. The more important aspect is student effort during instruction time.

Regarding student time, one approach which may be fruitful for economists, following Bishop (1996b), is to examine student effort levels within a competing choice framework.   Individuals devote effort to obtaining grades, conditional on the contributions of other factors (for example, teacher assistance, peer behaviour). Effort will be maximised to the extent that the education system either: assesses students in ways which yield substantial benefits or costs to the student; defines achievement 'externally' (rather than allowing the student or the class to define it); and/or that the system articulates an ostensible link between what is learnt and what is graded (Bishop, 1996b, 679–681). Proxied by attendance, classroom effort may be easily observable. Less observable, but perhaps equally important, would be individual effort on independent study outside school time. Bacdayan (1994, 1997) has modelled the deployment of effort (time) between individual study and classroom study in a single setting in US higher education; individuals trade off the time prices of learning either in school or outside. These time prices will vary according to the difficulty of the course, the quality of instruction and the learning environment within the school. As with any production function, students will invest in each mode of learning so as to equate the ratios of the marginal products to prices.

Some evidence on competing choices may be identified from combinations of education with work, the earnings from which may represent the opportunity cost of education. Here the individual faces an implicit trade-off between school work, that is, the accumulation of human capital, and paid work, which will preclude such accumulation and so have a negative effect on academic achievement. This is a trade-off which most students face (as do workers who are training) and it is likely to become increasingly important as fees are introduced for more educational services and borrowing constraints remain. Light (1998), for example, uses US longitudinal data on high school workers between 1979 and 1991 to look at whether or not out-of-school work is complementary with school performance in enhancing subsequent earnings. The mean work effort during the last year of high school, at around 10 hours per week, appears to be associated with a modest (2.4%) wage premium after graduation. The net effect of such work is positive and skill-enhancing in terms of wages (with the most significant effect on ensuring employment after graduation). Ehrenberg and Sherman (1987), also using US longitudinal data, find that weekly hours worked do not influence grade point average score but do reduce completion rates and extend the duration before completion, particularly if the work is off-campus. Up to certain threshold levels, work and schooling may be complementary activities.

6.3.2   Managerial and Physical Inputs

As well as the labour inputs of teachers and pupils, there are also managerial and physical inputs into the production of education. With a standard technology and scant product differentiation in schooling, however, there may be little scope for managerial inputs to influence the efficiency of educational enterprises. Plus, public sector education is generally criticised, perhaps in the belief that x-inefficiency is common, for being overly bureaucratic and for over-utilising administrative staff. Relatedly, schools are considered to be too rule-bound, with too much centralisation, overly formal operations and strict hierarchies (Chubb and Moe, 1988); again these serve to dampen the scope for innovative management. Such inertia may seem like a soft target and so it needs to rigorously tested. Moreover, mainstream micro-economics typically sidelines entrepreneurial skill as 'indivisible' to the expansion or contraction of a firm and the perfectly competitive model abstracts away much of the managerial role in dealing with uncertainty, technical change and the behaviour of competitors. Two aspects of the managerial role are noted here; Ross and Levacic (1999, 79) itemise other tasks.

First, managers will have a key role in the deployment of all other inputs and in particular in teacher selection, assignment and pay (Fidler et al., 1998). Ballou and Podgursky (1995), for example, consider how teachers evaluate the managerial productivity of principals. Such principals may have a positive effect on all other inputs with their general influence on the allocative efficiency of education enterprises and on reducing x-inefficiency by clearly defining the optimisation constraint under which the school operates. Specifically, they may impact on teachers' productivity (through the smooth management of staff) or student effort (as role models). However, managerial skills in education may be converged if salary scales and teacher allocation are set exogenously (by unions or by the imperatives from a standard pedagogy, from promotion rules or from professional autonomy). Notwithstanding these constraints, Brewer (1993), using evidence on 320 US public school principals, finds significant effects on student learning outcomes: both in terms of teacher selection and goal setting, high quality principals have a positive influence on student achievement. As well, learning outcomes for students and absolute pay levels of principals are correlated.

Second, the use of administrative resources is important, with some criticisms of an 'administrative blob' (Brewer, 1996). Certain types of educational administration – those that represent rule-binding behaviours most clearly – are most susceptible to these critiques. A strong version of this critique would be that the marginal product of administrative resources is negative, adversely affecting resources used in other ways. A weaker version would be that administrative resources have a lower marginal product than other expenditure items. In rebuttal, some non-instructional expenditures may involve resources used to improve peer or parent input rather than direct teaching; and these inputs would not show up on the schools' balance sheet. Brewer (1996) has looked at the allocation of expenditures across instructional and non-instructional expenditures within 700 New York school districts. From a generalised production function and a range of least squares estimations, US evidence suggest that both district and building administrators rarely have a statistically significant effect on achievement, relative to teaching inputs (Brewer, 1996, 118). More specific is the evidence of the greater proportion of expenditures spent in the classroom when the schools system has external assessments (Bishop, 1996b, 596).

As well as managerial inputs, physical inputs within the education provider should also be considered for their contribution to internal efficiency. These physical inputs may be divided into hardware, such as furniture and facilities, and software, such as instruction materials (Harbison and Hanushek, 1992). Reflecting the labour-intensive mode of production, these are typically given much lower priority than investments in teachers:

in 1998, UK per-pupil expenditure on information and communications technology for teaching and learning, for example, was approximately 1–2% of total expenditure (DfEE, 1998c).

In part, the lesser use of physical inputs reflects the (historical) ownership structure of state education: UK funding of schools and universities for physical capital maintenance has been borne by supra-institutional agencies, such as local authorities or funding councils. Placing such physical inputs outside the individual institution's command may dampen incentives to invest in such inputs (or perhaps reduce the investment's effectiveness), particularly if the teaching lobby is powerful. But it may also impair optimal resource allocation at school level. Perhaps unsurprisingly, therefore, the limited evidence on this – by Harbison and Hanushek (1992) – finds hardware and software inputs are highly cost-effective to introduce, especially if they reduce the number of years to complete schooling. Physical inputs may also be important if there are substantial difficulties in identifying and rewarding effective teacher inputs: without efficient teacher compensation, investments in hardware and software may yield relatively high returns.

6.3.3   Household Input

Extending the generality of education production functions, household environments and the characteristics of the community will contribute to the learning environment for individual students (community variables will also influence the expected pay-off from schooling). Education is partly produced through a vector of resources allocated by the household, such as parental time (which may be influenced by the number and age spread of children, Hanushek, 1992). Haveman and Wolfe (1995) develop a general framework for determining children's attainments, which depends on: (a) the choices made by society which determine the opportunities available to children (these include most policy instruments); (b) choices made by parents regarding the quantity and quality of resources devoted to their children; and (c) the choices which the students make. This choice-based approach is, in a sense, sequential, in that the environment is set first. It extends the production function modelling represented in equation (4.1) and indicates that formal schooling is only one of the inputs into education: circumstantial facts will affect human capital quality. Human capital levels may therefore differ across students with the same level of schooling.

Parental and home involvement in education may take a number of forms, for example, at school (as volunteers or assistants), in learning activities in the home, in school relationships (through communications) and in governance. Parents can participate in schools – through governorships or information-sharing – and in many cases may make top-up monetary contributions for differentiated provision. However, these contributions are likely to be swamped first by home effects – the provision of an effective learning infrastructure and complementary resources – and second by parental effort levels.

It seems likely that incorporating parental input would exacerbate the schooling investment differences observed across socio-economic groups. For the UK, Feinstein and Symons (1999) model the dependence of secondary school attainment on parental input using the National Child Development Study. They use an instrumental variable for parental input in secondary school, based on prior scores of teachers' impressions of the interest parents take in the education of their children. They find that for secondary school attainment, parental interest dominates influences of socio-economic class, parental education, family size and peer group influences (although parental input is itself strongly correlated with these socio-economic variables). Such evidence at the least makes clear that public sector provision is not the only input and may be substituted. Indeed parental input into education may be greater than that of a school (thinking of teacher–pupil ratios as roughly 20:1 and parent–offspring ratios as 3:1).

Further, it may be argued that parental input is under-supplied, perhaps because the parental contract with a free-at-point-of-sale school is not clear (Herrnstein and Murray, 1994). Bishop's (1996a) evidence may be cited on the relatively low priority US parents attach to education: despite a significantly lower investment in their children's education, US parents view that education to be of acceptable standard.[17] Hence, not only may parental input be substantial, but it may also have a higher marginal rate of return than government inputs.

Empirically though, parental input is largely an unknown variable: there are problems in estimating the amount and value of such input, although it should be possible to impute shadow prices or wages for parental time (see Rouse, 1998a). For example, family income might serve as a proxy for the quality of family effort into children's education. But this in turn may be inaccurate if wealthier families have less need to invest in human capital for the future or if parental effort in the labour market varies negatively with child-rearing effort. More generally, each of the individual, household and community variables will be only imperfectly observable; formal schooling's influence on behaviour may, therefore, be a result of measurement error or misattribution. Bias in the imputed significance of education is likely if there is substantial heterogeneity across individuals, households or communities. Behrman and Stacey (1997) give a long list of possible sources of such unobserved heterogeneity, where individuals are seeking both education and health. For example, some predetermined individual characteristics may influence the production of both health and education: healthy children may also learn better. Family endowments may differ as to their relative efficiency in producing individual education and individual health: some households may be better at making their children intelligent than they are at making them healthy. The tastes of households over child quality versus parental consumption may differ: some parents will allocate lots of resources to child quality (perhaps reflecting expectancies of family size), others less. Within the community, there may be differences in the expected returns to education versus health; communities will differ in their access to and prices they face for inputs which improve education as against those which improve health (perhaps marginal tax rates favour education accumulation over health preservation).

6.3.4   Peer Inputs

Education can be individualised, but it mostly takes place in classes: peer group effects may therefore be significant in influencing an individual's educational outcomes.   Again the endowment ability of peers is distinguished from how peer groups are composed and how they interact. In particular, students are competing with each other for the scarce resource of dedicated instruction. Glewwe (1997) presents an aggregated model to determine how peer effects should be input into the production process, where achievement is a function of ability. Representing students as low and high ability p_L and p_H on achievement A, then streaming a group of students where a proportion q are low ability yields:

$$A_{STREAM} = qA(p_L) + (1 - q)A(p_H) \qquad (6.1)$$

In contrast, mixing students will yield an achievement level:

$$A_{MIX} = A(qp_L + (1 - q)p_H) \qquad (6.2)$$

Figure 6.3 shows an individual student's achievement level against peer group ability. Here an individual's achievement is positively related to the ability of the group: so in a group with low (high) ability, achievement is A_{PL} (A_{PH}). Average achievement can be interpolated as the straight line joining these two achievement levels. Alternatively, mixing students will generate a peer group with low and high ability students, in proportions q and $1 - q$. If achievement levels increase in a convex form, as in Figure 6.3, and if the education provider is optimising absolute achievement additively, then streaming students yields a higher level of student achievement to mixing ($A_{STREAM} > A_{MIX}$).

Thus peers may have positive or negative effects on the own-student production function for education. Negatively, peers may be thought of as creating congestion for other individual students, perhaps through absorbing scarce teacher time at the expense of the rest of the class. Positively, peers may interactively teach each other, as well as allow the price (unit cost) of education to be reduced. With ability grouping or tracking, pupils may be able to progress at their own level and the mode of instruction can be adapted to the needs of the group; this may reduce failure, make education more interesting and make teaching easier. With pre-selected groups, education credentials at the end of the course may be more discriminating; this may be important in the labour market for allocating workers. As well, congestion effects may be lowered through pre-selected groups. There may also be economies of scale in education provision for homogeneous student groups. However, lower ability pupils may learn more effectively with higher ability pupils and stigma effects from tracking may arise (raising drop-out rates). Hence tracking is of interest because particular tracking systems will be more efficient than others (Gamoran, 1992); because tracking may impose externalities on other students or on other schools within a system; and because of how tracking motivates effort by students and parents. Glewwe (1997), for example, does find peer groups to be important, but his analysis is at district-level, rather than capturing within-school or within-class effects.

Figure 6.3 Mixed and Streamed Student Enrolment

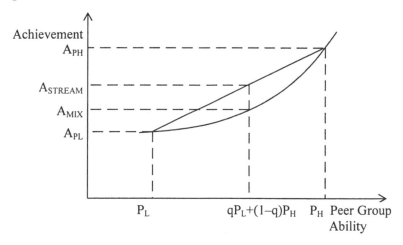

Generally, efficiency conditions for the partitioning of students depend on the interaction between achievement and average ability. If the interaction between an individual's ability and the percentage of high achievers in the class is positive, then all the best students should be allocated to the same class (Arnott and Rowse, 1987). However, the predictions from a customer-input technology are ambiguous: at the optimum, the net values of students of a given ability should be the same whichever track or class they are allocated to. In Epple and Romano's (1998) model, high income and low ability students would be willing to cross-subsidise low income and high ability peers. So mixing may be optimal, when these peer-input pricing rather than simple learning effects are introduced.

Moreover, several problems with such streaming models arise. First, the optimand for achievement may not be the absolute levels of performance but may instead be a compressed outcomes (for example, a 100% literacy rate). If so, then the superiority of A_{STREAM} over A_{MIX} need not be an ultimate objective. Second, peer group effects may operate through a number of variables – including household and socio-economic variables – which may not yield simple convexity of peer effects. Third, the interaction terms between peers may not be easily modelled: the dispersion of peer endowment may matter as much as the absolute amount. Finally, context effects and endogeneity should be distinguished: students are likely to choose peers who share similar educational objectives.

6.4   FACTOR COMPLEMENTARITY

6.4.1   Elasticity of Factors

Input-choice efficiency mandates that factors should be optimally combined in the production function. Both technical and allocative efficiency are important, in that the equi-marginal principle dictates that the ratio of marginal product to price be equal for each input. With a multi-product enterprise such as education, the marginal value product of the inputs toward each outcome should be equated. Technical efficiency may occur with any input combination on a given unit isoquant (Barrow, 1991). Allocative efficiency occurs where inputs are utilised in the correct proportions, based on their relative prices. Hence education enterprises can be technically efficient, but need not be allocatively efficient.

To establish how different inputs can be combined or substituted for each other, elasticities of factor substitution can be calculated. With data on 175 Michigan school districts, Gyimah-Brempong and Gyapong (1991, 1992) use a translog cost function to estimate elasticities of factor substitution between teacher input, instructional support services and non-instructional support services (including administration). Their estimates of Allen partial elasticities are shown in Table 6.3. The off-diagonals indicate how the use of one factor varies when the price of another factor changes; these are all positive and with statistically significant difference from zero. Hence each of these factors appears to be a substitute for the others.

Similarly, Chang and Tuckman (1986) calculate Allen partial elasticities of substitution for different grades of higher education faculty. Four ranks of faculty are identified – professor, associate professor, assistant professor and instructor (across four types of institution). Overall, Chang and Tuckman (1986, 200) find employment in most of the faculty ranks is not highly responsive to a change in relative prices (a 1% change in the price of full professors relative to associate professors, for example, leads to a 2% change in associate professors being substituted in). Multiplying such elasticities of substitution by the respective cost share of a given factor, a price elasticity of demand for that factor can be derived. Both the above sets of results show the own price elasticities of demand to be negative, significantly different from zero and less than unity: the demand for inputs is generally inelastic. This suggests that, as input prices rise, the cost of producing education is likely to rise more than proportionately. These elasticities are calculated for short run changes in the production function, however, and may be greater for changes over the long term.

Table 6.3   Allen Elasticities of Factor Substitution

	Teacher Input	**Instructional Support Services**	**Other Support Services**
Teacher Input	−0.70	0.73	1.02
	(0.17)	(0.31)	(0.21)
Instructional Support Services		−7.98	0.82
		(0.84)	(0.19)
Other Support Services			−1.96
			(0.04)

Notes: Elasticities are calculated at the means of the variables. Standard errors are in brackets. The Allen elasticity of substitution measures the cross price elasticity of demand between inputs i and j divided by the cost share of input i(j).
Source: Gyimah-Brempong and Gyapong (1992, 213)

Although these are the input-choice efficiency criteria for education enterprises, two operational difficulties arise. First, many of the above inputs do not have market prices or well-constructed shadow prices and so the relative prices of two inputs (for example, peer time and home input) may be difficult to calculate. Second, some of the inputs are outside the control of the educational enterprise, making it difficult to obtain or prescribe the optimal factor mix. Schools principals will have influence over teacher and physical resources, some influence over peer effects and student effort, but little influence over household inputs.

6.5   ISSUES AND CONCLUSIONS

This chapter has focused mainly on teacher inputs, following the substantial literature on the economics of teacher supply. Such teacher inputs are responsive to the market mechanism, with 'striking evidence of a significant positive association between the rate of adjustment of teachers' relative earnings and the level of market excess demand' (Dolton, 1996, 201). Relative earnings for other graduates are likely to have an effect on the supply of teachers, as is the dispersal of earnings; non-pecuniary factors are also important to those becoming teachers (with evidence that the 'tastes' for teaching as a profession are more well-defined than for other occupations). This responsiveness is important because a key conclusion from this chapter is that the factor mix is not important in practical terms. Most of the monetary (government) running costs are deployed on teachers and their performance is the foundation of the education production function. Other inputs are to a large extent either constrained in use or commanded outside the education provider. This then transfers research inquiry toward particular forms of teacher input, toward the role of unions and toward worker incentives as ways to enhance efficiency. More generally, Keep (1993) identifies the need for an overall strategy for teachers, where the general focus is on: teacher training; assessment and appraisal; reward systems; career structures; and use of other staff.

Yet as an efficiency criterion, factor mix is important and elasticities of substitution can be used to identify factor substitutes and complements. In general, evaluations of the returns from changing various inputs will be most useful if they translate the production relation estimates into standard economic metrics, such as cost–benefit ratios, internal rates of return and/or elasticities of substitution (Behrman, 1996). However, few stylised, plausible facts have emerged about factor inputs, leaving a theoretical framework about factor substitutability and complementarity which is as yet empirically modest.

Perhaps a more straightforward approach is to look at what direct barriers there are to changing expenditures and altering the input mix. Such costs may arise from fiat imperatives of a set (national) curriculum and policy inertia, so that spending on some inputs has been mandated and thus cannot be changed. For instance, teacher pay in the UK has been set by a different group to those making political promises about the pupil–teacher ratio (Dolton, 1996). As well, with split control of inputs, resources are not controlled by a single agency: government resources are managed at different levels (with running expenditures delegated to colleges and schools, but capital expenditures often not). Some of the most important inputs – parental effort and perhaps student effort – are only indirectly within the schools' control. Finally, some inputs are easier to manage and command than others (for example, capital versus students). There may be rigidities in the demand for educational outputs and in what is acceptable as an education production technology. General equilibrium effects may also be important: switching to a 'cheaper' input will of course raise the demand and so the cost of that input: factor prices cannot therefore be assumed constant (particularly if there is a relative price effect impairing productivity over time). On production functions, care needs to be taken that even if outputs are correctly specified, inputs are also and that proxies for inputs are not used instead (for example, family income is only an indirect proxy for home inputs). All these caveats suggest that economic re-engineering from theoretical principles should be cautious.

Finally, the equi-marginal principle implies that there is a knowable, optimal allocation of inputs; this may be hard to establish with cross-sectional data (although Moll, 1998, is confident that a cost-less reallocation of resources could improve cognition skills in a school system such as that in South Africa). Similarly critical to the economic method is the underlying assumption that sub-optimality can be easily identified. As Pritchett and Filmer (1999) note, a failure to reject zero marginal product effect of higher teacher wages or lower class sizes on student achievement may mean that in fact schools are at the optimum position.

7. The Theory of the Market

7.1 INTRODUCTION

The theory of the enterprise has been used to look at the supply of education by schools and colleges; human capital and enrolment choice models have been used to investigate the demand for education. Hence this chapter looks at the market structure, that is, how suppliers compete or co-operate to offer provision, and at the exchange mechanism, that is, how demanders and suppliers transact. The aim here is to see how education might be traded in conventional markets through the equilibration of supply and demand and trace the equity and efficiency implications of this.

In Section 7.2, the classical theory of the market is adumbrated, stylising markets from perfectly competitive to monopoly.. The perfectly competitive market remains the benchmark against which other structures are compared, although a form of strategic oligopoly is typically thought to be relevant across most industries (and in segmented markets). With the involvement of government, much education provision is casually thought to be a monopoly, although quasi-markets in education have developed, along with decentralisation and privatisation. Each of these market structures may be assessed with regard to education provision and Section 7.3 considers the evidence about these markets and trends toward marketisation. This evidence, which draws on both cross-sectional and time-series data from the US and the UK, is so far broadly supportive of enhancements to internal efficiency. The ultimate question is whether such efficiency gains from marketisation compensate for the effects on equity. In Section 7.4, exchange mechanisms are discussed: various mechanisms have been applied, including education vouchers and loans. Vouchers in particular attract persistent attention from economists. The efficacy of these is considered, drawing particularly on evidence from the UK nursery voucher scheme but also on international experiences. In practical terms, however, such schemes appear less efficacious than other forms of marketisation.

7.2   MARKET STRUCTURES

7.2.1   Perfect Competition

Markets may be considered as an efficient mode by which providers co-ordinate with consumers' needs. Competition in education markets means that students can choose superior providers (the more allocatively efficient) over inferior ones. This selection effect may lead to greater output-choice efficiency, although it need not if externalities dominate and if these externalities are not somehow internalised into individuals' atomistic decisions.   Markets work best if property rights are established and ownership is thought to be the best way of ensuring internal efficiency: if those working in schools own or control their budgets, for example, they should have an incentive to ensure efficiency, leading to improved provision. In terms of educational processes, choice and competition may have an effect on: the hiring of staff; on pressures for resources to be allocated more directly into the classroom; and on goal-setting in schools. Such imperatives to input-choice efficiency may also apply within tiers of government. Having fewer school districts or regional education authorities may inflate government spending beyond the optimal level because there is less inter-government competition.   Conversely, greater competition between districts may reduce per-pupil spending at the school level (perhaps by reducing union power, Hoxby, 1999). This may be interpreted as lower priced education (equal to marginal cost) for taxpayers.

Discussion below sheds some light on each of these pressures, as schooling provision may be evaluated against the characteristics of a perfectly competitive market structure.   If the following assumptions of perfect competition pertain to education, then such a market should be efficient in that education is offered, in the long run, with price equalling marginal cost.

First, enterprises should be small relative to the size of the market so that a dominant provider cannot raise price (lower quality). *Prima facie*, schools do appear to be relatively small and of reasonably equal size. But there are two caveats. There may only be a few schools within a given conurbation; although these regions are contiguous and so may constitute a linked market (Downes and Greenstein, 1996, model the locations of private schools in California).   The other caveat is that there are some niche or very high quality providers who may be dominant.   Generally, the evidence from earlier chapters suggests that schools may in fact be too small in efficiency terms. Second, factor prices should be given exogenously; this assumption may be plausible over the medium term (as discussed in Chapter 6). Third, technologies of enterprises are assumed to be identical: for schools operating under national legislation with a national curriculum, with prescriptions on class sizes and national assessments, this assumption may be maintained; and the education being provided might be assumed to be of reasonably standard quality, if there are not wide variations in per-student funding. These characteristics may fit with the education systems of countries such as the UK, Sweden or Norway. Fourth, demanders should be well-informed. Evidence on demand parameters suggests that this is perhaps plausible: as well as the evidence cited above, Woods et al. (1998, 119, 124), using three UK case studies, find a large proportion of parents and pupils could choose from three or more secondary schools and the majority 'got their first preference school'.

A general condition for competitive markets is that enterprises are assumed to be unable to influence the price (quality) at which they or others in the market sell their goods. But schools may be able to exploit the high switching costs that enrolled students will incur if provision is inferior, locking in students and progressively lowering the quality of their teaching. This lock-in is likely to be possible only in the short run, although it may be extended if there is national bargaining over the production function and over payments to inputs.

The final assumption is that there should be no barriers to entry and exit, and it is perhaps in this respect that schools and education providers are relatively insulated from the imperatives of competition (and also market contestability). High fixed costs, reputation and advertising are likely to operate as strong barriers to entry, especially for start-up colleges and universities. Substantial creative destruction is possible, however, and is particularly evident in the US private sector: Rothschild and White (1990, 33) count 33 public higher education institutions which closed between 1960–90; this compares with 242 privately controlled ones. In the UK, institutions faced with declining resource levels may more typically be merged (Dean and Gray, 1998; Chadwick, 1997). Often there is significant political pressure for a poor school to be kept open; the building of a new school may be motivated by political as well as economic concerns; and new schools may face start-up barriers (although these may be the high fixed costs, there are also likely to be regulatory or tax barriers).

Looked at broadly, schooling appears to have plausible conditions for trade in competitive markets (the test applied here is a rigid one, given that many private sector industries are not close to perfect competition). Moreover, market advocates emphasise the beneficial impetus of differentiated choice in schooling (Wahlberg, 1998; Friedman, 1997), even though this will move the market away from one where there is standardised provision. Finally, as evident in most industrial sectors, the competitive market may include substantial 'noise' as good and temporarily bad education are offered. Consequently, market provision of education may temporarily fail to satisfy equity criteria about equal opportunities and equivalent provision for all students (White, 1994). Although, as discussed in Chapter 8, uniform provision is not necessarily a characteristic of public sector education systems.

7.2.2   Monopoly

The polar contrast to perfect competition is monopoly. A monopoly may arise either where there are no substitutes for the good, for example, regional or subject-based specialist colleges; or for institutions with a government mandate; or for some intermediate goods in education markets, for example, curricula; and for examination boards deciding on assessment standards. With such constraints, the provider enterprise can then tie students because this is the only choice available (and/or there are high switching costs), allowing lower quality provision to persist. One important constraint on school choice is likely to be residency decisions and house prices: enrolment may depend on the school's exclusive catchment or territory. The opportunity to choose schooling (and housing) will be much greater to the extent that the market structure detaches the school choice from the residency choice. By forcing families to make a joint housing–education decision, education monopolies may be imposing deadweight losses. Lott (1987a) argues that the exclusive territories of schools will have an adverse effect on provision, allowing schools to over-supply socialisation or indoctrination benefits valued by governments and under-supply human capital valued by pupils. As well, the monopolist may have less incentive to innovate – either in terms of processes to lower the cost of existing products or in generating new products. This may have deleterious effects on internal and external efficiency over the long term.

Yet the cost function may be such that monopolies are optimal, if there are declining average costs at high rates of enrolment, that is, continuously increasing returns to scale. This may make atomistic competition among small providers inefficient. Monopolies may also be able to bargain with monopsonistic trade unions, lowering factor prices. A monopolist may be able to perform the quality checks on provision and act as an information intermediary or broker, where information services are subject to increasing returns to scale. Costrell's (1994) model of standards of assessment may be invoked here: national standards for assessment and the curriculum may be preferred to decentralised ones (a 'natural monopoly' in the production of standards). The rebuttal to this argument is that standards may emerge from and be adhered to by competitive schools (as in technology standards for cars). Within a monopoly structure, monopolists may none the less use multi-part tariffs for pricing of education provision, so that students are charged the marginal cost of production for particular items (for example, for music lessons), and they may price discriminate.

Such price discrimination may be common in education – pupils are identifiable and inter-pupil arbitrage is unlikely.   First-degree price discrimination, where individuals are charged different prices, may occur with scholarship awards. Second-degree price discrimination, where those who buy different quantities may be charged different prices, may occur if students are encouraged to stay with their education provider when there is an opportunity for change (for example, students staying on beyond 16 may move to a college or remain in the school sixth form). Finally, third-degree price discrimination applies to different groups buying education and may be widespread (for example, fees for overseas students). Thus, if significant opportunities for price/quality discrimination exist, then monopolies may replicate the outcomes of a perfectly competitive market.

To formally establish the relationship between returns to scale, equilibrium output and numbers of provider enterprises, reference should be made to the cost and production functions for such education institutions. Competitive conditions typically emerge from there being a U-shaped average cost curve: small enterprises can increase output to reduce average cost up to a minimum efficient scale, beyond which average cost begins to rise. The cost and production function evidence in earlier chapters is not conclusive, but suggests both that education enterprises may be too small and that monopoly provision is unlikely to be optimal.

7.2.3   Strategic Oligopoly

In most industries, provider enterprises need to take account of how their competition behaves. It may be in their best interests to co-operate or collude with their competitors and these arrangements are of interest to consumers and policy-makers. If education providers can collude or are encouraged to do so, as in UK higher education, then they may be able to simulate some of the beneficial characteristics of a monopoly market. One particular benefit might be the sharing of research evidence, for example.

Strategic oligopoly can take a number of forms, as providers make decisions conditional upon their expectations of the behaviour of other providers. (Given formula funding, for example, schools may typically prefer to fix prices and operate with flexible capacities). Alternatively, there may be a number of identifiable dominant strategies for some providers in the market: for example, the market niches of some of the older public schools or Ivy League or Oxbridge universities. Educational enterprises, because of their links to government, may co-operate more effectively. Within the public sector, there is likely to be substantial scope for cartelisation, either by autonomous competitor institutions or under the aegis of the local education authority. Cartels may therefore operate through agreements on quantities of students or through technologies, for example, the number of hours per accreditation. Because education is not generally sold through the price mechanism, the residual competition and collusion are therefore likely to play out in non-price forms, for example, through reputation effects.

However, cartels may be difficult to set up and maintain, particularly if there is excess demand for education. Providers' costs may differ, leading to disagreements on how education is to be priced: for schools with lots of pupils with special needs, costs will be much higher; in the UK further education sector, sixth form colleges and agricultural colleges operate under the same rules, despite very different pedagogies and intake. With many institutions in the bargain it may be harder to identify the reneging or under-performing party, raising bargaining and contracting costs. Such cheating may be difficult to notice in education: it may take the form of lower academic outcomes for the extra enrolees or non-equivalent accreditation. If demand varies significantly per period, providers will not be able to specify agreements about the quantity and quality of provision; this is most likely to threaten post-compulsory collusion: demographic demand for under-16 education may be reasonably stable. Cartels may also be harder to enforce if there is individual negotiation with students, for example, for scholarships or assessment, but easier because individual enrolments are small relative to the whole student cohort (meaning the relative positions of schools will not be rapidly destabilised). If product differentiation is common, then any agreement will be more complex and punishment more difficult (however, this also dampens the effects of reneging). Finally, there is no clear punishment strategy for violation of the cartel. These problems suggest that cartelised control of education providers (possibly through a government agency) will be difficult to sustain; remedies may be either to change the market structure for education to make it more competitive (through the creation of research hierarchies) or to introduce regulatory penalties.

7.3   EVIDENCE ABOUT THE MARKET

7.3.1   Market Reforms

A number of compromises between the command model and perfect competition have emerged in education. One approach is to develop quasi-markets in the provision of education. Such quasi-markets share some of the characteristics of the private market and some of goods provided by the public sector, with six key characteristics (Glennerster, 1991). First, suppliers are in competition – schools and universities may compete for students – but they are not profit-making. This promotes one sort of efficiency (output-choice) but not necessarily internal efficiency. Second, there is ambiguity over the entry and exit of providers – schools or colleges may be closed if their performance is deemed unfit but they may also be underwritten. Third, demanders in quasi-markets express their preference in terms of earmarked funds or vouchers, so parents and pupils choose their schools but revenues are obtained from government. Fourth, demand is highly inelastic for the total good – with education being compulsory. Fifth, regulatory costs and social effects may be substantial, necessitating some forms of government suasion. Sixth, there is no external optimisation procedure, that is, there is no obvious way to identify high-performing schools. This market structure suggests that some forms of efficiency are more likely to be promoted than others.

More generally, the success of these (quasi-) markets depends on the extent to which there is: potential for competition between schools; free flow of information about provision, so consumers can evaluate different schools and make choices; some element of pricing based on demand; effective billing and contracting; motivation toward consumers not providers; and a high cost to cream-skimming (otherwise the school system may be socially fragmented).

Another approach is for the extent of state involvement in education to be relaxed. Decentralisation, one broad strand, devolves state funding, regulation or provision to lower tiers of government, so that decisions are more closely related to the demands of pupils. Decentralisation has been applied across a range of countries and although there have been improvements in internal efficiency, schooling outcomes may not have been much enhanced: Peltzman (1996) finds centralisation reduces AFQT scores (for international evidence, see Bullock and Thomas, 1997). A second strand is for school districts to be allowed to merge or consolidate, in response to community preferences for public goods. Brasington (1999a) investigates the consolidation decisions of school districts in the US using the Tiebout model of public good provision: school districts decide on consolidation depending on their tax bases (property values), student cohorts and average costs of education provision. His evidence suggests that most consolidations serve to cut costs, rather than aim to raise educational quality. Two conflicting trends emerge here: the evidence that smaller (atomistic) providers have lower performance is being set against the evidence that monopolies of provision cushion against imperatives for internal efficiency. Perhaps reflecting this, little consensus appears to exist for the US: in a poll of 69 US economists to a question 'How would average student test scores be affected by centralising school finance at the state level?' the median response was zero (Fuchs et al., 1998).

Broadly, the precepts in favour of competiton, quasi-markets and decentralisation underpinned the market reforms in the education system in

England and Wales over the period 1980–97. Such reforms involved: fracturing of the Local Education Authorities' monopoly of schooling, with the introduction of grant-maintained schools and support for independent schools; liberalisation of the markets for services traditionally provided by Authorities; provision of more performance information; increased flexibility in school admissions to allow greater consumer choice; introduction of more business awareness through the composition of the governing body; and school inspections on the basis of competitive tendering (Bridges and McLaughlin, 1994, 3). It is an empirical question as to whether the benefits of these reforms outweighed the costs; the evidence reported below, at least on the existence of benefits, is encouraging.

7.3.2   The Competitiveness of Schooling

The potential effects of competition in schooling need to be assessed against the evidence. Several avenues are available: either the market could be described in market case studies; the competitiveness of the market could be measured; and/or particular characteristics of the perfectly competitive model could be tested. From Chapter 3, evidence on student choices in higher education indicated that tuition prices and enrolments were sensitive to the menu of provision from rival institutions. This finding suggests that choice will lead to improved outcomes, but more direct evidence is available. A more formal approach measures the competitiveness of the market between schools directly, using the Herfindahl index of competitiveness. With e as the enrolment at each institution and n the number of schools within the region, P is the enrolment share of the ith school:

$$P = e_i \bigg/ \sum_{i=1}^{n} e_i \qquad (7.1)$$

The Herfindahl index H for the region's market competitiveness is then the sum of the squares of these proportions:

$$H = \sum_{i=1}^{n} P_i^2 \qquad (7.2)$$

This index is bounded between 0 and 1, and the larger the Herfindahl index, the less competitive the market (Waterman, 1984, 166–171, discusses other measures of industry concentration and criteria for choosing each one.) Using this measure of competitiveness – either as an absolute measure or at particular critical values – at the school level within a district of

Kentucky, Borland and Howson (1992, 1993) then test for its significance in explaining student outcomes. They find for mild positive significance: schools facing more competition have improved outcomes.

Other US evidence is broadly supportive of market forces. Achievement scores rise as the local education market becomes more competitive, with such pressures obtained with reasonably few providers – perhaps below ten and even below five (Zanzig, 1997). Looking at competition effects between private and state schools, the proportion of students in private schools has a positive effect on high school graduation rates across districts, including those in state schools (Dee, 1998). Blair and Staley (1995), regressing fourth–eighth grade student scores against the average test scores in contiguous school districts, find neighbourhood test scores have a significantly positive effect on the test scores of a given school. Further, the existence of fewer school districts appears to raise government spending because there is less inter-government competition; this may be particularly notable in the US, with the consolidation of school districts (Marlow, 1997). Hoxby (1999, 40) tabulates the effects of competition for elementary and secondary schooling in the US: greater competition among public school districts has a positive effect on student achievement test scores, subsequent earnings and years of education; it also reduces per-pupil spending (the price effect of competition). Hence Hoxby (1994) finds a one standard deviation increase in the Herfindahl index to generate a substantively small increase in reading and maths scores, but that a much greater effect is on school efficiency as per-pupil costs fall (by 17%). In contrast, there appears to be no effect on the decline of AFQT scores from changing proportions of market share across public and private schooling (Peltzman, 1996, 108).

For England, the evidence of Bradley et al. (1998) for secondary schools also broadly supports the market: schools facing greater competition from non-selective schools tend to be more efficient; and more proximate rivals exert a stronger effect on a school's efficiency compared to its more distant rivals. There is also growing evidence on the benefits of local management, which may reflect a more atomistic school system (Thomas and Martin, 1996). And in Chile, education reform in the 1980s directly tied school revenues to enrolments and encouraged private school provision. Such private schools hence gained competitiveness because they could use resources more flexibly, in particular to reduce teacher pay; this led to a decline in the proportions of enrolments in public schools compared to subsidised and fee-paying private schools (Winkler and Rounds, 1996).

However, these correlations do not establish causality, and there are two necessary criteria for these (quasi-) markets to be effective (Levacic and Hardman, 1999). First, school performance should determine the recruitment of pupils: better schools should have higher (or better) enrolments. Second, the ability to recruit and educate pupils should determine the resources which a school obtains: funding has to follow performance. However, in the UK socio-demographic compensations are built into the funding allocation mechanisms, along with substantial central and local government interventions. Hence Levacic and Hardman, looking across 300 secondary schools between 1990 and 1996, find this second criterion to be undermined, with funding only loosely following performance. More positive (albeit substantively small) evidence for the first criterion is found: absolute and time series exam performance had positive effects on school enrolments, rewarding good schools with better student cohorts. In contrast, Bradley et al. (1998) cite the 900 000 surplus places in schools in England and Wales in 1995, notwithstanding one-third of schools having more pupils on roll than their stated pupil capacity. Choice appears to be compromised by the inability of popular schools to expand in response to excess demand (and the inability of under-performing schools to close).

Overall, competitive effects have a positive effect on performance within school systems. However it may be the case that increases in private schooling raise tax revenues for use in state schools (where private purchasers incur the deadweight loss). Also, little is known about how precisely market power is strategically wielded, the advantages of free enrolment and of incentives may be pertinent (when contrasted against the disadvantages of government provision, discussed in Chapter 8). Especially telling would be evidence that state schooling is better when faced with more private competition: intuitively, state schools would be expected to suffer from the cream-skimming away of their best pupils. Moreover, in a market with a number of enterprises, product differentiation may occur, with some school providers offering lower quality education to those of other providers and this may reflect responsiveness to differentiated demand.

International comparisons show the difference in private provision of education and so the possible variations in competitive effects: such provision is less than 10% in England, in Sweden virtually nil, in Australia around one quarter at the secondary level and in Ireland, Belgium and the Netherlands is very much the norm (Ambler, 1994). Such private provision in part reflects excess demand for education, beyond the government supply. However, as James (1987, 1993) points out, much private provision reflects differentiated demand, either linguistic or religious. This tends to support the concerns that privatisation and social stratification are conjoined, although it may also call into question the adverse effects of such stratification (if differentiated provision allows for, say, religious tolerance). Finally, the ideal competitive structure is as yet unknown, and so the level of concentration should not simply be minimised: mergers, particularly horizontally, may be beneficial if they lower costs, but not if they increase market power.

7.4   EXCHANGE MECHANISMS

7.4.1   Voucher Exchange Schemes

As well as the market structure, the exchange mechanism between pupils and schools will influence the standard of education provision. A variety of ways of clearing education markets are used: schools may be able to negotiate individually with pupils; UK universities operate a national auction house with bidding through a single agency in the first instance and then institutions complete unresolved trades individually (contrasting with individual applications to US universities). The exchange mechanism for most goods is through autonomous searching between suppliers and demanders; private schooling, firm training and much adult education constitute a large volume of trade and these are exchanged through this basic mechanism. This normally operates through a process of tatonnement toward the optimal exchange: providers and consumers bargain until an equilibrium position is reached which is mutually satisfactory. The other option is the command model: suppliers must educate specified groups of students; demanders must attend specified schools.

Either set of mechanisms should be efficient in linking consumers to providers, perhaps by facilitating choice and the opportunity for switching between providers or by saving individuals on inspecting schools before enrolment. As noted above, if education is complicated to purchase, then the effects of marketing may differ from those expected generally (that is, downward pressure on prices; on advertising for specialist, information goods in health, see Rizzo and Zeckhauser, 1992). An exchange mechanism should also be equitable, that is, allow for voluntary bargaining and negotiation by both sides; this voluntary aspect is of course undermined in a command model, but it is also problematic when education is subsidised and so students are only part-paying for their education. Both command and market methods have disadvantages: the conditions for tatonnement may not be ideally met in education markets, but the command model has a series of adverse effects on efficiency.   (Notwithstanding, the government does typically intercede to act as an intermediary purchaser or funder between the student and the school; these aspects are discussed in the following chapter.)

More generally, there are various ways of introducing choice into education: at its most basic, students can be given opportunities to attend any state school (with quotas or exclusive territories relaxed); more liberality would allow choice of state or private schooling; government-funded privatisation would involve vouchers; and outright privatisation would eliminate all government subsidies (Cohn, 1997). For example, the funding of schooling in the UK operates through an age-weighted pupil unit formula, which is akin to a 'voucher' system. This is not directly equivalent to the voucher most economists like to call 'money' (in part because of who has ultimate control of the voucher), but it is an attempt to simulate some of the conditions for trade through voluntary tatonnement.

Vouchers create a market in education by establishing an exchange mechanism and the price is the nominal value of the voucher (Levin, 1992). Such vouchers, as an entitlement to an amount of schooling, may then allow pupils to choose their education, but, because of government funding of the voucher, the inequities which come with choice would be ameliorated. Hence, vouchers should stimulate greater freedom of choice, with competition between providers (Rouse, 1998a); and provision may be diversified so that differences in demand can be accommodated. Also, providers should receive signals about the quality of their provision so that rewards and incentives are embedded; the vouchers, representing revenues, should impose budget constraints on providers and simplify the tax effects on private schooling (West, 1997). Although Carnoy (1997) is critical, these attributes seem theoretically appealing, thus leading to repeated exhortations for their use (for a survey of a wide variety of voucher schemes internationally, see West, 1997, 88–90).

But there are considerable problems with implementing voucher schemes. An immediate problem is the setting of the value of the voucher: one option is to issue a flat nominal value, but this may not cover the costs of a school place. The value has to relate (a) the revenue the voucher represents to the provider to (b) the quantity of provision offered to the pupils. Typically, a pledge voucher is issued, prescribing the content of the education, but this pledge prescription may be no different a problem from setting a funding formula. This pledge option allows uniform consumption – with the intention of giving families equal opportunities for common access to a standardised good – and may stimulate competition through enrolment choices. Indeed, the second main element of a voucher system is the terms of enrolment for students across the school district (at different schools). If demand for education is not homogeneous, the most effective exchange mechanism should cater for this, by either allowing vouchers to be supplementable and/or good schools to earn extra revenues (ameliorating possible deadweight losses, as considered in Chapter 8). Because institutions are likely to face different costs and because better pupils (either higher ability or putting in more effort) are likely to be 'lower cost', then under a flat voucher system providers will have an incentive to cream-skim. This will entrench inequalities of provision, meaning that compensatory vouchers may therefore be necessary. Also, a flat voucher is unlikely to yield many of the putative benefits because it does not allow for differentiated demand – a simple open enrolment policy would do equally well. However, cream-skimming may itself serve as an incentive for students to put in more effort if only at the point of enrolment (if so, this may again reveal an equity–efficiency trade-off).

As well as cream-skimming, marketising educational choice (through vouchers or other non-governmental exchange mechanisms) may stimulate grade inflation, as institutions attempt to purvey quality. Narrow self-interest may be destructive of social values, with discrimination against certain groups and some parents denied their first choice, although West (1997, 95) contends that these all occur in the state system anyway. Inequities may arise because of windfalls to parents who previously sent their children to private schools (although this can be addressed through means-testing). An alternative set of criticisms depicts a market system with too much stasis: there may be insufficient factor mobility to stimulate new modes of provision or respond to excess demand; the benefits of choice may be constrained as students may hedge against uncertainty and so all demand the same courses (making the idea of choice otiose). This latter set of arguments conflicts with concerns that education through the market will lead to social stratification.

7.4.2   Evidence on Vouchers in Education

Plenty of evidence on the efficacy of voucher systems is available, although the findings are somewhat mixed. In part, this may be because it is hard to disentangle the effects of an open enrolment policy from a full voucher scheme, as well as because of the heterogeneity of the voucher schemes in practice. In particular, key distinctions across the schemes are: (a) the acceptability of the voucher across types of school; (b) the extent to which the voucher can be supplemented; and (c) the competitiveness of the provider market.

Model-based approaches may offer a comprehensive picture of the benefits of vouchers. Epple and Romano (1998) simulate the introduction of vouchers, using a peer group model of schooling. They map the simultaneous effects on achievement, the tax rate and welfare from variations in the value of a voucher. Achievement gains are generally increasing as a voucher increases in value, because more students in the private sector allows for greater student partitioning by ability and for greater synergies from peer group effects (that is, an allocation of schooling which recognises the differing input costs of students). These achievement gains are increasing until around 90% of the student cohort attends private schooling. The tax rate is also affected by the introduction of vouchers. When vouchers are low in value, their costs are offset by the effects of students attending private sector schooling and the tax rate falls; as the voucher rises in value, it covers the costs of most of the students in schooling and so causes the tax rate to rise. This suggests that government expenditures may rise sharply in a non-linear fashion – more per-student government expenditure encourages a higher rate of take-up – and this may inhibit the introduction of vouchers. Finally, Epple and Romano (1998) find welfare gains from vouchers to be positive, albeit small as a proportion of (parental) income.

Further direct evidence is available from the introduction, over the previous century of state schooling, of voucher mechanisms into a range of education systems. Overall, school choice does appear to have been responsive to provider quality, but social stratification and the erosion of a common culture have been identified as adverse by-products. Evidence is available on schemes in Scotland, New York State and Victorian England (collected evidence is in Cohn, 1997); the large scale voucher experiment in Richmond in the US (1987–90) appeared not to have improved outcomes measured in terms of absenteeism, drop-out, test scores or school desegregation (Chriss et al., 1992). More recent evidence is available on schemes in the US and the UK.

In the UK two overt voucher schemes have been applied. The Assisted Places Scheme was set up in the UK in 1981 to allow high ability pupils from low-income families to attend independent schools. However, the scheme was small scale (applying to less than 1% of students in 1995) and is particularly open to criticisms of inequity in rewarding academically able students, whose life-cycle income prospects are likely to be good regardless of the schooling they receive (West, 1997, 94). A more substantial voucher scheme was introduced in England and Wales for 4-year-olds for the academic year 1996–97 (following the Nursery Education and Grant Maintained Schools Act, 1996). Both its inception and abandonment were strongly politicised decisions, but it offers an important test case of the efficacy of voucher systems.

Prior to the nursery voucher scheme, there was concern over the standards of education: Sparkes and West (1998, 172) describe provision for children under statutory school age as having been 'patchy and diverse'. Although there were a number of modes of provision (private providers, nursery centres, reception classes in school), there was regional differentiation, with ability to pay an important component of access to provision. Under the new voucher scheme, parents received a voucher book, which they could then use in exchange for places offered by validated providers. If the providers charged higher fees than the nominal value of the voucher, then parents could pay the surplus to private providers; in the state-maintained sector, top-ups would be provided by the Local Education Authority. The funds for the vouchers were taken from Education Authorities: based on the previous year's enrolment (1994–95), £1100 was taken from each Authority per 4-year-old. In aggregate, assuming no switch between Authorities and private providers, such a system was intended to be revenue neutral (although the actuality of this was disputed).

A number of substantive problems arose. A flat rate voucher was selected, regardless of variations in costs across the country and variations in local need. Hence, in some regions the value of the voucher was insufficient to cover the costs of nursery provision, with Authorities underwriting the difference between the school's expenditure and its voucher revenues. The system may also have incurred a high dead-weight loss: the voucher was paid to all, subsidising parents who would have paid for their children's nursery education anyway (although these parents may have been using private nurseries because of the standard of provision in the state sector). Another criticism was that the voucher specified an amount of provision, rather than a price of provision: the voucher was linked to a 'daily session of not less than 2.5 hours'. This form of voucher – favouring some providers and some parents over others – further limited the flexibility needed from providers. Information on providers – key to maximising the benefits of choice – was poor: partly this was because the scheme was complicated, but there was little incentive for Authorities to publicise information on competitor private providers. In addition, Authorities could vertically integrate nursery provision to subsequent schooling, locking parents in to choosing their provision.

Administration and implementation difficulties also arose. In order to get compliance from Authorities, the government pledged specific grants up-front to state nursery providers, along with administrative grants. This pledge in effect severed the link between performance and funding, one of the main anticipated benefits of voucher schemes; private providers were therefore at a disadvantage in not receiving front-loaded, underwritten funding. State-run providers were subsidised in the medium term. Combined with an ambiguous call for co-operation by providers, this litany of difficulties suggests against the forceful imposition or creation of the market from this scheme. Finally, Sparkes and West (1998) argue that the voucher scheme failed in promoting parental choice; parents behaved very similarly to how they had done in the past. This inertia is perhaps not surprising: the scheme was not operating for very long, with an uncertain future (with changes in government) and with choice limited in the short run (with immobile factors of production). Nevertheless, the voucher system was fundamentally hampered by the overwhelming complexity of imposing competitive market conditions on education providers, the majority of which were state run.

As well as in the UK, the US education system frequently entertains the possibility of implementing voucher schemes. A range of such schemes are surveyed in Peterson and Hassel (1998), with generally beneficial effects from choice. For the US, Witte et al. (1995) and Rouse (1998b) describe the Milwaukee Parental Choice Program, begun in 1990. This Program (also small-scale, with less than 2% of the enrolment in the public schools system eligible) gave state-aid vouchers to low-income students to attend independent private schools. The intention was that these low-income students would benefit from the educational quality, teaching style and school environment of the private sector. By 1995, 12 private schools were participating and they could accept these voucher students up to 65% of their total enrolment.

Unfortunately, not only was the Program small-scale, but it also allowed choice to be exercised only by the pupils – schools could not reject specific applicants unless they were at capacity – and only in non-sectarian schools. Also, schools' budgets (both those participating and those not) may not have been fully determined by these choice effects, muting any market forces. As a basis for evaluating the general efficacy of voucher systems, this scheme too has some imperfections. Looking at methodological aspects, the evaluations of this Program – comparing the voucher students' performance with that of other students – highlight the difficulties of selectivity of enrolment. In their evaluation of the Program, Witte et al. (1995) compared three groups' achievement: a random sample of Milwaukee school children; a sample of low-income pupils; and those participating in the Choice Program. Their results yielded no evidence that the Program had raised test scores. An alternative approach is to compare those who did participate with those who applied to participate, but were unsuccessful (by chance). Rouse (1998b) does this, compensating for endogenous enrolment and for continuation in the Program, as well as for the fixed effects of students' characteristics. For maths scores, this comparison yields small but positive effect sizes of 0.08–0.12 standard deviations per year; for reading scores, no significant differences were evident. Alternative measures of performance, particularly parents' views, suggest that the Choice Program did raise educational quality, albeit not by any substantial magnitude. Across their evidence on choice-based programmes, Peterson and Hassel (1998) do find parental satisfaction to be much enhanced.

7.4.3   Loans for Education

As well as vouchers, a range of different exchange relationships may be created to make trades in education. These may include mortgage loans with independent grants, graduate taxes and income-contingent loans (Oosterbeek, 1998a, 230–232; on auctions, see Johnes, 1993a). Relatedly, education may be subsidised in a variety of ways, such as through: direct payments to institutions to cover costs; unconditional grants; ability-tested scholarships; means-tested scholarships; repayable loans (at subsidised interest rates); employer subsidies for education release; or tax concessions either to students or parents (Woodhall, 1995). Most education systems use a mix of these methods, which are differentiated primarily by the proportions of full costs which are covered, the conditions under which the scheme is made available (for example, by age, income or achievement) and the spread between the market and the student loan interest rate.

Charging for education is an important way to reveal willingness to pay and students' preferences: course pricing serves a financial function in generating revenue, a rationing function (determining access), a distribution function (relating prices to subsidies) and an information function (reflecting the equality of marginal costs to prices). Yet it may be difficult to ensure these in education. In the UK, for instance, higher education fees are flat-rate and therefore only serve the first of these four functions; the last function is most evidently violated, given the differential costs for subjects. After the introduction of fees in 1998 in the UK, the ratio of undergraduate fees in medicine to those in the humanities was 1:1; the marginal cost ratio was approximately 8:1.

Rather than pay-per-use prices, discretionary loans represent the most obvious way to simulate the disbursements incurred through life-cycle human capital investments, and also ameliorate capital constraints. In UK higher education, for example, undergraduates can access an income-contingent loan, in addition to the means-tested contributions to tuition fees. In Australia, higher education contributions are through an income-contingent repayment scheme, based on flat-rate fees during study (Chapman, 1997). Contingent loans, where no interest accumulates when the individual is unemployed, may be an effective way of ameliorating the problems of under-investment because of irreversibility and employer hold-up. If no interest accumulates when the individual is unemployed, then the interest payments are part of the surplus which individuals and firms bargain over and hence education costs are not irreversible to the individual (Moen, 1998). One benefit of such income-contingent loans is that, because they are conditional on the earnings of each graduate, they represent 'individualised prices' for higher education. Hence the equality of marginal cost and price can be obtained at the individual level, rather than across faculties. The problem here is to define the utilisation of human capital which would incur interest payments, without it having substantial disincentive effects on labour supply.

Whereas grants are more likely to encourage enrolment from low-income students with greater price sensitivity, loans are more likely to stimulate efficiency because the students are directly bearing their own costs (and resources are not being transferred to those who are already endowed with high developed ability or who can simply buy more education). However, few other loan markets are run principally through the state and such loan systems may have high administrative costs – particularly if there are high default ratios. Student loan schemes also typically have low interest rates, which may distort incentives away from investment in other economic activities (and represent a subsidy to wealthier families).

As well, there is only limited means-testing, which reflects a neutral position regarding the current income distribution (but also the administrative complexity and political unpopularity of such testing); and repayments which are responsive to earnings (thus placing a disincentive on work). Similar disincentive effects arise with graduate taxes: these are levied on all parts of income, not just that attributable to the extra education, generating a general disincentive to pay and borrower default. Dynarski (1994), for example, reports a 17% default rate on higher education loans in the US. Johnes (1994), in a study of UK students' loan take-up, finds support for implicit higher education pricing as loan take-up reflects the expected rate of return to graduation – along with a tilting of student choices toward more vocational subjects. The method of funding, particularly higher education, has significant implications for student enrolments, subject choice and levels of provision.

7.5   ISSUES AND CONCLUSIONS

The above comparison of education provision against the notional characteristics of the market suggests that education does have a number of properties which are conducive to efficient marketised provision. The main area where market forces appear muted is in the freedom of entry and exit. This may, however, in part reflect the high fixed costs of provision. Monopoly provision may be possible, although there is no explicit and clear evidence from the cost function or the production function to support this market structure as being optimal. Of more relevance is the way in which, through government links, education institutions can co-operate strategically to offer provision.

Evidence on the market – both in the UK and the US – suggests that there are beneficial effects from competition, either in terms of performance or productivity of schools. However, the causal steps by which competition enhances performance should be identified and established. Although Woods et al. (1998, 200) recognise the positive benefits of the market in terms of accountability and the impetus to continually raise standards (as does Barber, 1996, 68), they point out some disadvantages. These include: significant financial resource and teachers' time and energy diverted to marketing; a relationship between parents and schools which is about image rather than substance; and more weight given to quantifiable (examination results) than to what is important. These may, however, be necessary information costs incurred for the market to work, that is, for greater specificity of pupils' demands and greater clarity of the optimands of the school. Although this may not be the case for education, in other markets advertising typically has the effect of reducing prices. Nevertheless, even if the market is established to provide education more efficiently, the trade-off between that greater efficiency and its effects on the equity of provision still needs to be articulated and formalised.

In education systems across the world, many market reforms and liberalisation are already developing, both on the consumer and supplier side. The range of solutions includes: encouraging direct private provision; greater pay-per-consumption, which should reveal preferences; the creation of capital markets for students to raise funds to pay fees; improvement or better apportionment of property rights or ownership of assets; and exhortations for institutions to compete for students. In the UK this liberalisation was being applied across all sectors. The Dearing Review of higher education (NCIHE, 1997), for example, stylised the professionalisation of the workforce and exhorted universities to respond supportively. It also placed the onus on higher education to seek new and alternative sources of funding. On the consumer side, there was an expectation that individuals would increasingly pay for education directly, with less subsidy.

Although these developments reflect the move away from a command model of education, the evidence on voucher schemes and the administrative costs of student debt management are not fully comforting. Looking at the exchange mechanism of vouchers, a number of new costs arise and these may outweigh the expected benefits of introducing greater freedom into the provision of education. Fundamentally, voucher systems are still subsidies – so many of the difficulties of ensuring efficiency remain – and they necessitate government setting the value of the voucher, that is, the price of education. It may be difficult to separate the task of setting the price of education from dictating the exchange mechanism. The experience of such schemes suggests an important role still for government, a role which is taken up in the next chapter.

8.   The Role of Government in Education

8.1   INTRODUCTION

Governments are heavily involved in education, its provision, funding and regulation. Specific reasons for this have been advanced over previous chapters, for example, capital constraints and/or concerns over the equity of the allocation of provision. Indeed, it might be argued that compulsory education should always be decided collectively, with the goals of government deriving from a political value function which includes more than just maximising individuals' examination scores (Carnoy, 1995). It is therefore desirable to evaluate governments' success in specifying and satisfying this value function. Although the evidence from the previous chapter indicated the effects of the market in enhancing efficiency, a number of equity–efficiency trade-offs have been adverted to. Government's role is therefore to acknowledge these trade-offs and create education systems and modes of funding which reconcile them.

Section 8.2 considers directly the rationale for government intervention in education, taking a demand and supply approach (this rationale builds on the discussions of the demand function for education from sub-section 3.3.1). Having plausibly established government intervention, a particular application is discussed, namely higher education subsidies, and an efficiency condition is established under which subsidies across worker groups can be defended. Section 8.3 explores in more detail the funding of education, considering social and fiscal rates of return and the funding burden. Formula funding is considered, particularly in terms of equity, along with mechanisms for the creation and dissemination of performance information and indicators, to ensure superior regulation of education. Section 8.4 considers the difficulties with government intervention in education, distinguishing the criticisms of government provision from those against government funding. Three aspects are considered: the costs of political suasion, the welfare costs of public schooling and the distortionary effects of taxation on the accumulation of assets to pay for education.

8.2   THE GOVERNMENT IN EDUCATION

8.2.1   Government Intervention

Government funding of education may be simply justified for efficiency reasons either with asymmetric information, increasing returns to scale or because there are externalities. These topics have been discussed in other chapters; here the focus is on government provision itself. A useful distinction, building on previous chapters, is between demand and supply aspects. Augmenting these, it is then possible to consider the argument that government provision is appropriate because education is a collective aim of society.

The demand for education, it is contended, is somehow different from the demand for other goods. First, there may be problems for children in expressing a demand for education; individuals may not realise the benefits of education until it is 'too late' – for any choice to be meaningful requires an awareness of what is being chosen – and there may be an information asymmetry between the educated (who 'know' what the education is worth) and the uneducated (who cannot be sure). Government may embody past wisdom about the benefits of education (and how best to generate human capital) and so may have a role in reducing this uncertainty and ignorance. Second, incomplete contracts typically arise when there are difficulties in measuring the quality of the good (for example, how schooling might inculcate social mores), leading to a sub-optimal allocation of resources. Government may therefore write and enforce these incomplete contracts. Third, education demand is not like that for other consumables in that resale markets are limited. The government may underwrite outcomes, by guaranteeing medical jobs, for instance, for graduates in medicine. Finally, capital markets to borrow may not exist because it may be hard for individuals to persuade banks that education is worthwhile and insurance markets may be missing (particularly for education at lower levels). If there is a gap between the borrowing rate and the lending rate in capital markets, then children of wealthier parents will be more easily able to borrow from within the household. Here the government may offer loans, perhaps on socially redistributive terms.

On the supply side, government may offer education more efficiently than the private sector. First, it may provide services which it is efficient to bundle together along with education: society through government underwrites unemployment so unemployment-reducing education will have a fiscal effect on welfare payments, allowing provision of education and other public services to be merged (Davis, 1998). Second, the longer term horizon of government may allow it to be a credible provider of education, as a government's reputation can be trusted. Third, there may be economies of scale or standardisation in gathering information and organising provision, which the private market would under-provide. The key example here is that of organising a curriculum, where schools may benefit from using a common curriculum and firms may find it easier for screening workers. Fourth, the efficacy of the market depends on some equality of bargaining power, and private providers may have 'too much' influence over pupils; governments can arbitrate. Fifth, it is not easy to raise the efficiency of labour-intensive goods, such as education, because of the relative price effect – it may be hard, for instance, to automate teaching or to speed up pupil–teacher interaction. Government may therefore enforce an intergenerationally equitable contract of education provision against an increasing relative resource burden. Finally, it may be that government support for education acts as a form of compulsory saving, which (myopic) individuals would not commit to.

Relatedly, Shleifer (1998) specifies a set of supply conditions under which government provision – to complement government funding – might be preferred. These would be where: innovation is relatively unimportant – because without market incentives and hard constraints it is unlikely that innovation will take place; reputational mechanisms are weak – so good providers cannot generate greater demand; competition is weak and consumer choice is ineffective – so poor providers would not be eliminated by competition; and opportunities are significant for reducing costs which lead to non-contractible deterioration in quality – because then the market will under-supply education. These conditions, applied to education, prescribe a rather more limited role for government to play in the economy.

Perhaps more importantly, the social benefits of education may be sufficiently large that government should subsidise education to ensure it is not under-provided, that is, at amounts where marginal social benefit still exceeds marginal social cost. (The specific social benefits which education may generate are considered in more detail in Chapter 9.) In this case, the rationale for government provision depends on the size of the externalities relative to the private gains (for example, better health is a fiscal gain but also a private one) and on whether or not the government can subsidise only the externality-generating element of the education. Little evidence is available on the ratio of social to private gains and disentangling the two is problematical. Hoxby (1996b), for example, considers that these externalities need not be large before government provision is favoured. Given the levels of government involvement in other sectors of the economy, this argument seems persuasive. Heaton (1999) factors in the tax burden of provision of higher education in Fiji, finding high social returns beyond those for the individual.

More generally, society may express a collective desire for education. A social imperative for non-exclusion posits education as a merit good or a public good, perhaps in the belief that social stratification may occur if education is freely chosen. Government may be more effective at ensuring fair allocation and distribution of resources; equal access to services – as redistribution is easier to 'sell' to taxpayers when it is tied to specific services; non-profit oriented decision-making for the interests of the customer; stakeholder personnel policies; and co-operative industry relations (Davis, 1998). Each of these may suggest that government intervention in education is appropriate, but each needs to be established empirically in terms of the efficiency–equity trade-off. Historically, state ownership has served less to promote the social ownership of goods but more because prices and competition were not felt to be applicable to the provision of commodities such as education (or health). Similarly, the argument that education is a public good should be regarded cautiously: in most cases it is both rivalrous and excludable.

Set against this collective view, moreover, might be an individualised one that contends that choosing a school or a type of schooling should be an individual's right – state education may be doctrinaire (or a form of 'despotism over the mind', as John Stuart Mill described it). Lott (1990) argues that schooling may be used as an instrument of persuasion to reduce the costs to government of making wealth transfers to groups it prefers. This argument may explain Lott's evidence: (a) that the pattern and mode of government expenditures on schooling appear to mirror those on state radio and television; and (b) that schooling is typically allocated territorially. Relatedly, if government is to control an individual's education, in doing so it may then feel justified in extending control over a span of family environments because these have a knock-on effect on an individual's school achievement. Opponents of public sector schooling may also draw attention to the fact that many of the benefits of education are independent of who is providing it, and so if private schools are more efficient then they should be subsidised. Redistribution may be separable from provision.

8.3   HOW GOVERNMENT FUNDS EDUCATION

8.3.1   Social and Fiscal Rates of Return

The above arguments do not readily suggest the form of government intervention: governments can provide education, subsidise it or regulate it. Alternatively, governments can write contracts for outsourcing provision, but only if the government knows what it wants will these contracts be straightforward to write (Shleifer, 1998). If educational goals are not clearly known but have to be discerned through the preferences of students, however, private ownership with limited regulation may strengthen the incentives to make investments. Hence a clear rule on the optimal government investment in education is necessary.

Governments may subsidise education on external efficiency grounds, and to assess the benefits of this, private rates of return (as described in Chapter 2) can be modified into 'social' rates. Such 'social' rates incorporate transfers and the costs borne by the taxpayer to support education (the costs of any grants and the difference between the price to the student and the cost). Earnings premia will differ because extra tax payments from higher earnings should be included; costs will differ because private individuals do not bear the full costs of education. However, such social rates should also include the external benefits of education because these are part of the governments' motives for subsidising education in the first place. Typically, though, these rates do not include externalities and might be criticised as narrowly conceived. Even less rarely do such rates include the deadweight loss of government intervention (West, 1991). If gross pre-tax earnings are used, then some externalities are being incorporated, it might be argued, through an individual's contribution to government provision of such externality-generating activities.

Looking at available evidence, narrowly conceived 'social' rates of return are often found to be below the private rate of return by a few percentage points (because of the subsidies). Ashworth (1998) estimates the social rate of return to the average UK graduate after expansion (with an alpha factor of 60%, 2% economic growth and 4% graduate unemployment) at 6.7%; for the marginal graduate, the estimate is 3.1%. Given the arguments for government intervention resting in no small measure on the positive externalities of education, though, these rates appear insufficient as investment criteria for education. Aggregate GNP rather than individual earnings may include the externalities of education. McMahon (1999) does calculate macro-economic social rates of return for the UK and US, using the correlation between GNP and education from a regression model extrapolated 35 years ahead. Controlling for changes in population, physical capital and government policies, this macro-economic rate is around 14–15%. This estimate is substantially above the narrower measures of the social rate of return.

Hence a more accurate nomenclature is needed to replace 'social' rates (and 'private' rates) where only earnings effects are included. Instead, full-social rates would include both earnings effects and all externalities; and full-private rates would include earnings and individualised, non-pecuniary or non-marketised benefits. To complete the definitions, fiscal rates would be the returns to education investment for the government, where the effects on all government revenues and expenditures are taken into account (Nonneman and Cortens, 1997). For example, if education improves health levels or lowers crime, this reduces the costs to a state committed to full health insurance or to comprehensive policing. Again, these also are not included in standard 'social' rates.

A high full-social (or fiscal) return may prompt governments to encourage or fund education. However, the concern should be with the disparity between this rate of return and the full-private rate: government intervention is only justified on efficiency grounds if there are differences between the full-private and the full-social rate of return. If the former rate is high, individuals will undertake education for themselves and pay for it themselves: the government need not subsidise this activity (on external efficiency grounds). The critical value for government should be the full-social rate; if that is above a test discount rate, education should be expanded. However, an individual's full-private rate of return may be low and yet the full-social (or indeed fiscal) return may be high, as with the example of reduced health disbursements or lower law and order expenditures. In these examples, government intervention would be cost-effective, although there are obvious problems in coercing students into such education.

For the UK, rate of return estimates in actuality have had a rather simpler relation to government policy on funding education. The logic may be stylised as one where the higher the 'private' rate of return, the greater the contribution by the individual and so the lower the government subsidy. The high private rates of return to university education during the 1980s, identified in Chapter 2, along with the relatively lower social rates of return led to the government mandate (DES, 1988, 1) to 'share the cost of students more equitably between students themselves, their parents and the taxpayer'. Evidence on greater pay-per-use for graduates referred to the high per-student expenditures in the UK and low share borne by UK students compared to other countries, as well as earnings premia for (male) graduates (DES, 1988); similar arguments were made for reform of funding of higher education in Australia (Chapman, 1997). This prompted the reduction in student living grants and subsequently an imperative that UK students pay part of the average tuition cost (NCIHE, 1997). The Teaching and Higher Education Act of 1998 introduced this new funding scheme, abolishing student grants for maintenance, imposing means-tested contributions to tuition fees (of £1025 p.a. in 1999–2000) and enhancing the income-contingent loan scheme, which is one quarter means-tested.

As an alternative, governments may reduce the disparity between the social/fiscal rate of return and the private by, for example, reducing academics' pay or increasing student numbers with the same level of resource (Ashworth, 1998). However, part of the logic which prompts government intervention – the existence of possible non-contractible deterioration in quality – also means that efficiency gains are hard to enforce. Moreover, these strategies, even in narrowing the differential, may reduce all rates together. The result is a more equitable burden of funding, but an efficiency loss in that intensive margin investments are forgone.

Nevertheless, using these critical investment rates elucidates clearly the benefits of education, clarifying the merits of special interest calls for more graduates in particular subjects. A common canard in the provision of education may be used in illustration: the shortage of engineering and sciences graduates. *Prima facie*, graduates in these disciplines might be thought to have obtained strongly vocational skills. However, the analytical skills of these graduates are prized in other occupations; as a result, many will not move directly into subject-associated occupations. This mismatch may generate a form of market failure, prompting calls for an expansion of engineering and sciences provision. For graduates, market failure may arise because the rewards from these subject-related occupations may be perceptible only imperfectly (and if these occupations require long or difficult training with barriers to promotion, graduates who are risk-averse or face borrowing constraints will avoid them). Skills shortages may be compounded as firms themselves fail to train graduates into careers in the sector and if higher education providers deliver insufficiently relevant instruction. For the broader UK economy and society, the number of workers in these subject-related occupations may be sub-optimal in the long term with their highly technological skills misapplied in generalist occupations, impairing economic growth and innovation.

Yet there is only indirect evidence of a positive relationship between the numbers of scientists and engineers in an economy and its economic growth (Gemmell, 1997). There is some evidence that engineering graduates earn relatively higher private rates of return than graduates from other subjects, but engineering courses are also relatively expensive to provide. Moreover, the rate of return to scientists is not clearly above that of the returns to other degrees (particularly if ability is not adjusted for). Most evidence shows the pecuniary returns to a law or medicine degree are higher than to science degrees, and the differential spill-overs from science degrees remain to be identified (Weale, 1992, 1993). Other work has identified the accuracy of market signals, suggesting graduates do not make systematic errors in deciding which course to take (Dominitz and Manski, 1996; Betts, 1996b; Belfield, 1999).

But even here there is a danger of being too specific in advocating law or medicine degrees. The relative return to other education investments, for example, at primary or secondary level, needs to be considered: investment can either be made intensively (more resources for those already attending) or extensively (extra resource to allow individuals to stay on in education). This extensive/intensive margin is particularly important, as it is unlikely that externalities from education – the types of externalities which government would seek to capture – will be equivalent across all sectors and current international evidence generally indicates economic growth effects from expanded primary and secondary education. The primary criterion for such investment by government should be the full-social (or at least fiscal) rates of return from marginal expansion, when applied across all types of education provision.

8.3.2   The Burden of Funding for Education

The above investment criterion establishes how much should be invested in education and in which sectors. Yet it is also necessary to establish who should fund this education. Broadly, the burden of funding should be placed on those who benefit, but this of course need not only be the individual student.

In Johnson's (1984) model, individuals are motivated to borrow to attend college as the increase in the post-tax earnings exceeds the costs of attendance (Kodde and Ritzen, 1985). A workforce L_i is therefore composed of those L_u who are unable to pass college examinations, who become unskilled workers at a wage w_u, and those who are able to go to college. Of the latter group, some L_h will enrol and become highly skilled workers at w_h; others L_m will not enrol and become medium skilled workers at w_m. The net output Y_N of the economy is gross output Y_G minus the college enrolment L_h times the per-unit cost of college γ:

$$Y_N = Y_G - \gamma L_h \qquad (8.1)$$

Net output is therefore maximised with respect to college enrolment under the condition that:

$$\partial Y_N / \partial L_h = 0 \qquad (8.2)$$

Differentiating the net output function yields:

$$\partial Y_N / \partial L_h = \partial Y_G / \partial L_h - \gamma \qquad (8.3)$$

The first term on the right-hand side of equation (8.3) is the rate of change of gross output with respect to a marginal increase in the skills of the workforce from more college education. This rate of change will be the discounted difference between the wage available to the highly skilled as against that to the medium skilled ($w_h - w_m$). Combining equations (8.2) and (8.3) at the maximum of net output, this wage difference should be equalised to the per-unit cost of education:

$$\gamma = w_h - w_m \qquad (8.4)$$

College education may be subsidised via the government. College students each pay $(1 - p)\gamma$ and the government collects taxes to pay the remainder of the costs of provision $p\gamma L_h$. The key differential is between the wages of the highly skilled workers and the medium skilled workers: both groups could have gone to college, but only the highly skilled workers did so. The question of interest is what sort of funding constraint needs to be imposed such that ratio L_h/L_m is optimal, that is, of the college-able students, how many should enrol to maximise net output. If taxes T are lump sum on all workers, then:

$$(L_h + L_m + L_u).T = p\gamma L_h \qquad (8.5)$$

Lump sum taxes reduce both w_h and w_m, preserving the differential between them, but because the costs of study have fallen from γ to $(1 - p)\gamma$, there is an over-investment in college. The relative benefits (wage differences) are undiminished for attending college and the costs have been reduced. Hence L_h/L_m, when funded by lump-sum taxes, is greater than would be optimal. If taxation is progressive on income of the form $t(w_i - k)$, then the optimal condition is:

$$(1 - t)(w_h - w_m) = (1 - p)\gamma \qquad (8.6)$$

This condition can be used to ensure that the post-tax earnings differential equals the costs of attendance. To preserve the first equality between costs and wage differentials, optimal tuition subsidies occur where $p* = t$.

This framework may also be used to describe the burden of funding, which need not fall entirely on those enrolling at college. There may be scenarios under which unskilled workers would be willing to pay for education for those able to go to college. Assume government revenues are collected through a tax of θ on each of the L_h and L_m workers and a tax of $v\theta$ on L_u workers $(v < 1)$. Unskilled workers L_u would want a higher subsidy value for p than the group L_h and L_m if:

$$\partial w_u/\partial L_h > v(\partial w_m/\partial L_h) \qquad (8.7)$$

Here the left-hand side of equation (8.7) describes the increase in the wages of the unskilled workers due to the inducement of another possible college student becoming an actual college student. The right-hand side of (8.7) is the ratio of the tax rate on unskilled workers compared to those who could attend college, multiplied by an increase in the wages of medium skilled workers when the numbers of high skilled workers increases (Johnson, 1984). The likelihood of this condition holding (such that v does not equal zero) depends on the substitutability across the three types of labour.

Nevertheless, if college places are controlled by the government, it is possible that the unskilled may pay part of the educational expenses of the skilled, to mutual advantage.

The above discussion omits two important factors, however. The first is that the electoral choice regarding education will depend on the proportions in each group (where groups are differentiated according to their benefit from education) and/or the characteristics of the median voter. Assuming household ability drives the choice of education, then if median ability is lower than mean ability, the voting system is likely to generate under-investment in education. (If education is the main source of income generation, then the salient relationship is between the incomes of the mean and median voters.) Peltzman (1996) offers a variant of this argument: states with high proportions of mobile, educated graduates as taxpayers will be more tolerant of ineffective education provision – the graduates themselves do not benefit from the education delivered to other groups. Alternatively, Director's Law may hold: public expenditures are made primarily for the middle and higher income groups. This may be the case if the higher income classes decide only to part-subsidise education, with the indirect consequence that the credit constraints to accessing education will impact more on the lower income classes.

A second pertinent factor is that operationalising and estimating these marginal returns across worker groups may be difficult (see also the comparative static analysis of the elasticity of substitution in Chapter 2). There are difficulties in extrapolating from current values of demand parameters to those which would hold under alternative regimes or for marginal enrolments. Because individuals know that an increase in subsidies will increase enrolment and reduce skill prices, enrolment response effects may be small when looked at in general equilibrium. Considering an education system planning to raise tuition subsidies, Heckman et al. (1999) indicate that the move to higher tuition subsidies produces a two-way flow: as well as more students enrolling, some students who would have attended no longer do so (because of the skill price effect). Depending on the burden of taxation, on the elasiticity of demand for particular skill types and on the size of the subsidy, those not enrolling under either tuition-subsidy regime and those who would enrol under both regimes are also affected. Heckman et al. (1999) estimate any educational effects (for example, on earnings) to be magnified tenfold when only partial equilibria are analysed, that is, when only inflows are considered. Similarly, Schultz (1999) looks at rates of return for South Africa across demographic groups, in relation to the proportion of each group with a given schooling level; this relationship, which is clearly negative, illustrates the trade-off between returns to education and proportions with each schooling level.

8.3.3   Formula Funding

The above discussion suggests that funding of education needs to be conditioned on many varying economic parameters, some of which may only be identifiable after school attendance and completion. Rather than reflect skill differential effects (and other such parameters) in funding education, much government funding is presently based on simple formulae. These funding formulae build up resource allocation amounts per-student, with supplements for specific educational needs and differential site costs for example (Ross and Levacic, 1999). In UK schools, for example, funding typically regards individual pupils as age-weighted pupil units and resources flow to institutions on a per-enrolment basis (although successive layers of government will control or top-slice particular amounts of resource). For higher education providers, funding is via an amount for teaching (taking account of numbers, subject and staffing levels) and an amount for research (based on research quality). The funding system for further education identifies a core (basic funding unit allocated on the basis of class size; student taught hours; student characteristics; average lecturer costs; type of course; and prior attainment). In addition, marginal funding, an attempt to stimulate efficiency gains by being set year on year, was available with institutions bidding for funds at marginal costing. To cover possible inequities, a redistributive element is also included for special needs, particular pedagogies and institutional mission (Barrow, 1997).

Alternatives to such formula funding may be used, such as historical funding (based on previous levels of provision), discretionary systems or through competitive tendering (for example, for capital funds in schools or research funding). But these are less common. Instead, this simpler formulaic approach to funding satisfies some equity criterion in that it treats all pupils broadly alike. However, it limits the scope to treat different pupils differently (Le Grand, 1982). As discussed in Chapter 4, non-separability across the arguments of the production function is probable, where pupils' effort depends on that of teachers. Funding systems which fail to reflect these customer–input technologies are unlikely to be efficient.

Nevertheless, such simple formulae do have the advantage of being transparent and may allow for greater decentralisation of funding (Bullock and Thomas, 1997), with some advantages to internal efficiency. They may also allow purchaser–provider splits, separating government provision from funding. However, such purchaser–provider splits are often only partial, not applying to all the costs (such as capital financing); and they may not generate real budget constraints. Moreover, to satisfy horizontal equity, redistributive elements are needed and the amounts of these may not be easy to estimate (with compensatory funding made at both central government and Local Education Authority level in the UK). As formulae treat particular elements of the education system as equivalent (for example, maths courses are equivalent to computing courses), this will be satisfactory to the extent that there is little heterogeneity across those elements. For example, in UK higher education, standard pricing (and to extent standard costing) may be justified because: any degree is thought to be equal to any other; costs are regarded as all the same; and prices may be bid up very high, because agents care about relative quality rather than absolute quality. Yet none of these arguments is either fully persuasive or substantiated with evidence. The concern with such standardisation is that it is likely to reduce the opportunity set and so impair the matching of supply to heterogeneous demand.

Two other concerns are noted here. One is that, because formulae may be significantly altered in a short period of time, and are derived from government fiat, resourcing levels may be volatile (evidence from UK further education is pertinent here), which is detrimental to planning by education officials and school managers. Second-guessing politicians may be harder than predicting the market demand. As well, many formulae serve multiple ends: the New Funding Method in further education, for example, aimed both for convergence in funding for colleges and for expansion of student numbers.

Given the complexities and problems of funding, it should be conceded that such allocation mechanisms may be difficult to evaluate and efficiency criteria for them not readily derived (Hoxby, 1996b). A simple distinction is between cost-plus and fixed-price formulae. If cost-plus funding formulae are imposed, then profits or rents will be limited (because only legitimate costs are paid). However, such formulae give no incentive for efficiency or cost-saving, with possibly deleterious effects over the longer term (the consequences of which are considered below). If fixed-price formulae are used, this should encourage efficiency, but is also likely to yield high rents to institutions with low costs (and exacerbate other resource differentials between providers).

For institutions such as universities, intra-institutional funding formulae will also be applied and these may differ from the sectoral funding formula. Within universities, block allocation or responsibility budgeting may be applied at the departmental level (Johnes, 1999). With block allocations, university departments bargain over an amount of resource and then utilise that as they decide; the difficulty here is that such allocations may depend on bargaining powers which are only indirectly tied to performance. With responsibility budgeting, departments retain revenues from their incomes; this method has built-in incentives, but may cause problems if one department competes for revenue at the expense of another.

In general, to ensure value for money, such formula funded education systems may often have complex accountability mechanisms and there is no obvious manner in which to weight modes of provision (beyond historical costing or activity-led funding; and these need not reflect relative scarcities). For the state to measure educational outcomes may require either unwieldy bureaucracy or a lot of performance indicators or some distortion of incentives.   For research funding in the UK, for example, there are substantial costs in identifying high quality research (through research assessment exercises); for UK further education, the tariff for funding units must be regularly monitored.

A further level of complexity is added when students can migrate across tax bases. Interactions between the funding mechanism and the allocations of students may then have more generalised effects. If formula funding from a local tax base is combined with an open enrolment policy, then inequities may arise if students choose schools outside their tax community. In Lee's (1997) model, students may be enrolled in schools outside their local community, where such schools have excess capacity; these schools would then receive a transfer of state aid from the home funding body. This state aid is likely to be greater than the marginal cost of the provision for the transferring student (because of the surplus capacity effects), leading to positive welfare effects in the outside community and lower post-tax incomes in the home community.   Under this funding regime, open enrolment allows families to consume education in a different community to the one they pay taxes in and these families are not considering the negative externality they impose on the home community government budget.

As well as being efficient, funding mechanisms should be equitable. One measuring stick would be if the education system is 'wealth neutral', that is, the wealth of a local education authority and its per-pupil expenditures have a low or zero correlation (Cohn, 1984). However, this may be overly homogenising and conflict with an appreciation of education as a normal consumption good with demand rising with income. At the per-pupil level, Johnes (1993a) articulates the utilitarian position, where equity is served when the rate of change of students' utility with respect to education is equal. With a Cobb–Douglas utility function, to satisfy this equity criterion then allocations of education expenditure should be ability regressive: those students with more ability should be allocated less expenditure.   In contrast, simple efficiency conditions suggest allocations are likely to be progressive in ability, giving concerns over such efficiency-driven education provision.

Relatedly, another equity test might be the responsiveness of the system to reducing evident regional differences either in inputs (to ensure equality of opportunity) or outcomes. It might be expected that government would compress differences across students. Any spreads which do exist therefore represent the government benchmark against the counterfactual of a market system.   The difficulty in making such comparisons is that internal efficiency levels cannot be assumed to be uniform (in part because of differences across intake abilities). Central school districts typically spend relatively more per-pupil on education, within a part-historical funding formula, even as their academic outcomes are lower (Hoxby, 1996b, 53). Under such circumstances, to ensure full equality of outcomes may necessitate extreme differences in resource inputs.

For the UK, Bradley and Taylor (1996, 6) tabulate the educational achievements of the most and least prosperous education authorities in 1992, showing substantial differences in skills levels and economic performance in terms of GCSE attainment or proportion of students in education beyond 17. Even with a national funding system, some regions with very low levels of human capital face a low-skill poverty trap, as evidenced by the threefold proportions of pupils with five or more GSCEs in Surrey (44%) compared to Knowsley (16%) and the significant gaps in the percentages enrolled in post-compulsory schooling (61% compared to 28%, respectively). For the US, Burke (1999) uses the teacher–student ratio as a measure of resources and compares 1204 school districts across 37 states; Gini coefficient values reveal substantial variation within and across districts (with differences greater at the school than the student level). McCarty and Brazer (1990) compare per-pupil expenditures across three US states to reveal large differences in amounts allocated: funding for the 95th percentile school was 1.8 times the funding for the 5th percentile school. Finally, Murray et al. (1998) catalogue the effects of court-mandated school finance reforms, which have served to equalise (upward) school funding within US states. This evidence indicates that neither equality of opportunity or of outcomes is automatically obtained within the state schooling systems.

One way of ameliorating these inequities and disparities is to improve transparency between students' characteristics and funding formulae, perhaps through using detailed tariffs. Other allocation mechanisms are possible, such as those based on vouchers or sporadic bidding competitions. Funding mechanisms which are non-distortionary (loans or fees) may be applied increasingly across provision, although vouchers appear to have limited success (as discussed in Chapter 8). One approach would be for expansion to occur through different ownership mechanisms; this was the logic behind the expansion of UK further education through outward collaborative provision ('franchising') during the 1990s; or through charter schools in the US (Peterson and Hassel, 1998). One general, widespread approach which maintains a role for government has been to introduce more information about providers' performance into the public domain. This information may enhance consumer choice and so improve the demand side of the exchange.

8.3.4   Performance Information

A performance indicator is 'an item of information collected at regular intervals to track the performance of a system' (Fitz-Gibbon, 1996). Such performance indicators may improve resource allocation and improve consumer choice (another use would be for schools to advertise or market their provision). Another option is to strengthen the reputations of good schools and universities – this was favoured by Adam Smith, who considered that inspection systems were 'liable to be exercised both ignorantly and capriciously' (Ortmann, 1999).

Fundamentally, the utility of such indicators depends on the quantity and quality of the information available and this quantity may need to be substantial. Information flows cover many different facets of education of interest to government and their regulatory agencies; institutional planners and managers; demanders of education, such as pupils and parents; and 'end-users', such as employers and subsequent education institutions. Since it is impractical and inefficient for all agencies to satisfy their information needs independently; open and transparent cross-sector performance indicators may therefore be cost-effective.

In the UK, the Office for Standards in Education (OFSTED) has a remit to improve standards of achievement and quality of education through regular independent inspection, public reporting and informed independent advice. Composite inspection judgements are made on the pupils' standards, educational quality, the attendance rate, the school climate and the management and efficiency of the school. For 'failing' schools, conditions for improvement are then set down. Although the information is open to the public, with an aggregate list of top and failing schools published each year, the principal impact appears to be motivation for staff and reputation effects for the school. There are few pecuniary rewards. The indicators may also influence consumer choice (in case study regions, Woods et al., 1998, found them to be used as supporting information). Finally, such performance indicators can also help enforce public sector accountability, by checking on the financial status of semi-autonomous institutions; by facilitating the redistribution of resources; and by giving the system a range of comparative information on performance to promote competition.

Performance indicators are more likely to be accepted if they embody the systemic relationship between performance and reward, and can be understood within the goals and production function of the institution. This understanding might be developed in a number of ways. First, indicators might be made directly pertinent to the process of teaching and learning in such a way as to be related to school development. Second, the indicators might cover a significant number of a school's activities, yet also reflect the existence of competing educational priorities. Finally, the indicators should allow meaningful comparisons between schools or over time and allow institutions to produce a higher level of performance, based on the inspection information.

However, such performance indicators need to be sufficiently precise to take account of the heterogeneous provision of education. There may be substantive inaccuracies, as the inputs, processes and outputs of education are not properly modelled. There are multiple outputs from education, with heterogeneous provision both across and within schools; a key variable, the student, may be hard to track; the effects of teachers cannot be easily measured; and the effect of one particular educational programme may not be easily identifiable. Also on substantive issues, there is limited consensus on school improvement and effectiveness (Coe and Fitz-Gibbon, 1998) and no obvious predictive theory of learning within which the data can be incorporated. Finally, the indicators do not readily answer questions about education management and/or resource allocation, with few value for money or efficiency measures (Audit Commission, 1996).[18] This substantive ambiguity is especially pertinent to national targets in education: unless these are a way of holding government accountable, they have no constitutive meaning at the school level (or even at the aggregate economy level, Robinson, 1995).

Ideally, the inputs to the education system need to be related to the outputs. Examination scores are an output measure and so represent an improvement on student–teacher ratios, an input–input measure long used, but mistakenly, as a performance measure. (Similarly, because leisure is a normal good then conditioning universities' funding on a performance indicator such as graduate earnings, for instance, will be inappropriate.) However, the use of examination scores as indicators of performance by individual schools is critically dependent on the assumption that inputs are broadly consistent across schools. It may be plausible to assume this if teacher pay and teacher qualifications are regulated; if the (national) curriculum standardises the education process; if pupils are not allocated to a given school by merit and so make the same contribution to the learning process; and if funding is via a common formula. If these can be assumed, then an output measure may be justified as a performance indicator; however, more desirable are outcome measures which are productivity-based (input–output). These indicators must then be tied sufficiently to funding and so generate binding incentives.

Also, measurement error may be a source of inaccuracy: schools are composed of groups of classes and aggregation bias may arise, with components of variance at four levels: the individual, the class, the school and the education authority district (Goldstein and Spiegelhalter, 1996). Because education programmes have an incremental effect, evaluation should recognise that the effectiveness of programmes depends on the value-added effect on students' performance. Complex (multi-level) statistical measures may be needed to isolate the effects of individual programmes, otherwise performance measures may fail to distinguish between schools and fail to take account of differential effectiveness (Gray et al., 1995; Goldstein and Thomas, 1996). More conceptually, it should be noted that education scores are not a 'natural' measurement scale; the scores may be skewed in a particular way, making normalisation inappropriate; equal interval scoring of responses may mean that linearity and additive effects are inappropriate; and there may be floor and ceiling effects in exam grades (Fielding, 1997).

Reflecting these difficulties, UK performance indicators in education were slow to have an effect on education management. The actual indicators used were an over-extensive mixture of quantitative and qualitative measures yet not fully adequate for answering questions about education management or resource allocation. There is some evidence of management closely tracking to the designated performance targets: outcomes which are not designated as 'desired' are prone to 'opportunistic strategies', where agents behave so they appear to be high-performing when measured on designated performance indicators. Also, performance indicators may be contentious to introduce (Gray and Wilcox, 1995, 1996); there is dispute over the indicators to use; and in practice very few indicators are used. Finally, with government performance indicators, the disadvantage is that information flows to the regulators rather than students, necessitating an indirect feedback loop from government back to students.

8.4   THE COSTS OF GOVERNMENT PROVISION

8.4.1   Political Suasion

In part, the above arguments may justify government intervention because markets, which provide many other goods efficiently, may fail to produce an optimal amount of education. However, there may be numerous difficulties with general state funding of education. First, the state has to be able to identify the market failure appropriately: even if there is market failure, it remains to be proven that policy-makers can ensure a better outcome. Second, government underwriting is likely to be a problem for ensuring efficiency, both external and internal. Third, x-inefficiency may also arise. These last two aspects are discussed subsequently, but there may also be political suasion of the allocation of resources in education, causing deviation from optimal investment strategies.

Political concerns may sway the allocation of investments in education into sub-optimal areas. The same logic which presumes that parents are unable to choose their children's education appropriately, and so justifying a role for government, might also suggest that they are unable to choose their legislators (Lott, 1987b). But there may also be some more specific influences. First, there are numerous pressures for overspending, particularly with entrenched distributional coalitions (Olson, 1982). Lobby groups may benefit from the 'dispersed costs' faced by others; politicians may be self-serving (although there can be tax revolts), with governments spending to signal something; or there may be inertia in public spending (but individuals have this too). Second, the public may have little idea of the true costs of spending, partly because distributional coalitions make government allocations highly complex (and the public often mistakenly focus on the tax rate rather than the amount of tax paid, Davis, 1998). Third, resource allocation is held to be more efficient where information about the merits of a good is embodied in its price: by removing the price mechanism for education, government obscures this information and maintains control over provision. Fourth, incentives may be distorted when a government has policies to transfer resources to its supporters and where there are significant opportunities for government corruption because few people are held accountable (Shleifer, 1998). Instead, it may be plausible to model educational outcomes in terms of teacher utility: the principal–agent model suggests that teachers know more than parents and so can 'sell' them teaching; unionised teacher power may have strong influence over how budgets are spent; and the patronage of politicians may favour teachers' unions, who have a disproportionately strong influence on political outcomes.

Evidence from practitioners and policy analysis may also be cited: Barber (1996, 57–59, 114) illustrates the difficulties of implementing education policies, in particular the real difference between a policy idea and a practice; and Collier and Gunning (1999) chart the problems of implementing education policies in Africa. Yet these distortionary effects may be hard to estimate – they need to be scrutinised as part of a proper cost–benefit analysis of government intervention in education – and the full costs of alternative regimes may not be accurately known. These possible political decisions may simply be the costs of a net beneficial structure of provision. More tractable and relievable sources of distortion are the welfare burdens and potential x-inefficiencies from government; these are discussed next.

8.4.2   Welfare Burdens from Government Financing

With government underwriting, subsidies may cause deadweight losses across a number of domains. First, subsidised students may have been willing to undertake education even without a subsidy, so the government funding is sub-additive. Second, subsidised individuals may be simply displacing others on education or training programmes. For training programmes, these substitution and displacement effects have been approximated at half of the total expenditure (Dolton, 1996). Third, subsidies may dampen incentives for schools to be efficient and encourage over-spending on education, particularly for those students not subject to capital constraints. Fourth, there are deadweight loss effects in the public school system from raising tax revenues and because of welfare costs of tax avoidance and tax evasion (West, 1991; Steuerle, 1996). As well, government intervention may compound risk. As government may pre-commit future generations of workers to an investment in education during their childhood, the returns to this investment are going to be highly correlated with these workers' earnings from which future tax revenues will be drawn. This could exacerbate any adverse effects: if the investment in education yields a low (fiscal) return, taxes will have to rise just as workers' earnings are low.

Distortions from the tax system may arise because not all inputs into human capital generation are tax-deductible and because progressive tax systems reduce earnings' differentials. For example, depreciated human capital on retirement is not declared on tax returns. And if the costs of investment in human capital include both forgone earnings and forgone consumption of direct goods that are not tax-deductible, tax increases on earnings discourage human capital accumulation because they reduce the benefits of education disproportionately compared to how they reduce costs. Education accumulation will also be reduced if greater investment in human capital – with expenditure incurred at a low tax rate – pushes earnings into a higher tax bracket. Finally, government demand for skilled labour (for example, for defence industries) may crowd out the employment of skilled labour for research and development in the private sector (Cronovich, 1998, provides some evidence of this crowding out effect).

As a corollary, standardised government schooling will impose welfare burdens on those whose optimal amount of education differs from the uniform level of provision. This welfare burden is the cost of state schools minus the maximum willingness to pay and has two components (Sonstelie, 1982). First, some parents choose a state school because otherwise they would lose their subsidy, even though this means choosing a lower quality of education than desired. Second, there will be a welfare cost where private schools are more efficient than public schools (Lott, 1987b, 476). Such welfare burdens will differ with variations in demand and factor mobility (for example, if households face high costs in moving residence to a high spending education authority).

Following Sonstelie's (1982) model, the family's general utility function

U(X, E) is a function of amounts of educational quality E for the child and of other goods X (for a parameterised model along similar lines, but using ability differences rather than income differences, see Johnes, 1993a, 77–79). State schooling is chosen with utility of family income Y and the state schooling amount q:

$$U^* = U(Y, q) \qquad (8.8)$$

However, where private schooling is chosen the optimal utility derives from family income less the amount expended on school fees $P_E E^*$:

$$U^* = U(Y - P_E E^*, E^*) \qquad (8.9)$$

The state school surplus S(q) arises for a family which uses state schooling of quality q rather than a private school:

$$U^* = U(Y - S(q), q) \qquad (8.10)$$

Sonstelie derives an average level of per-pupil expenditure on low quality state schooling, q', as a reservation quality above which families choose private schooling. This demand function for education expenditure will depend on the proportions of students enrolled in state schooling, the tax base for providing that schooling, and the income levels of families. As the reservation level of education quality demanded by families rises with income, there is a unique income Y' at which families are indifferent between state and private schooling. For those with incomes above Y', private schooling will be chosen; for those with incomes significantly below Y', they may favour a lower level of state expenditures than is currently provided. As incomes increase toward Y', then the demand for expenditures on state schooling will rise (assuming plausible values of the income elasticity of demand for state education). Hence there are two groups who would prefer a decrease in state expenditures on schooling – those favouring private schooling and those with incomes below the threshold Y' which justifies the expenditure q'. The sizes of these groups and the divergence of their desired expenditures ($P_E E^* = q^*$, for those using private schooling, and $q^* < q'$, for those with low incomes) will determine the deadweight loss from standardised state schooling.

Figure 8.1 pictorially illustrates this welfare burden on groups wanting high and low spending on education and the trade-off between efficiency and equity (McCarty and Brazer, 1990). With a constant cost of education at MC and with high and low demand curves for education given as D_H and D_L, a government mandate of E_G is imposed. The welfare loss for each group, as the mandate diverges from their optimal demands for education, is given as the shaded area (with its size depending on the spread between the demand curves). A potential solution is to levy a tax on the high-demand group or simply to fix education levels by fiat. The tax will reduce the higher demand for education, compressing the differential in desired education ($E_H - E_L$) and the revenues may be transferred to the low-demand group. Another route to compressing education amounts occurs as education expenditures in the state system are reduced. This causes some pupils to switch to private schooling; the lower participation rate in state schools then means higher per-pupil expenditures and so higher quality state provision. But in turn these new higher expenditures are devoted to households composed of an even greater proportion where $Y < Y'$; these households would prefer income transfers and proportionately less schooling. In summary, whereas the state-run system eliminates differentials arising from parental choices, which in part reflect parental incomes, it does not eliminate differentials from student ability (Biggs and Dutta, 1999). Moreover, in distorting education choices – both for high income and low income families – there is an obvious efficiency–equity trade-off.

Figure 8.1 Government Prescriptions on Demand

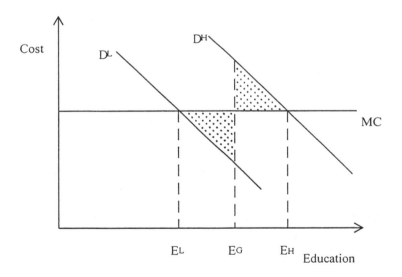

A second source of distortion arises from behaviour in response to potential subsidies. For higher education, a welfare burden may arise if there is parental means-testing of government aid. Currently in the UK, financial aid for university is applied across all students (over 95% of first degrees are eligible for mandatory awards), and is partly means-tested. Where financial aid is closely means-tested, as in the US, then each additional increment of assets that parents accumulate raises their expected contribution and decreases their expected financial aid. This will affect the demand for assets prior to university enrolment because if interest income is taxed, an increase in income of dm raises tax payments by tdm. So for an interest rate r, the after tax interest rate is $(1 - t)r$. Hence means-testing is equivalent to a tax on parents' saving for their children's education: any savings are taxed in the form of reduced eligibility for education grants. Given that education is a large proportion of a family's lifetime expenditure, and that the college participation rate in the US (UK) is around 40% (30%), there may be significant distortionary effects from such a tax.

Feldstein's (1995) model estimates these distortionary effects. For US higher education, parental contributions are calculated depending on discretionary income: the higher this income, the lower the eligibility for tuition subsidies. This reduced eligibility acts as a tax on earned income, which Feldstein bounds at 22–47% (and this rate is in addition to income tax). The educational tax will encourage families that would be eligible for financial assistance not to accumulate assets before their children enrol at college. This pre-enrolment period is a large part of most people's working lives (as children reach college age their parents have probably completed 20 working years), with an additional effect on retirement expenditures and savings. Set against this effect of lowered saving, the subsidy should make it more likely that students will attend college and/or that the college attended will be of higher quality. This may raise the need to accumulate assets.

Using a two period model, with family incomes of Y_1 and Y_2 an individual family faces a tuition subsidy function:

$$S = \alpha(E - \theta A) + \beta \qquad (8.12)$$

Here scholarship aid S depends on the amount spent on education E less accumulated assets A taxed at a rate θ, that is, the amount of the expected parental contribution, which is subsidised at rate α; there may also be a financing gap β. Hence $\theta\alpha$ is the effective marginal tax rate on educational capital. The household wishes to maximise utility which depends on first period consumption C_1, education E and retirement expenditure R, subject to a budget constraint:

$$\text{maximise } U = U(C_1, E, R) \qquad (8.13)$$

$$\text{subject to } E - S + R = A + Y_2$$

The budget constraint says that education spending less the scholarship plus retirement spending has to equal earnings in the second period Y_2 plus accumulated assets. For this analysis, maximisation occurs with respect to A and E, which can be substituted in, from equation (8.12), the tuition subsidy function:

$$U = U(Y_1 - A, E, (1 - \alpha\theta)A + Y_2 - (1 - \alpha)E + \beta) \qquad (8.14)$$

The first order conditions for a maximum are:

$$-\partial U/\partial C_1 + (1 - \alpha\theta)\partial U/\partial R = 0 \qquad (8.15)$$

$$\partial U/\partial E - (1 - \alpha)\partial U/\partial R = 0 \qquad (8.16)$$

These conditions solve so that:

$$(\partial U/\partial C_1)/(\partial U/\partial R) = (1 - \alpha\theta) \qquad (8.17)$$

$$(\partial U/\partial E)/(\partial U/\partial R) = (1 - \alpha) \qquad (8.18)$$

An increase in the marginal rate of accumulated tax $\alpha\theta$ impacts on the marginal utility from first period consumption C_1 relative to that from retirement consumption R. It is likely that first period consumption will rise relative to retirement expenditure: intuitively, less is saved or more of the accumulated assets are spent on education. Similarly, an increase in the rate of subsidy α will raise gross education spending E relative to retirement consumption R. Combining these conditions gives:

$$(\partial U/\partial C_1)/(\partial U/\partial E) = (1 - \alpha\theta)/(1 - \alpha) \qquad (8.19)$$

An increase in the marginal rate of educational tax θ and a decrease in the subsidy rate α are both likely to raise spending on first period consumption relative to education. There are straightforward price effects, albeit expressed in an intertemporal framework. However, the disincentive effects of such means-testing depends on the effects of θ and α on the level of asset accumulation. Feldstein (1995) differentiates the first order conditions (8.17) and (8.18) with respect to A, E, θ and α:

$$\partial A/\partial\alpha > \text{ or } < 0, \ \partial A/\partial\theta < 0, \ \partial E/\partial\alpha > 0, \ \partial E/\partial\theta < 0$$

Each of these partial differentials has implications for the effects of means-testing and subsidies. First, an increase in the rate of subsidy may cause accumulated assets either to rise or to fall depending on whether the individual wishes to save more to obtain more education in response to a rise in the subsidy (that is, whether income effects dominate substitution effects).   Second, the increase in the tax rate on education will unambiguously reduce the level of capital accumulation.   The last two conditions are straightforward: an increase in the marginal rate of educational subsidy α raises spending on education whereas an increase in the education capital tax θ reduces it.

To estimate the effects of this, Feldstein (1995, 561) regresses the family's financial assets against income and this educational tax rate (adjusting for age of head of household AGEH and number of children under 18):

$$A_i = -8785 + [-2.12 - 1.71\theta_i + 0.077AGEH_i + 0.041CHILDREN_i]*Y_i$$
$$(1.16) \quad (0.48) \quad (0.026) \quad (0.104)$$

The sign and significance of the coefficient for the marginal tax rate θ indicates its strongly negative effect on asset accumulation (standard errors are given in brackets).   In aggregation, Feldstein proposes the effect to be substantial: reduced eligibility for means-tested subsidies may depress asset accumulation by approximately one-third of the existing stock of financial assets.

Although not all students at public universities might qualify for such aid and expected family contributions may not always be met (Dick and Edlin, 1997), back-of-an-envelope figures suggest that such implicit tax rates may be high.   In the UK the resource expenditure on a university degree is around £6 000 per annum (1999 prices).   If it is assumed that this is paid in full, tax progressivity would necessitate steep tax rates: if families with asset incomes below £15 000 were to pay nothing and those with asset incomes above £40 000 were to pay full cost, the removal of a £6 000 benefit over £25 000 would require this supplementary marginal tax to be rated at almost one quarter (Kane, 1999, 58).

8.4.3   X-inefficiency

The third and final source of inefficiency which may be associated with government intervention to be discussed here is more general: inefficiency in the production of education may be inferred if decision-makers are not guided by profit-maximisation or cost-minimisation incentives.   This is x-inefficiency, a broad term which may apply to an enterprise which either finds it hard to enforce a budget constraint or does not have clear optimands. Without specified optimands (perhaps because education is a multi-product enterprise) and if budget overspends are underwritten by governments, such enterprises will find it difficult to ensure efficiency (on defining x-inefficiency and operationalising the economic-rational model, see Levacic and Glover, 1997, 1998).

Ownership problems may also arise – it is not clear who 'owns' a university, for example, and so is ultimately responsible for it; deans and chancellors may not be able to take the same types of decisions as CEOs in private companies. This lack of ownership denudes any opportunity to claim the residual reward for extra achievements. A lack of competition may have analogous effects: Fels (1996) and Hoxby (1999), for example, juxtapose the declining standards in US public schools, which are state-run and fully subsidised. with the excellence of US higher education, which is competitive.[19] Articulating a counter-factual superior market education system is difficult, however. Instead, a narrower, more conceptual approach to identifying and estimating such inefficiency may be proposed. For US schooling, two possible sources of x-inefficiency have been considered: low effort and a lack of incentives.

Low effort, Bishop (1996a) maintains, is likely to apply across many of the agents operating within education provision. There may be low student effort. This may be manifest in actual time, either measured in total, as a percentage of time in school or as a percentage of time lost through absence, lateness or inattention by students. Low effort may also be manifest in the amount of homework undertaken, the use of other time in school and of other leisure time, the avoidance of 'hard' courses by students and a general lack of psychic energy to engage in learning. There may also be a series of implicit contracts between teachers and students to do less: if students and teachers collude, this low effort is likely to be unobserved in the medium term by parents, by funders or by firms. In addition, there may be low parental effort. At least for this US evidence, parents appear easily pleased (giving high approval ratings to teachers relative to the approval ratings such teachers would get in non-US education systems); they give relatively low tutoring to their children; and offer a relatively ineffective home infrastructure for learning. Finally, there may be low public and government administration effort across a number of spheres. Such effort may be manifest in an easing of graduation requirements (grade inflation) and a pressure on teachers to pass more students; Brasington (1999b) gives some evidence of this. Most clearly, the low public effort is manifest in relatively declining spending levels on education, met with voter apathy or even encouragement: over the two decades 1980–2000, there has been little political reward to governments which petition for higher taxes to raise education expenditures.

A second tranche of inefficiencies may arise because there are few rewards for learning, with incentives being insufficiently strong. A number of reasons for this may be offered: easy and entertaining courses may drive out rigorous ones; achievement in school may be of only imperfect benefit in subsequent education (or subsequent career); and admission to university may be based on class rank (or wealth) rather than achievement. Also, there are difficulties in signalling upgraded standards to colleges and employers: only those students who want to progress to more education have an incentive to demand higher quality at their present level of education. There may also be systemic breakers on incentives, with local monopolies in the provision of schooling. With difficulties in assessing teacher performance (because students' education is fractured between classes and across teachers), it may not be possible to generate improvements in quality. As well, there are peer group norms: students who work hard get low respect among peers and the winners are so few that incentives to compete are weakened. Bishop (1996) also questions the extent to which the US labour market rewards high school achievement, as segmented labour markets may reduce the returns to human capital or discourage its accumulation; similar arguments have been made for the UK for medical degrees, where access is tightly constrained (Zweifel and Eichenberger, 1992).

Exchange mechanisms will also have different consequences, depending on how the incentives are structured. Both secondary and higher education are state-subsidised, yet the latter may encourage more efficient provision. First, higher education subsidies are more obviously fungible across different universities, whereas schools may adopt greater exclusive territories. Second, undergraduates are contributing a larger proportion of their own resources to study with higher opportunity costs during study, making universities more accountable (Hoxby, 1999, 38). Also important is whether subsidised provision is time-limited: higher education or schooling may be available as open-ended contracts, diluting the incentive to graduate. These arguments should be considered in the light of perhaps the most important incentive: competitive pressures from new entrants. Nevertheless, changing incentives may be regarded as areas for real efficiency gains, in that these involve changing the education process rather than raising education inputs.

An alternative approach to assessing the inefficiencies of government enterprises is to compare schools in different systems: Chubb and Moe (1988) contrast public (state) and private education providers by comparing public, catholic, private and elite schools in the US across a variety of characteristics. They itemise the (unavoidable) incentives for policy-makers to impose their views on schools, in a manner destructive of autonomy and flexibility. This imposition is manifest via: influence by the school board; influence of the administration on school policies; and constraints on the deployment of personnel. For each of these factors, there is greater inflexibility and imposition within public schools. As well, Chubb and Moe considered the role of the parents (their expectations, involvement, co-operation and monitoring of the school); the characteristics of the principals, including their experience; and staff relations. For each of these, more beneficial environments were found in the private sector, leading Chubb and Moe (1988, 253) to conclude that private schools have 'simpler, less constraining environments of administrators, school boards and parents', being 'more autonomous and strongly led'. In contrast, Brown (1992) finds the production patterns of private and public schools to be very similar.

Such differences may lead to private school efficiencies in resource use outweighing the social gains from a uniform provision level. Importantly, these are process aspects and the critical question is whether these processes determine higher outcomes of non-government education providers or whether the differential intake policies necessarily change the technology or delivery of education. If the latter, such schools should be evaluated under different terms to those in the private sector.

Table 8.1 Performance across Sectors of the UK Economy (%)

	Private sector	Education sector	Public sector (other)
Managers responding yes:			
Dispute over pay and conditions within last 1 year	6.0	2.2	4.3
Labour productivity gone up within last 5 years	80.3	78.5	66.7
Managers (strongly) agree:			
Workers asked to help in ways not specified in the job	55.2	49.1	43.5
Employees are fully committed to the values of the organisation	67.0	94.0	74.9
Employee absence (workdays over last 1 year)	4.5	4.9	4.6
Number of establishments	*1404*	*244*	*543*

Notes: All frequencies weighted for sample selection.
Data: Workplace Employee Relations Survey (1998)

In this coruscating critique, it is nonetheless important to remember that these results may apply across other endeavours or within other sectors of the economy (and that such inefficiency may reflect preferences). It is important to get a measure of relative efficiency of the education sector, compared to other sectors. This allows for differences between general critiques ('low effort') and more telling relative critiques ('low effort compared to others'). For example, it is argued that incentives in education may not be possible because education providers optimise many variables. Yet many enterprises and industries do that also: all firms face inefficiencies when there are joint production of services, high transactions costs and consumer uncertainty.

As a final comparison, Table 8.1 shows survey data on some performance measures collected from 2191 UK enterprises, divided into three sectors: private, education and (other) public sector. Information on absences, on disputes and on changes in labour productivity do not suggest relative inflexibility within education providers; there is some evidence that the public sector generally is bound more by rules and job specifications, but not especially or perhaps solely in the education sector. The most striking (statistically significant) difference is the collective commitment of employees to the values of the organisation, which is much heightened in the education sector.

8.5   ISSUES AND CONCLUSIONS

In this chapter, the need for government intervention has been considered, both on efficiency and equity grounds. The latter principally dominate because of capital constraints which impinge on the least well-off, but there may also be spill-overs which the government incorporates into its value function. Yet these spill-overs are not typically incorporated into the 'social' and fiscal rates of return. More sceptically, it remains to be fully argued that these external benefits render education either as a merit or as a public good. Exposition of the production function for education suggests only some types of education are a public good – much learning is excludable in use and rivalrous (Oosterbeek, 1998a, 221); and economies in standardisation (for example, all schools using the National Curriculum) does not mean that there are economies of scale in production, such that only one supplier of schooling is appropriate. The outcomes of research may be considered as a public good, but their generation may in turn be separated from education provision. On Lott's (1987b) reasoning, the arguments in favour of public subsidies for education fall significantly short of being arguments in favour of public provision of education.

Abstracting out provision of education by government, conditions on the optimal rules and modes of funding have been discussed. In particular, it is readily plausible that, on efficiency grounds, lower skilled workers may be willing to part-subsidise those enrolling at college. The difficulty is in substantiating this empirically. More simply, funding of education is allocated according to formulae; the effectiveness of these depends on the heterogeneity of the education system, the extent to which incentives are embedded and the match between the formula weights and the education technology. Another approach to improving public provision of education is to create markets in information about providers. Students can then use this information to make choices. These performance indicators may be a way in which the quality of education is established.

Alternatively, some of the anticipated difficulties of government provision may be ameliorated. For education, three distortions have been considered. First, the costs of political intervention have been suggested (although no full cost–benefit analysis is attempted). Second, there are likely to be distortions if standardised public sector provision drives a wedge between possible qualities and amounts of education available for students. Here more persuasive conclusions can be drawn: it seems unlikely that a uniform allocation of schooling will be optimal for a heterogeneous student cohort. Both the discontinuity in provision (with no middle grade of education between private and state schooling) and the homogeneity of schooling generate this distortion. Finally, x-inefficiency may be prevalent if there are soft budget constraints and underwriting of inefficient providers.

A more solid rationale for government intervention is then to look at possible market allocations of education and base subsidies on *ex ante* rates of return. Here a key distinction is between allocations which favour the educationally able (who, in an economy of cognitive partitioning, are likely to be winners anyway) over the less able (who may be more expensive to educate); and between allocations which allow those with higher incomes to purchase and consume more education. Two points of discussion appear salient. First, Herrnstein and Murray (1994, 434) argue that the emphasis on redistribution has gone too far in the US and that the rate of return to society from educating the highly able is presently the highest. In desegregating the US Elementary and Secondary Education Act expenditures, 92% of the discretionary resource goes to disadvantaged children, 6% does not distinguish between ability levels and only 0.1% is allocated to gifted students. Herrnstein and Murray (1994) appear to be alone in calling for more ability-regressive allocations of expenditure: they argue, however, that the highly able students have been the ones whose performance has declined relatively over recent decades. Second, if funding for schools is linked to property taxes, that is, local wealth, then this may entrench inequities: poorer districts have a lower tax base but also need more funding for education, a dual effect which Slavin (1999) refers to as 'overburden'.

In evaluating the efficacy of subsidies to students, it should not matter what the initial position of the student is, but instead their dynamic life-cycle prospects. Hence this allocative role increasingly emphasises identification of the relative rates of return to education both for the individual and government. Unfortunately, these life-cycle prospects may be hard to observe, as may be the effects of education for the high-skilled on the earnings of the low-skilled. Moreover, up to this point only individual labour market effects have been considered, yet education evidently has effects outside this individuated realm and these may offer greater justification for government intervention. In the next chapter, these more general effects of education are considered in detail.

9. Aggregate Effects of Education

9.1 CONCEPTS

Education is not only useful for subsequent employment and raising earnings; individuals operate in a social milieu and behaviour after a dose of education is likely to differ across a number of realms. The workplace – as detailed in Chapter 2 – is only one such realm: the effects of education are likely to extend across to consumer behaviour, health levels, activities within the household, in social settings and across the economy. The underlying logic is that education changes information sets and so influences preferences and behaviour. Learning may increase the precision of information in that it embodies more information sources, although experience may be a substitute way of increasing such precision. Education may also enable an individual to obtain more information from each experience, with education and experience looked at as complements. In influencing preferences and so behaviour, education may have pervasive effects, many of which are non-marketised and/or non-pecuniary but do of course involve resources.

This chapter considers the economic effects of education in these more general spheres and two sets of externalities to the human capital model are explored. First, the non-marketised realms where education has an effect are identified in Section 9.2 – proceeding from individual to household to aggregate effects. Attempts at measurement for the individual are also made. Perhaps most important are the aggregate, macro-economic effects of education. Models for this are given in Section 9.3, along with discussion of the evidence on the effects of education and economic growth. For the individual and the macro-economy, the evidence is illustrative of the importance of education rather than conclusive; there is both clearly favourable and clearly unfavourable evidence. As well, in both spheres, inference about education is sensitive to identification and calculation problems. These are considered directly in Section 9.4, that is, whether education causes higher incomes or greater wealth permits more education vice versa.

9.2   SOCIAL EFFECTS

9.2.1   Individual Non-marketised Effects

To complement the private earnings premia, the effects of education within non-marketised realms may be substantial, covering how people understand, as Adam Smith put it, 'the ordinary duties of private life'. Here, these can be decomposed into three. The non-pecuniary outcomes of education primarily affect the individual person, that individual's household and the broader society (macro-economic growth effects are considered in the subsequent section). The first two of these may be amalgamated – own-household members are likely to be part of a given individual's utility function. They should be juxtaposed against the third, which is the realm of pure externalities, and is considered in the next sub-section. Many of these individual effects, it should be noted, may have implications for labour market participation; they may therefore already be reflected in the earnings premia identified as the private returns.

A substantial amount of research finds education to be strongly correlated to family fertility and household composition. Education may raise the age of both marriage and first pregnancy: this is because it either raises the opportunity cost of time spent in child care or improves the efficiency of contraception, or because it changes lifestyle expectations (Greenwood, 1997). However, higher incomes also mean that a couple can afford to have more children, perhaps with a higher productivity of child care. The evidence tends to support both these arguments, with a general world-wide trend of higher income resulting in fewer children per family but higher expenditures per child. Such education effects may be most obvious in developing countries (Sullivan and Smeedling, 1997), but links between education and out-of-wedlock births have also been investigated in the US (Herrnstein and Murray, 1994; Haveman and Wolfe, 1995).

A second set of non-pecuniary effects of education are more obviously linked to the labour market. Job conditions may be more pleasant for the educated, in that less intensive monitoring is undertaken, with workers instead being trusted (Meer and Weilers, 1996). Such non-wage labour market remuneration (fringe benefits, working conditions and status effects) may augment the observed earnings premia.

A third set of effects of education may arise from more rational behaviour, in that education may be useful for stabilising or processing information flows. Consumer choice may be enhanced and preferences may be better ordered, that is, transitive and consistent. Education may help individuals avoid costly actions or may improve their general decision-making skills. If education makes workers trainable, then they may be more innovative, respond better to technological or social change and be more willing to tolerate diversity. For instance, looking at the rate of adoption of cost-saving innovations in farming, early adoption of new technology appears to be positively related to education levels (Wozniak, 1987).

A related set of effects is evinced in healthier behaviour: Sander (1995) reports on the effects of education in reducing cigarette or drug addiction. These effects might be considered more readily attributable to education because the consumption of most goods varies positively with income, which in turn is strongly correlated with education. Education's effects on crime, on views about the environment, risk management and family structure may also be substantial and, for most value frames, positive (Behrman and Stacey, 1997). Indeed, the range of behaviour changes may appear endless, including: changes in the value of leisure; more patience and higher savings rates (Becker and Mulligan, 1997); better asset management; and even marital choice efficiency.

Finally, it is also appropriate here to itemise the specific consumption benefits of education provision. These benefits include the enjoyment of classroom experience and of school-community activities. Parents may also reap childcare benefits. These consumption benefits are typically not incorporated into private rates of return, even though they may allow for a substantial 'discount' on the costs.

If these effects are attributable to education, life satisfaction might be expected to be increasing in education levels. Unfortunately, this does not appear to be unambiguously or at least monotonically so. Separating measures of IQ from years of schooling, Hartog and Oosterbeek (1998) find substantial positive effects from education on health, happiness and wealth for a sample of workers in the Netherlands. On health, males with lower vocational education are almost six times more likely to have very poor health status than those with higher general education. On happiness, similarly, the former group are five times more likely to self-report the lowest happiness value. Yet their evidence also supports findings for the UK: those with the highest levels of education are neither the healthiest, happiest nor wealthiest (Clark, 1996; Clark et al., 1996). Beyond a certain education level, schooling seems to have an adverse effect on these outcomes. Perhaps there is costly information obtained from education or beneficial misinformation from no education (although whether these can be established *ex ante* is disputable).

9.2.2   Generalised Societal Effects

Such individual and household behavioural changes from extra education may also spill over into society's welfare function. Public education may therefore perform an important function in generating social capital. Yet this extrapolation from the individual to the societal should not double-count any effects which are attributable to the individual.   Consequently, education's broader societal effects may be hard to estimate, but Usher's (1997) model provides an exposition of the key concepts in relation to crime.

Assuming that the crime rate can be represented by the proportion of 'bandits' in the economy, denoted as n. All other workers (the proportion 1 – n) are farmers and their output is constant, regardless of how many there are. Bandits steal from farmers, although the more bandits there are, the harder it becomes to find farmers to steal from. The consumption levels of the two groups are:

$$c_f = w(1 - s) \qquad\qquad (9.1)$$
$$c_b = D.s.w.(1 - n)/n \qquad\qquad (9.2)$$

The consumption of farmers c_f depends on the output of grain per farmer w less the share of grain s stolen by bandits. The consumption of bandits c_b depends on the output of the farmers, the relative proportions of farmers to bandits and the share of grain not destroyed during stealing Ds. In turn, the share of grain appropriated depends on the technology of banditry F(n), which depends on the numbers of bandits. The optimal solution for society would be for the proportion of bandits to be zero, but as this proportion tends to zero, the returns to banditry rise sharply. The numbers of bandits and farmers are determined by the returns to each pursuit up to equal consumption levels of farmers and bandits ($c_f = c_b$). There should be a positive output because as the number of bandits rises, their consumption levels fall sharply, making it unlikely everyone will be a bandit.

Introducing education E into the model influences the consumption of farmers:

$$c_f = w(E).(1 - s).(1 - E) \qquad\qquad (9.3)$$

Productivity is positively affected by education (w is a function of E), but obtaining education reduces the time available to produce grain, hence the last term on the right-hand side of equation (9.3).   More importantly, education reduces the destruction effect; perhaps bandits realise that aggregate consumption levels are raised if the proportion of bandits n falls – as exemplified by the initial circumstances in equations (9.1) and (9.2) – and so they desist. Instead there is a propensity to banditry P(E), which depends on education. The consumption of bandits now becomes:

$$c_b = P(E).w(E).s.(1 - E)(1 - n)/n \qquad\qquad (9.4)$$

The optimal value of education is that which maximises the value of c_f

(equal to c_b). Education has three effects on the consumption of farmers: $w(E)$, the productivity effect; $P(E)$, the deterrence effect; and $(1 - E)$, the cost effect. The last of these should balance against the benefits of the first two. Typically, only $w(E)$ minus the cost effect is recorded in the economic benefits of education, although the effect through $P(E)$ should also be considered. With education, the returns to banditry have fallen and the equilibrium value of c_f should be higher.[20] In this model, education is therefore of merit because it influences the choices individuals make, raising the 'price' of crime. This effect is different from a simple preventative education programme or one which seeks to raise incomes and so lower crime.

A unique societal welfare function which incorporates effects such as those on crime is difficult to posit, but a number of socio-political indicators may illustrate the possible social benefits of education. Corruption, quality of bureaucracy, enforceability of contracts, incidence and prevalence of civil war, fractionalisation of society, social development and inequality; all these may be ameliorated by greater education levels, allowing individuals to internalise in their behaviour the spillovers described in equation (9.4). Using international aggregates, McMahon (1999) considers such effects through comparisons of human rights, homicide levels and the quality of the environment across education levels (Gemmell, 1996, and Appleton et al., 1996, summarise the gains to developing countries of raising education levels).[21] There may be a positive relationship between education levels and voter turnout; trust and social capital may be enhanced with more education (Shachar and Nalebuff, 1999; Fukuyama, 1999, 50).

Simple correlations again suggest that these elements and education are linked. But inferring causality is problematic, particularly if education is state-funded with government (which may promote these values) and education proceeding together. More generally though, democracy (or tolerant social values) and state education are not always conjoined: dictatorships and command economies typically have state education systems; also, the histories of the US and the UK show that democracy preceded state intervention in education (Lott, 1987b).

Also, education need not have beneficial effects in each of these realms; it may have adverse ones. Education may lower burglary rates as it raises occupational fraud; if education boosts output, this may also raise pollution levels. More specifically, education may fail to reduce inequalities: this depends on the returns to human versus physical capital and the initial allocations of these two forms of capital (Ram, 1989, 1995). Overall income inequality should decline only if income from non-human sources is more unequally distributed than that from human capital and if the rate of growth of human capital exceeds the rate of growth of physical capital. Yet a rapid expansion of education levels may reduce earnings to those accumulating human capital, offsetting any positive equity effects. Whether or not these conditions obtain can be answered empirically: for example, Goldin's (1999) review of the 'great transformation' of US high schools between 1910 and 1940 shows how earnings inequalities were substantially reduced as education provision expanded.

Finally, if there are both consumption and production externalities, then these are typically solved in most economic exchanges through the appointment of property rights. To the extent that property rights can be apportioned, this means the dispersed social effects of education may not be high. Network externalities – as distinct from network effects – need to be substantiated with direct evidence (as Liebowitz and Margolis, 1994, argue, these externalities may be less common than imagined).

9.2.3   Estimation of Positive Externalities

Because many of the social effects of education occur (almost by definition) outside the market, it is difficult to establish their magnitude and so they remain poorly quantified (Haveman and Wolfe, 1984; McMahon, 1997a). But cost–benefit decisions on whether to undertake education – from the individual perspective – or to subsidise it – from the government view – depend on all the effects, not just the earnings premia.

Most attempts at measuring these social effects impute the costs incurred, were the effect to have been bought, using shadow prices. For example, Gramlich (1986) undertook cost–benefit analysis of the US Perry Pre-school Education Programme for 58 matched pairs of students. The pre-school group was found to have a lower crime rate and the resultant savings to the potential victims and to society were calculated by multiplying the average costs of particular crimes by the differences in the probability of such crimes being committed across the groups.

A more general approach uses the equi-marginal principle to estimate the social benefits of education (Wolfe and Zuvekas, 1997, 496–497). For any given agent in equilibrium, the ratio of marginal product (or possibly marginal utility) to price will be equal across education E and other goods X:

$$MP_E/P_E = MP_X/P_X \qquad (9.5)$$

Simple transformation yields:

$$P_E = (MP_E/MP_X)P_X \qquad (9.6)$$

In order to calculate the willingness to pay for education, therefore, estimates of the marginal products of education and of other goods, along with the prices of the other goods, need to be estimated. For example, Wolfe and Zuvekas (1997) assume that an additional dollar of household income reduces the expected number of times a child will repeat a grade by 0.0002 (this coefficient is taken from a regression equation explaining the probability of repetition). Evidence is also available that if the child's mother has a high school diploma then this reduces the expected number of times the child repeats a grade by 0.062. As income is measured in money terms, the marginal value of a high school diploma in producing educational achievement (that is,, a non-repeated grade) is derived at (0.062/0.0002) = $310. Similarly, Shachar and Nalebuff (1999, 533) find that a $1000 increase in US per capita income raises political participation by 0.00969, and a 1% increase in the percentage of people with at least four years of high school education raises political participation by 0.002211. Hence the marginal per capita value of a 1% increase in the population percentage with at least four years of high school is $228 (1970 dollars). Aggregating these effects and collecting them together may yield a substantial effect. Table 9.1 gives some more examples of how extra schooling improves consumption efficiency, raises household income and, with indirect effects on health, raises net family assets, lowers smoking and reduces the risk of heart disease.

Table 9.1 Estimates of the Annual Value/Impact of Additional Schooling

Realm of gain	Amount of gain
Consumption efficiency	$100 in household income (per extra year of schooling)
Net family assets	$8950 in increased net family assets (per extra year of schooling)
Lower smoking	1–2 fewer cigarettes smoked per day (per extra year of schooling)
Lower risk of heart disease	1.25–1.37 greater relative risk of death (8–11 years of schooling compared to 12+)

Source: Wolfe and Zuvekas (1997). 1996 prices.

Individually, these estimates may seem small, but taken together Wolfe and Zuvekas (1997, 497) estimate the non-market effects of education to be approximately equivalent to the market effects. In other words, the full-private rate of return to education (described in Chapter 8) may be double that typically estimated using earnings equations (as given in Chapter 2). This implies that policy discussions are missing about half the information needed to assess the efficiency of education investments.

One obvious approach for testing this contention is to examine education which ostensibly has no labour market value. Data on this are sparse, but Corman (1986) has examined whether non-credit adult education enhances home productivity. Such education, undertaken by around 5% of the US population, includes courses in car repairs, cooking, money management and gardening. These types of education have different implications from schooling: they may be invariant to unemployment or labour market discrimination; and they may be useful beyond the working life. Corman (1986) finds reasonably-sized positive effects from such education, but limited corroborating evidence is available regarding the scale of these non-market effects.

9.3   ECONOMIC GROWTH EFFECTS

9.3.1   Macro-economic Models of Education

A macro-economic approach to the generalised effects of education involves modelling economic growth. Aggregate production function and growth models may be used to capture some of the social benefits and productive spill-overs of education. In these models education may affect economic growth in representing either an enhanced labour input or a separate factor of production (Blundell et al., 1999; Romer, 1994). Following Benhabib and Spiegel (1994), the production function for per capita income Y_t may rendered in Cobb–Douglas form:

$$Y_t = \Lambda(t). K_t^{\alpha} . H_t^{\beta} . L_t^{\gamma} \varepsilon_t \qquad (9.7)$$

Here Y_t depends on physical capital K, labour L and human capital H; $\Lambda(t)$ is a growth coefficient over time (with a residual error term ε). Growth regressions can then be estimated using log differences across the base period X and current time period T:

$$(\log Y_T - \log Y_X) = (\log \Lambda_T - \log \Lambda_X) + \alpha(\log K_T - \log K_X) +$$
$$\beta(\log H_T - \log H_X) + \gamma(\log L_T - \log L_X) + \varepsilon_{TX} \qquad (9.8)$$

The coefficient of interest here is then β, the impact of the difference in human capital on per capita income growth. To extend the model, a law of motion or trajectory for human capital can be generated (as in De Gregorio, 1996; Glomm, 1997). These trajectories for human capital accumulation map the possible effects of education on economic growth as the two grow together. Benhabib and Spiegel (1994), for example, model the effect of human capital as a way either of raising productivity through innovation and endogenous growth or allowing nations to catch up with designated 'world-leader' economies. Alternatively, these leading economies may experience positive feedback in investing further in education and so growth rates may diverge. Another chain of causation may occur where an educated workforce is a pre condition for foreign investment of physical capital; this may be either directly because of the educated workforce or indirectly because education is correlated with political stability. Instead of direct influence as a factor, though, education may boost total factor productivity, through innovations and through the speed of adoption of technology from abroad. Also, human capital may be rivalrous in individual workers or non-rivalrous as a shared level of knowledge about new designs and methods.

Unlike labour and capital, factors which may be inelastic in the short run, education may be a more immediate way to raise economic growth. In Eeckhout's (1999) model, where inputs are not readily substitutable and ability levels are heterogeneous, education serves as a way to move the economy on to a higher growth path. De Gregorio (1996) traces through the effects of borrowing constraints on human capital accumulation and so economic growth, finding the removal of such constraints may boost growth. If the stock of human capital produces growth, then innovative workers are in effect generating economic growth and may do so over long periods of time.

Thus the growth of output may be attributable either to the level of education or to its growth (or both), with flows of human capital raising technical progress. To test this, two measures of human capital are typically used. The stock of human capital may be proxied by years of education per worker or literacy rates. The flow of human capital may be rendered as enrolment rates in schooling, that is, the net proportion of the age group which is in schooling. An enrolled student cohort is therefore the flow which augments the existing stock of years of education. The difficulties with using such variables are that, typically, developed countries have literacy rates which are narrowly spread and very high, tending toward 100%, and so leave little room for 'growth'. As an alternative, Pritchett (1996) uses the wage increment from years of education across the working population to represent the present value of a given stock of schooling.

Before looking at the evidence of the effects of education on national economic growth, such models may be applied to regional development. Economic growth effects may be estimated from looking at the multiplicative effects of education institutions, particularly universities. Such institutions are important loci of expenditure and economic activity and may have spill-over effects on the skills mix and industrial structure of a local economy. The effects of such institutions may be significant for regional economic growth and research effort (see Harris, 1997; CVCP, 1997; for a single university, see Battu et al., 1998). On the benefits side, a larger host community of education providers is likely to: attract and retain workers; provide low cost access to education for the local population; possibly offer some resistance to economic cycles (although increase sensitivity to demographic cycles); and allow for economies of scale in labour markets. On the costs side, congestion and higher tax burden may suggest against increased education provision in a region.

9.3.2   Macro-economic Evidence

Although there is plenty of evidence of the individualised benefits of education, evidence of the benefits of education at the aggregate level is less conclusive.

Growth regressions indicate countries with higher average years of education across the labour force do grow faster and countries with faster growing rates of education grow faster, with human capital significantly more important than manual labour. In expenditure terms across countries, Barro and Sala-I-Martin (1995) find a one standard deviation increase in the ratio of public education spending to GDP (1965–75) would have raised the average growth rate by 0.3 percentage points, with strong higher or tertiary education effects; using a different metric, they report a 0.9 year's increase in average secondary schooling would raise the annual economic growth rate by around 1.5%. McMahon (1999) extrapolates forward the effects of gross enrolment rates and expenditures on GDP growth per capita: through education, endogenous development is generated because (a) it raises physical capital investments (akin to the skill-biased technology change, discussed in Chapter 2); (b) it influences fertility and participation rates; and (c) because education enhances law and order, democracy and political stability. Overall, his evidence suggests a long run beneficial stimulus from education. For the UK, Gemmell (1997) finds increased enrolment from 70% to 95% (1960–85) to be associated with 0.6 percentage point per year faster productivity growth. Contra-positively, Bishop (1989) charts the continued depression of test scores and its deleterious effects on US productivity.

Yet there is also some critical evidence that the macro-economic effects of education are weak or indeed negative. There are very long lag and duration effects, with limited evidence of contemporaneous changes in education passing through into economic growth; the macro-economic effects appear stronger for males than females, contrary to micro-economic rates of return and perhaps unexpectedly in the context of the non-marketised benefits described above (Barro and Sala-I-Martin, 1995, 437). McMahon's (1999) model when applied only to Latin America shows few of the education investment coefficients to be statistically significant from lagged economic growth and higher education does not significantly raise GDP per capita (for East Asia, this last relationship in fact appears to be negative).

Less equivocally, Pritchett's (1996) growth regression evidence suggests that human capital accumulation has not raised economic growth. Although there are positive effects from growth regressions using enrolments rates and using levels of schooling (rather than growth in schooling), Pritchett (1996) rejects these models to regress educational capital per worker on per annum growth of GDP per worker. Using this specification, education is negatively, not positively, associated with economic growth. In their main model, Benhabib and Spiegel (1994) too find that human capital growth has either an insignificant or occasionally negative effect on economic growth. In relation to the above log differences equation (9.8), the parameter estimate for β is typically negative. In their extensions, human capital is predicted both to raise productivity through innovation and to allow lagging nations to catch-up with a designated 'world-leader' economy. In these extensions, Benhabib and Spiegel (1994) find per capita income growth does positively depend on average levels of human capital, with economies closing the gap, although again the effect is not statistically powerful. They also find human capital is a way of attracting physical capital. Their evidence suggests it is the human capital stock in levels rather than its growth rates which affects the growth of per capita income; this points to human capital augmenting labour's role, not as a separate factor.

Related, indirect evidence may also be considered. At the regional level, Phelps (1998) establishes a positive relationship between both US state employment and income with the absolute size of the education provision; Rauch (1993) presents evidence of a positive correlation between all individuals' earnings and the average education level of a region. In contrast, there is the relatively poor GDP growth rate of Africa over the last few decades, despite relatively high levels of investment in education (Collier and Gunning, 1999).

9.4   MACRO-ECONOMIC EFFECTS RECONSIDERED

9.4.1   Over-estimation of the Benefits of Education

For individuals, the broad evidence points to education's importance. Even if causality has not been established, there is plenty of circumstantial evidence and the imperative for individuals investing in a substantial duration of education appears strong. Yet there appear to be several difficulties both in estimating the non-pecuniary social effects and in substantiating the macro-economic gains from education. Along with the equivocal macro-economic evidence, some more direct criticisms have been offered, however, and these merit serious consideration.

Levin and Kelley (1994) offer a critical evaluation of the economic benefits of education on a number of fronts, arguing against the 'educational optimists' who simply presume that more education will mean higher economic growth. First, they argue that neither the connection between test scores and earnings nor the connection between test scores and productivity measures is strong. Workers may need to satisfy a threshold level of skills, but beyond this the returns to education are small and education does not boost economic growth. Second, although education may have a positive effect, a number of other complementary inputs must be in place: these might include new investment in capital goods, better management processes, and better organisational ways of working (the absence of complementarity may have impaired the 'Green Revolutions' in Africa, Pritchett, 1996). Third, the strongly persuasive cross-sectional evidence, which has been amassed above, needs to be contrasted with the less persuasive and more sparse longitudinal evidence. Looking at black women between 1967 and 1982, Levin and Kelley (1994) point out that although education has insulated these workers from being unemployed, this is in the context of greater unemployment over time. This leads to the problematic conclusion that unemployment had become more education-dependent over the period. Similarly for voter participation, where in two decades (1968–88) of rising education levels the numbers voting has fallen, even though the pattern of voting is still segmented by education level. Patterns over time, they maintain, do not readily seem to bear out the cross-sectional evidence.

On equity and education, Ram (1989) challenges the argument that increased schooling is linked to reduced income inequality for less-developed countries: the distribution of education itself may become less equal. For less-developed countries schooling inequality increases with average schooling, yielding inequalities across education levels. This may generate a negative feedback to some of the other expected benefits of education: wider income distribution across an economy may raise crime levels, for example. Perhaps inequality within education levels may be reduced: higher education does serve to ameliorate gender inequity as female graduates earn near-equivalent salaries to male graduates. Nevertheless the benefits of such education will depend on whether access is equal across income groups. Overall, if economies partition individuals based on their schooling and their cognitive ability, education may polarise social groups.

Country-level estimates of the benefits of education may also be problematic. Both for regions and countries, there may be 'brain drain' effects, with out-migration of skilled workers. Carrington and Detragiache

(1999) use evidence on migration to the US from 61 developing countries: these immigrants were more highly educated than the average for their home country. More importantly, the proportions of those with tertiary education in developing countries who do migrate are very high, at the least 10% and in some countries 50%. These endogenous movements in response to wage premia heighten the complexity of estimating the benefits of education to a particular economy.

Given the inconclusive aggregate evidence, there are plenty of explanations for why education does not raise economic growth. Pritchett (1996) suggests that screening and signalling effects simply serve as a way of re-distributing wealth; subsidies for education may lead to over-investments; and under-employment may be tolerated through under-written jobs in the public sector. Perhaps investment has been on the wrong sort of education – either higher education, investments on the intensive margin or training programmes with high deadweight losses may be suspects here. Relatedly, Collier and Gunning (1999) identify the low rate of implementation of education policies in Africa, with less than 10% successfully enacted.

Finally, Behrman (1987, 1996) contends that there is limited evidence on how durable education's influence is on behaviour. It is possible, but not well investigated, that a high school diploma or a degree enhances all life experiences, but it seems an optimistic proposition. Belfield et al. (1999) present evidence from 11 000 UK graduates on the contribution their degree made to their personal development; the evidence suggests that a degree is only a temporary boost, as other life events supersede.

9.4.2   Mismeasurement of the Benefits of Education

Another set of criticisms relates to the correlation approach used to establish the gains from education, which may cause them to be exaggerated. In this sub-section, three more aspects are considered.

First, Behrman and Stacey's (1997, 28) example shows why the gains may be overestimated using conditional demand functions, for health H and education $\dot{E}$:

$$H = a_{11}P_H + a_{12}P_E + a_{13}X + \varepsilon_1 \qquad (9.9)$$

$$E = a_{21}P_H + a_{22}P_E + a_{23}X + \varepsilon_2 \qquad (9.10)$$

Here P_H and P_E are the prices of health and education and X other variables (the ε_i terms are error terms). Such demand functions are often not fully specified. Estimating the following reduced form equation will not yield an appropriate measure of the effect of education on health:

$$H = a_{31}P_H + a_{32}E + a_{33}X + \varepsilon_3 \qquad (9.11)$$

Mathematically, a_{32} is the ratio a_{12}/a_{22}, that is, the ratio of education price coefficients determining education and health from (9.9) and (9.10). This parameter a_{32} cannot straightforwardly be interpreted as the relationship between education and health (as discussed in equation 9.6 above). To the extent that education is an input into health it is the (relative) price of education that matters.

Second, Behrman (1987) is also sceptical that human capital augmentation can be identified with increases in schooling, because there are other ways in which human capital can be generated, such as reading. Instead of schooling, individuals may also accumulate human capital through independent home study (Bacdayan, 1994) or through observing others' behaviour. Depending on the prices for each investment and the form of the production function, there may be a strong correlation between investments in schooling and in, say, reading. If there is a strong correlation, it may not be possible to identify the unique contribution of schooling to the outcome; any estimation which just includes education as an explanatory variable is omitting the effects of reading and all other such human capital variables. As Behrman (1987) shows, this correlation depends on the relative prices of each investment, which should differ in order for the correlation between the two investments to weaken. Yet if access to parental loans for schooling is easier for rich children than poor, then access to loans for other human capital investments is likely to be so too. Also, the more that child behaviour depends on genetic and some family-determined outcomes, the more likely it will be that relative time-prices (of schooling and reading) are constant.

A third issue is that the result of low or negative macro-economic effects may be contested as being dependent on the sample of countries chosen for investigation. Temple (1999) finds that Benhabib and Spiegel's (1994) results are significantly modified when outlier nations are removed. Regressing the log of the difference in output DY between 1965 and 1985 against the log of the difference in, respectively, physical capital DK, average years of schooling as the measure of human capital DH, and the labour force DL:

$$DY = 0.10 + 0.553DK + 0.165DH + 0.241DL$$
$$(1.95) \quad (13.2) \qquad (4.0) \qquad (2.2)$$

Reducing the sample to 64 countries, Temple (1999, 132) finds the coefficient on the log of the difference in human capital DH to be positive and statistically significant (t-ratios in brackets). However, human capital remains less potent than changes in the physical capital or the labour force.

Inevitably, there are significant difficulties in separating the effects of high education levels from their causes; rich economies may be able to afford more education provision. Also problematic are the modelling of the lag effects of education; the assumption that augmented human capital is of equivalent quality and type across countries; and the use of enrolment levels as proxies for human capital. In rebuttal, Pritchett (1996) points out that these arguments should also apply to tests on physical capital, yet this variable is consistently positively correlated with economic growth (as in Temple's estimates given above).

Essentially the problem is how to establish that these externalities and growth effects are caused by education: disentangling correlated from contextual effects is essential if the benefits of education are to be identified. To counter this disquiet, a number of estimation techniques are used to identify the social effects of education as per those for earnings in Chapter 2. First, instrumental variables, that is, variables correlated with education but not other collinear variables, could be used. These are however difficult to find and so have only been infrequently applied to estimating the social effects of education. Second, attempts may be made to adjust or control for other circumstances. One way to improve estimation of the non-labour market effects of education is through inclusion of more of the 'unobserved' variables. Endowments, such as IQ or more details on parental status, may help to identify the effects of education; sibling and twins data have also been used. Finally, longitudinal data may be used with information on individuals over time to hold some unobserved social characteristics constant. Unfortunately, because many individuals stop education in their early twenties, education itself may be differenced out of any such estimation.

9.5   ISSUES AND CONCLUSIONS

This chapter has considered aggregate and social benefits of education in two realms. For the first set of effects – those for individuals in non-market realms – there is evidence of the benefits to health, household management, fertility and other non-pecuniary behaviours. However, education needs to be modelled as an input to these individual outcomes. Simple correlation cannot serve to establish causality, and without a theory of how education changes behaviour, questions will remain over the efficacy of education in raising socio-economic outcomes or ameliorating social inequities.

Externalities from education at the aggregate level also need to be clearly identified. Although many of the social benefits of education are non-marketised, that does not mean that they accrue to society's welfare function. Better household management, health and consumer efficiency may all be reaped by the individual and not society. Nevertheless, there is likely to be a divergence between the social and the private rate of return to education, either because the social marginal cost is less than the private marginal cost or social marginal revenue is greater than private marginal revenue. If this divergence between private and social parameters is substantial, individuals are facing the 'wrong' prices for education and (Pigovian) subsidies can be used to ensure optimal levels of education. Perhaps one approach to ensuring the externalities are 'captured' is to merge the services, for example, bundling vocational education with health instruction, if schooling improves health. The tasks are then to specify these social effects, separating individual/household gains from pure externalities, and to estimate the size of these gains. A range of estimation techniques may be used, applying equi-marginal principles or instruments for identifying the effects of education. One important metric is the marginal utility of education. Another is the elasticity responsiveness from education compared to other interventions. For instance, crime may be reduced either by higher incarceration rates or by more education: to assess the cost-effectiveness of each approach, estimates are needed of the elasticity of crime in response to (expenditure on) incarceration compared to that in response to (expenditure on) education.

The second set of effects are those education has at the macro-economic level. These are arguably the most important, particularly if the individualised effects of education – be they earnings or non-pecuniary – are zero-sum. The evidence here is not conclusive though: interpretation of these models is also difficult when few of these macro-economic effects have been expressed in rate of return metrics or cost–benefit ratios. This comparability with individual effects of education identified above is important none the less: individualised data may not be sufficient to show education investments to be externally efficient, that is, for the private marginal product of education to be equal to the social marginal product. For this efficiency condition to be established, aggregate data must also be incorporated and interpreted so as to cohere with the more robust micro-economic evidence that education raises earnings.

Yet even if this last tranche of macro-economic evidence is nugatory, this need not suggest that government should invest less in education. Perhaps education has significant effects in the other non-pecuniary realms which offset these null growth effects; and if education is a merit good and GDP is not society's ultimate maximand, then education can still be justified with non-economic reasoning. Policies which embody each of these issues are considered in the next and final chapter.

10. Education Policy Using Economics

10.1 ECONOMIC CONCEPTS IN EDUCATION

This final chapter offers a general discussion of how economic theory and evidence can be used to inform and direct education policy, drawing on the arguments of the previous chapters. One usage for economics – prompted by the economist Friedrich von Hayek – is to help to make policies possible by making them acceptable. A prime example of this for the UK is the plethora of estimates of the rate of return to higher education. These empirical estimates legitimised increased access to higher education, as well as the shift in the burden of payment from the taxpayer to the individual student. Another example, drawing on the economics of public choice, is the liberalisation of public services through contracting out, local management and open enrolment. These are part of a general trend towards the creation of atomistic markets in education, increasingly substantiated by economic evidence.

In most instances, however, the motivation for policy appears to be as much ideological as evidential. Hence a more potent usage for economics might be in advancing the evaluative criteria for implementing policy in education and so remaining ahead of policy agendas. The foregoing chapters show how raising the status of key economic concepts would help in directing the policy agenda towards economic analysis. Each chapter may be taken in turn.

From Chapter 2, the human capital model is found to have strong explanatory power. Supported by copious private rate of return and earnings premia studies across practically every country, the evidence remains that education is an important and worthwhile investment for a large proportion of each age cohort. These gains hold even when the endogeneity of decisions to invest are accounted for and when ability has been factored in. This does not mean that education is ever and always a good investment – some individuals will make poor investments in their education, particularly when the opportunity costs to education, such as unskilled wages or other investments, fluctuate. Further scepticism arises if education is held simply to reduce signalling costs in the labour market; available micro-economic evidence largely refutes this, verifying human capital accumulation as an important determinant of wages. Also, subsidies and taxes are likely to distort economic decisions, yielding over-educated workers, and economic analysis can show the sizes of these distortions. To extend the economic analysis, it should be possible to substantiate closely and robustly the effects on firms' surpluses from training and rate of return to different modes of education.

In Chapter 3 the demand for education was considered, in analogous form to the demand for standard commodities. There are a number of difficulties in purchasing education both from the individual consumer's and from the provider's perspective, indicating the divergence of private from social costs and benefits and so market failure. Nevertheless, there is a persuasive mass of evidence that education is responsive to its tuition price, to income levels and to other costs; it also seems plausible to model non-completion of education as a rational cost–benefit decision. Institutional and government policies should reflect these demand parameters and elasticities, particularly as the education demand function appears to shift outward with higher income levels and individuals' rates of intertemporal substitution vary. However, access to education, that is, effectual demand, may need to be constrained in some way. For policy a critical distinction is between efficient and equitable access rules: efficiency is enhanced by investing in education for those who learn fastest (a form of cognitive partitioning) but this may be inequitable if compulsory schooling threshold levels are set too low. Wealth effects on access may also be efficiency-reducing: there are lots of reasons why the demand for education may be differentially affected by the net cost of education and by initial wealth (such as endogenous labour supply, consumption aspects of education and uncertain future incomes and employment propensities). Generally, though, a society would seek to 'mine' all its human capital, not simply that which is free from borrowing constraints. These equity and efficiency trade-offs need to be identified and calibrated.

Turning to issues of internal efficiency, the operations of educational enterprises are mapped in Chapters 4 and 5. Education enterprises are assumed to be maximising a composite achievement function, subject to a budget constraint. The cost function is described, where the particular technology of education suggests emphasis on class size and, relatedly, on capacity utilisation and school size as a way of reducing per unit costs. Linking revenues to costs is problematic, because the returns to education are not simply 'sales', reflecting the specific contributions of students as non-price inputs into the technology of provision. Albeit as yet only partly explored, this customer-input technology model may have wide-ranging implications for the management of education enterprises, with its stress on the student body as a determinant of both school performance and mode of delivery, as well as a source of revenue.

Direct investigations into internal efficiency have produced less than promising evidence, however: on the whole, greater resources do not seem to lead straightforwardly to improved outcomes. Yet unless this link is identifiable, policy-makers should be sceptical about the claims by institutions and by funding bodies that they can straightforwardly deploy extra resources in ways which improve outcomes. But there is broadly consistent evidence that larger institutions have higher outcomes, suggesting economies of scale (if not of scope). Together, these findings are useful in directing policy away from certain routes – expecting straightforward pricing for education, or unconditional increased tranches of funds to all providers – rather than toward specific policy initiatives. Government policies emphasising resource allocation rather than resource levels seem justifiable on this evidence.

In Chapter 6, more details on input allocation are further considered: here the research stresses the optimal usage of teachers, because of their dominance in standard education production functions. Manpower planning, salary setting (both relative to other occupations and within the teaching profession) and unions all play a central role in the deployment of teaching staff. A role for government here is to structure the market for teachers so as to minimise disequilibria of supply and demand and to maximise the efficiency-enhancing role of unions. Other inputs should also be evaluated for their contribution to education provision, using the equi-marginal principle. The tasks here are: first to ensure that enterprises internalise this principle in resource allocation – a practice which is acknowledged to be difficult with multiple or conditional funding streams and where some inputs are more malleable than others; and second to ensure that output-choice external goals are compatible with these efficiency conditions. Overarching these inputs is managerial control, stressed by successive governments and national education agencies as fundamental to improving education provision.

Internal and external efficiency will both be affected by the market structure in which education providers operate, and this is discussed in Chapter 7. Subtly and variously, the extent of the market is increasing, with evidence on its efficacy accumulating to support this trend. The main barrier in schooling and higher education for command systems may be the restriction on entry and exit of providers, although even here marketisation appears inexorable (as schools either increase or decrease enrolments or obtain new, differentiated status). More generally, providers can compete, co-operate or collude, and it is perhaps avoidance of collusion rather than direct stimulation of competition which is necessary. Also important here is the exchange mechanism – how schools and pupils trade. From subsidised loans, vouchers, learning accounts and top-up fees, a range of options exist between the command nexus and the straight pay-per-use nexus, but evidence from international and UK studies on voucher schemes illustrates the difficulties of imposing new exchange mechanisms within existing command structures.

In Chapter 8, the role of government is addressed directly. The difficulties of ensuring efficient provision and imposing effective funding formulae are identified, and again a slew of liberalising trends has emerged to undermine the command nexus. One recent policy which has been successful has been the use of performance information in education: ideally such information should go to consumers (pupils and students) rather than government, but if government is funding the education, then it too should collect performance indicators and make funding conditional on them.

Following this, potential inefficiencies in government provision, funding and regulation have been examined, particularly x-inefficiency and the scope for policy failure. On the subject of x-inefficiency, it has been noted that: decision-makers may not be guided by profit-maximisation or cost-minimisation incentives; decision-makers may not know the education production function and are therefore unlikely to ensure efficiency; and it may be hard to incorporate incentives when education is 'free at point of sale'. Finally, two areas where ostensibly innocuous policies may have substantial indirect effects are in the hidden tax on savings from means-tested student loans and the welfare costs of having a substantial wedge between the prices of private schooling and state schooling.

Thus, numerous difficulties in ensuring an efficient funding mechanism and government provision have been identified. Yet as different institutions promote different syndromes, public schools cannot simply have private school values supplanted on to them. However, general liberalisation of services has been encouraged, reflecting the belief that private rather than state schooling is more efficient. This range of solutions has been considered over the previous chapters and is eclectic. That all those options exist and are put into practice suggests that the consumption of education is rivalrous and excludable and therefore education is not a simple public good.

To fully articulate the benefits of education, effects outside the individual need to be considered. Two areas are discussed in Chapter 9: those pertaining to the individual in non-pecuniary markets and to the aggregate economy. With a social capital model, again education yields a stream of post-investment returns, non-pecuniary but still individualised in the form of better health, greater consumer efficiency or enhanced well-being. As well, such returns may also apply outside an individual's own utility function, where greater education leads for example to greater social cohesion, respect for human rights, lower pollution and lower crime. These returns may be substantial (if emerging evidence is borne out) and perhaps are even equivalent to the earnings premia derived from the human capital model. If so, government policy should acknowledge these in its direct funding of education: the key here is to articulate the link between the investment and the net returns, through estimation of full-private and full-social rates of return. A role for government may be more appropriate in structuring incentives for the accumulation of such social capital rather than human capital; this may mean, for example, favouring investment in younger age groups if externalities diminish with the level of education. Finally, general equilibrium economic effects also need to be considered. The evidence presented above suggests that the strong individual effects from education may in part be transfers from those without education to those with, consequently without proportional increases in economic growth.

10.2   DIRECTIONS FOR POLICY

From this petition, three micro-economic policy aims stand out. First, policies can influence the stream of costs and benefits within any investment appraisal. For individuals, subsidies to instruction will influence the marginal pay-off to study. For numerous reasons, such students may be particularly sensitive to such subsidies, probably rapidly driving them away from their optimal investment strategy (Hoxby, 1996b), but possibly toward it. The directions of partial effects can be plausibly identified: the transition to work from school will be improved through inducements to study, career counselling and better quality education; alternatively, work may be made more attractive, through cutting hiring costs for youths. But the general equilibrium interactions across these partial effects have to be resolved empirically. If the optimal level of education has not already been accumulated, the latter policy – of making it easier to employ young workers – will drive educational outcomes away from optimality. Also for workers in training, there may be opportunities to relax credit constraints or to improve property rights over the ownership of skills. Tax policies need also to be structured to encourage optimal investment (which may be less, rather than more, investment in human capital). Unfortunately, although rates of return currently appear high, many of the increases in enrolment in (UK) higher education in the 1990s (but also in previous decades) are on such a historically large scale that existing evidence may be inadequate, particularly when general equilibrium effects need to be accounted for.

An underlying mandate appears to be to make those who reap the benefits of education also bear the costs of provision. This has influence at all levels: individuals in higher education reap most of the rewards; regions may also reap rewards from having a highly skilled workforce; institutions may also benefit from highly motivated inputs; and businesses benefit from workers with particular skills. Decisions should be devolved to those best able to internalise all the costs and benefits of an investment in education; this should encourage 'profitable' investments, as well as prices which reflect relative scarcities.

Yet equity effects also need to be considered and the main difficulty here is that these will depend on individuals' life-cycle outcomes rather than their on-entry status. The three inequalities considered are: of inputs, both from the state and within the community/household; of abilities; and of outcomes. Not only do individuals have heterogeneous skills and abilities; but they also differ in their access to education (perhaps through constraints in the capital market). Hence it is desirable to identify which (socio-economic) groups face returns which differ from the general average. Careful distinction between *ex ante* and *ex post* returns has to be made: if there are barriers to entry for enrolment for group x, then any actual group x enrolees will have higher ability and so *ex post* rates of return higher than the average (unless the same barrier pertaining to enrolment affects earnings). Ashenfelter and Rouse (1999) do, however, claim that the rates are already all but nearly indistinguishable for the US; evidence on studies of access do indicate some inefficiencies in human capital markets for the UK. (Another, more simple way is to look at the amounts of funding available for particular groups, as Herrnstein and Murray, 1994, do). Further, it is necessary to distinguish between the rate of return being equalised as individuals accumulate education until they reach their reservation rates of return and the rate of return for a given qualification across ability levels. High ability students may have a higher rate of return to high school than low ability students, but their rate of return to university might be the same as the low ability students' rate of return to high school.

Governments can operate on both individuals' supply and demand functions for human capital, especially in reducing differences in costs for different education programmes. But with only formula funding it may be harder to ameliorate inequalities of inputs linked to household income and community context; and it may be undesirable to limit those inequalities associated with outcomes from education provision. Otherwise there will be significant disincentives.

A second aim for policy would be to enhance internal efficiency of education providers through the use of incentives. Several steps would be effective here, to include improving educational optimands; hardening budget constraints; raising efficiency-enhancing rather than rent-seeking behaviour; and allowing expansion where marginal cost is less than average cost. Within educational institutions, however, expansion of one activity will ultimately lead to contractions in others. The equi-marginal principle may be used here, in that the timetable or school year, for example, should be rescheduled until all study programmes generate equal returns. Yet within an existing enterprise, lengthy contracts, prior investments and political interests are all likely to compromise the ability to utilise the equi-marginal principle. Moreover, even if redistributing resources within an enterprise were straightforward for managers in practice, there is considerable uncertainty over where resources should be redistributed to or from.

Evidence on the relative efficiency of large schools prompts the obvious question as to what savings could be made from restructuring schools into equal units of the same size or from allowing schools to evolve into the optimal size; back-of-an-envelope calculations suggest such savings could be large. Also possible is the modelling of enrolment demand functions (so that universities, for instance, do not remain geared to the needs of school leavers, when the corporate training market is growing), as well as liberalising factor input usage to apply equi-marginal principles. A greater use of incentives may reward those who are efficient or productive – these may be teachers or education managers, but may also be pupils, whose greater effort in the classroom should be rewarded in assessments and beyond. For institutions, separating capital expenditures from current expenditures changes the incentive to invest in different resource inputs, with possibly substantial long term effects. One difficulty here is for the education system to create exchange mechanisms which reveal individuals' willingness to pay and so create marginal revenues from enhanced provision.

A third broad aim for policy is to encourage analysis of provision and performance within the sector for use by government, by students and by taxpayers/voters. Education is more like an experience good than an inspection good, but this may be increasingly less the case: highly specific information on rates of return to higher education are available; pedagogies and curricula are stated; and contractual agreements between education providers and students are codified. Greater use of this information would help the specification of demand. But because there are high initial fixed costs and because of their financial accountability, governments may play an initial catalyst role in setting up such information systems, which can then be traded away to consumers.

Rather than more descriptive information, however, a better understanding of the expected costs and benefits of education should be cultivated; to encourage efficiency, taxpayers, students and government need to be persuaded that more resources will lead to better outcomes and shown how this might be achieved. This may allow a consensus for investment decisions to emerge. Such information should be expanded to address efficiency as well as simply performance outcomes, clarifying the burden of costs: for taxpayers, the appropriate evaluation of an education system is not its effectiveness, but instead its cost-effectiveness or indeed the full rate of return. For individual students, debt should not be avoided: it is simply the borrowing necessary for any investment. For taxpayers, funding decisions should internalise all the relevant societal benefits. However, the link between education and the local tax base is often oblique, with mixed local and central government funding. Moreover, the outcome measures need to be appropriate: although most education is undertaken to boost earnings, it is likely to be impractical to hold teachers accountable – through funding formulae – if their students turn out to be low earners. Yet this earnings effect represents a key indicator for students where education is traded in open markets. Reflecting all these issues, Bishop (1996) argues for better signals of learning; external assessment of achievement to determine college admissions; and greater certification of competencies for releasing student records. Unfortunately, such requests are perennial (as in O'Keefe, 1981).

At the aggregate, macro-economic policy level there is less which is certain. Education probably contributes to long term economic growth, and the diffused, widespread effects through endogenous development are charted by McMahon (1999). But the specific investment strategies which underpin this cannot be readily inferred. For government's optimal investment strategies, looking at both economic and social benefit streams, a ready consensus on where to invest is absent. Any shift toward a 'knowledge economy' might either mean more investment in those already highly skilled (to invent and innovate) or in the unskilled (to produce with new technologies). Similar ambiguity might apply to the trend for the professionalisation of the workforce. As another example, Psacharapoulos (1996b) challenges Birdsall's (1996) emphasis on higher education, by stressing the returns to extra skills learnt at school over those gained from research. Of particular interest are the relative expenditure ratios across different sectors of schooling, further and higher education, as these reflect current priorities for investment. From this, marginal expansion can be undertaken, although the scale of investment necessary to effect change may be prohibitive: Hanushek (1998) argues that it would take a massive investment to improve secondary education in the US and Heckman (1999) finds that educational investments of the order of a year's gross salary per unskilled worker would be needed to reset the divergences in earnings over the last two decades. With these estimates, micro-economic changes may be the most effective over the longer term, even as they are unlikely to redress major shifts in economic structures.

Finally, economic concepts can be used to look across educational research. Fitz-Gibbon (1999) sets out an agenda for education which includes: challenging the imposition of unproven policies; solving problems and avoiding harmful practices; and creating improvement. These of course are easily endorsed (as are the multivarious anodyne lists of the characteristics of effective schools, see Barber, 1996, 129–130); but one proposed way to develop that agenda is to use a rigorous nomenclature for educational improvements. Such terms or metrics (for example, effect sizes, cost–benefit ratios or multiplier coefficients) would allow educational policies and interventions to be compared; an important way for economic appraisal to progress. Fitz-Gibbon's particular citation favours cross-age tutoring over computer-aided instruction for maths education, over reduced class sizes and over more time on basic education. Yet each of these interventions had a positive effect size and so presumably each one should be implemented (assuming their independence of effect). What is needed is in fact a way of deciding amongst competing claims, when more than one effect size is positive. The only logical way to do this is to acknowledge that resources – be they time, money, energy or will – are scarce and that the appropriate evaluative criterion is the relative cost-effectiveness or rate of return to each intervention.

The above prescriptions may lead economic criteria to be used more in policy – there are very few rigorous cost–benefit analyses of education programmes – and used more persuasively. This stress on the ideas as much as the evidence is an acknowledgement that governments need to present and represent policies in changing circumstances and with inevitable trade-offs between gainers and losers. The translation from evidence to policy is far from straightforward, no matter how intuitive or substantial the evidence. Krueger (1999), for instance, argues that a rigorous randomised trial should dominate over n pieces of circumstantial evidence; but if those circumstances reflect actual behaviour, then it remains to be established that a workable policy can be created from the rigorous inferences of a randomised trial. In the abstract and despite the evidence of Chapter 5, more resources must mean better outcomes; but there are plenty of confounding variables and impediments (as well as policy inertia) to impede this relationship in practice. As Herrnstein and Murray (1994) point out, educational environments are complex milieux and most (intensive margin) interventions will at best generate small improvements. And this presupposes there is agreement over what the evidence means – a recent survey of economists is not particularly encouraging on this, finding high levels of disagreement on policy questions, disagreements which largely reflected differences in values rather than in the estimates of parameters (Fuchs et al., 1998).

None the less, economic theory and argument should be adopted to meet the aims of education policy. The above chapters – using a set of concepts and models, embedded in theory, together with empirical evidence which can be used for education policy analysis – hopefully illustrate this.

Notes

1. Sutherland's (1992) amusing book considers the 'efficacy' of instinct and intuition over models and frameworks. The latter are simplified expositions and, although model-building unavoidably abstracts away much of the educational environment into the catch-all of *ceteris paribus*, this has its merits. The clause may help as a frame of reference for the diverse phenomena which cannot be well specified, formalising the model. And the absence of a *ceteris paribus* condition may in fact make little difference to the inferences drawn: understanding the interaction of supply and demand advances the study of participation rates in education quite significantly, for example, notwithstanding unobserved changes in tastes.
2. Hopefully, this exposition yields both a wider and more detailed role for the economist, compared to previous stylisations. No obvious consensus emerges on the economics of education from Becker and Baumol (1996), Cohn and Johnes (1994), Johnes (1993a) or Cohn and Geske (1990). Turning to two papers with promising titles, the economics of education is substantially circumscribed. Psacharopoulos (1996a) looks at policy and reduces the research agenda to rate of return analysis; screening; and externalities. Hoenack (1994) advocates research inquiry into behaviour within educational organisations.
3. A general example may make the case. There is a wealth of literature on teacher payment systems, but little on resource allocation to other factors such as class materials. Yet teachers represent only one factor of production in education, albeit a large commitment. The elasticity of substitution between teacher inputs, student inputs and physical resource inputs is critical. Estimating teacher retention and recruitment is not useful, for example, if teacher input is already over-utilised. Inserting research on 'the market for teachers' into the theories of factor inputs makes it clear that teachers are only one factor and that an efficiency criterion requires each factor to be considered. Barber's (1996, 130) observation – 'common sense tells us that the only thing that really matters is the individual teachers' quality' – illustrates why this point is worth labouring.
4. Of course, these decisions may be uncertain: one may not be able to put new skills into practice; what one finds out may not be worth knowing; and one may never understand certain phenomena. But the same is true for physical capital: new machines may not produce anything worthwhile; new techniques may not be worth applying; and technologies may fail to function.
5. Female graduates' earnings in education in the UK (US) are around 75% (83%) of those of male graduates. These are raw differences of course and may reflect different tastes of male and female workers for pecuniary returns to labour market participation. For example, when Hecker (1998, 69) standardises earnings to take account of an individual's subject of study, the observed gap in earnings falls by around 9 percentage points.
6. Participation in a training programme is also likely to be correlated with economic conditions: areas with higher unemployment are likely to get 'better' recruits. Individuals may select themselves into the programme for reasons which may be unobservable, such

as declining demand for their original skills. If programme administrators are evaluated on the basis of the performance of their trainees, they may have an incentive to cream-skim. Heckman and Smith (1999) present an evaluation of a large scale US training programme, based on the Job Training Partnership Act, highlighting the difficulties of such evaluations. In particular, most evaluations either compare trainees' before-and-after performance earnings, as would make sense from a cost–benefit approach, or contrast trainee performance/earnings growth with that of non-trainees. Unfortunately, the before-and-after comparison is impaired because of the so-called 'pre-programme dip' in earnings – trainees' earnings are often falling as they enter the training programme. And the differences-contrast approach is biased if the decision to enrol is motivated by a change in the opportunity cost of forgone earnings. Again, estimation of the marginal rather than the average trainee's outcomes may be most appropriate if the decision is whether or not to expand the programme. These problems may be overwhelming: in her evaluation of the Comprehensive Employment and Training Act of 1973, Bassi's (1984, 40) conclusion is stark and still pertinent: 'selection of white males into the program is so non-random that none of the estimation techniques developed in this paper are adequate to eliminate selection bias for this group.'

7. The Michigan Panel Study of Income Dynamics asks 'How much formal education is required to get a job like yours?' In the UK, the Social Change and Economic Life Initiative asks 'If they were applying today, what qualifications if any would someone need to get the type of job you have now?' Battu et al. (1999) have estimated graduate over-education in the UK using responses to the question: 'Was the degree gained a requirement in the job specification for your main employment (including self-employment)?' This categorisation is not informative about the extent of over-education, in contrast to questions about the formal requirements for one's job.

8. Perhaps a better target measure for public funding of, say, the higher education sector would be how many graduates have ever had jobs which require degrees. Battu et al. (1999) estimate this to be around 70%. At ten percentage points above the respective cross-sectional figure, this suggests a non-trivial entry to and exit from 'matched' work. Although most graduates get matched work, around 30% never have a job which requires a degree. This fits with the view that there exists a hard-core of 'low-achievers' (in terms of the labour market) emerging from higher education.

9. An additional reason is that individuals are uncertain about their longevity (within which period to pay back for their education), although this presumably applies to any capital good.

10. Kim (1988) uses the indirect utility function, assuming a translog constant elasticity of substitution and uses Roy's identity to derive the demand curve and expenditure shares for durables, non-durables, education and other services. Kim's (1988, 180) modelling shows many of the simpler, restrictive functional forms for the demand curve fail mis-specification tests, particularly ones for auto-correlation.

11. As well, these customer-input technology models need to address the assumption of profit maximisation; capital market imperfections; informational asymmetries; the incorporation of other outcomes such as research; and technologies other than constant returns to scale (for a full discussion, see Rothschild and White, 1995). Customer-input technologies are also general as to the form of pricing, that is, whether particular individuals or particular groups of students should be subsidised, and how much the wage should be, compared to the tuition fee. Some extensions are developing of customer-input technology, however: Epple and Romano's (1998) model of priced peer inputs – considered in the main text – reflects a similar organisational logic.

12. University funding council grants – which are largely formula-driven at a flat rate for teaching and by performance-assessed research – remain the largest source of income (42%), but these are supplemented by academic fees and support grants (23%), research

grants and contracts (15%) and endowment income (3%). The use of tuition fees to determine enrolments is as yet limited, but is growing in importance.

13. As Behrman (1996, 350) concludes: 'most of the existing studies do not control well for the behavioural decisions that determine who goes to what type of school for how long with what type of success.' As emphasised elsewhere, two individual controls which are critical are those for family background and prior achievement; their omission may over-estimate the rate of return to education by over one third (Griffin and Ganderton, 1996).

14. Hanushek et al. (1996, 111) simplify the production function to illustrate the problems of aggregation and measurement error. Ignoring variation across family background and across pre-test scores, achievement A_{ij} can be cast as a function of school quality or resource common to all environments R_{ij} and a single measure of community environment C_j, with the marginal impacts of these two variables being the same: $A_{ij} = \theta C_j + \psi R_{ij} + \varepsilon_{ij}$. If there is no information on C_j, then the school quality coefficient ψ will be biased as ψ' $= \psi + \theta \phi$. Here ϕ is equal to the school expenditure coefficient in a regression of community environment on school expenditure. Aggregation affects the coefficient ϕ if both C and R are driven by a common factor, such as a community's tastes for education. These tastes are possibly reflected in property values, with educational quality depending on both the average tastes and the difference of each school's average from the overall state average. When only state average effects are included, ϕ and so ψ are likely to be pushed upward, erroneously suggesting that state-level resource effects have a positive effect on outcomes. Measurement error may also be a problem. If the observed school input is measured only imperfectly, again the estimate of ψ (and other coefficients) will be inconsistent and biased toward zero. These errors may however bias the research toward finding positive resource effects, rather than not finding them.

15. Gibbs et al. (1996) study performance at one UK higher education institution of 6075 students on modular courses. As modules have increased in size over time, average student performance should have declined. They find a negative relationship between module enrolment and average marks, although a substantial spread between the sizes of groups is needed before such effects are evident.

16. Yet there are obvious problems in having self-regulation: Adam Smith, for example, noted that a faculty member will allow other faculty members to neglect their duty 'provided he himself is allowed to neglect his own'. Barber (1996, 58) euphemistically refers to 'the producer stronghold on policy'.

17. Bishop (1996, 110) cites data from Stevenson and Stigler (1986) on the US and Japan. Respectively, 63% versus 98% of fifth graders have a study desk; 21% versus 58% purchased workbooks for additional homework in maths; 1% versus 29% purchased workbooks for additional homework in science; but 91% versus 39% of parents believe their school is doing an excellent or good job.

18. Yet of all public sector realms education performance indicators might be expected to be particularly effective. They can be regularly staged (during examinations) without intervention into the education process. UK schools are funded under a common formula and with a common National Curriculum, so differences might reflect differential performance rather than differential circumstances. Analogously to business, however, there are many ways of measuring the performance of a company, despite enormous effort to identify a magic variable. This suggests an eclectic approach to performance indicators in education.

19. This inefficiency has been a common and perennial criticism of public sector providers as 'mired in their history and traditional modes of operation', with under-utilised physical resources, inflexible faculty, inconvenient pedagogy and insufficient information about provision (Sperling, 1998). Yet state-run universities have, over the last decade, responded vigorously to enormous changes: in their student number; the profile of students recruited; modalities of provision; relationships with corporate and public sector

clients; and their financial and regulatory environment (Daniel, 1996). In recent years and through a range of collaborative ventures, higher education has moved progressively into knowledge and technology trades; human resource exchange; business advice and consultancy; and a range of educational services, such as accreditation schemes (PREST, 1998).

20. Inserting some simple functions for these three aspects, Usher (1997) estimates the optimal level of education, finding that education – if measured by public sector disbursements – is under-provided.

21. Adam Smith (1776), for example, believed an 'instructed and intelligent people besides are always more decent and orderly than an ignorant and stupid one ... They are more disposed to examine, and more capable of seeing through, the interested complaints of faction and sedition.' Looking at current UK legislative documents, there are some explicit government objectives set for ameliorating social inequality through education: one of the anticipated outcomes from effective target-setting is for schools to take 'practical steps to raise the achievements of ethnic minority pupils and promote racial harmony' (DfEE, 1998d). How such targets are operationalised at the school level is however undetermined.

References

Acemoglu, D. (1996), 'A microfoundations for social increasing returns in human capital accumulation', *Quarterly Journal of Economics*, **CXI**, 779–804.

Acemoglu, D. (1998), 'Why do new technologies complement skills? Directed technical change and wage inequality', *Quarterly Journal of Economics*, **CXIII**, 1055–1090.

Acemoglu, D. and J-S. Pischke (1999), 'Beyond Becker: training in imperfect labour markets', *Economic Journal*, **109**, F112–142.

Akerhielm, K. (1995), 'Does class size matter?', *Economics of Education Review*, **14**, 229–241.

Alba-Ramirez, A. (1993), 'Mismatch in the Spanish labor market: overeducation?', *Journal of Human Resources,* **27**, 259–278.

Alpin, C., J.R. Shackelton, and S. Walsh (1998), 'Over and under-Education in the UK graduate labour market', *Studies in Higher Education*, **23**, 17–34.

Altonji, J.G. (1995), 'The effects of high school curriculum on education and labor market outcomes', *Journal of Human Resources*, **30**, 409–438.

Altonji, J.G. and T.A. Dunn (1996a), 'The effects of family background on the return to education', *Review of Economics and Statistics*, **42**, 692–704.

Altonji, J.G. and T.A. Dunn (1996b). 'Using siblings to estimate the effect of school quality on wages', *Review of Economics and Statistics*, **42**, 665–671.

Ambler, J.S. (1994), 'Who benefits from educational choice? Some evidence from Europe', *Journal of Policy Analysis and Management*, **13**, 454–476.

Angrist, J.D. and A.B. Krueger (1991), 'Does compulsory school attendance affect schooling and earnings?', *Quarterly Journal of Economics*, **CVI**, 223–245.

Angrist, J.D. and V. Lavy (1999), 'Using Maimonides' rule to estimate the effect of class size on scholastic achievement', *Quarterly Journal of Economics*, **CXIV**, 533–576.

Appleton, S., J. Hoddinott and J. Knight (1996), 'Primary education as an input into post-primary education: a neglected benefit', *Oxford Bulletin of Economics and Statistics*, **58**, 186–211.

Arabsheibani, G.R. and H. Rees (1998), 'On the weak versus strong version of the screening hypothesis: a re-examination of the P-test for the UK', *Economics of Education Review*, **17**, 189–192.

Arnott, R. and J. Rowse (1987), 'Peer group effects and educational attainment', *Journal of Public Economics*, **32**, 287–305.

Arrow, K.J. (1973), 'Higher education as a filter', *Journal of Public Economics*, **2**, 193–216.

Ashenfelter, O. and A.B. Krueger (1991), 'Estimates of the economic return to schooling for a new sample of twins', *American Economic Review*, **84**, 1157–1173.

Ashenfelter, O. and C. Rouse (1999), 'Schooling, intelligence and income in America: cracks in the Bell Curve', Cambridge, Mass.: National Bureau of Economic Research, Working Paper 6902.

Ashenfelter, O., C. Harmon and H. Oosterbeek (1999), 'A review of estimates of the schooling/earnings relationship, with tests for publication bias', *Labour Economics*, **6**, 453–470.

Ashraf, J. (1992), 'Do unions affect faculty salaries? *Economics of Education Review,* **11**, 219–223.

Ashton, D. and F. Green (1996), *Education, Training and the Global Economy*, Cheltenham, UK; Edward Elgar.

Ashworth, J. (1997), 'A waste of time? Private rates of return to higher education in the 1990s', *Higher Education Quarterly*, **51**, 164–188.

Ashworth, J. (1998), 'A waste of resources? Social rates of return to higher education in the UK', *Education Economics*, **6**, 27–44.

Audit Commission (1996), *Trading Places: The Supply and Allocation of School Places*. London: HMSO.

Audit Commission and Office for Standards in Education (1993), *Unfinished Business: Full–Time Educational Courses for 16–19 Year Olds*, London: HMSO.

Bacdayan, A.W. (1994), 'Time-denominated achievement cost curves, learning differences and individualized instruction', *Economics of Education Review*, **13**, 43–53.

Bacdayan, A.W. (1997), 'A mathematical analysis of the learning production process and a model for determining what matters in education', *Economics of Education Review*, **16**, 25–37.

Ballou, D. (1995), 'Causes and consequences of teacher moonlighting', *Education Economics,* **3**, 3–18.

Ballou, D. (1996), 'Do public schools hire the best applicants?', *Quarterly Journal of Economics*, **CXI**, 97–133.

Ballou, D. and M. Podgursky (1995), 'What makes a good principal? How teachers assess the performance of principals', *Economics of Education Review*, **14**, 243–252.

Barber, M. (1996), *The Learning Game*, London: Victor Gollancz.

Barro, R. and J. Lee (1996), 'International measures of schooling years and schooling quality', *American Economic Review*, **86**, 218–223.

Barro, R.J. and X. Sala-I-Martin (1995), *Economic Growth*, New York: McGraw-Hill.

Barron, J.M., M.C. Berger and D.A. Black (1997), 'How well do we measure training?', *Journal of Labor Economics*, **15**, 507–528.

Barrow, M. (1991), 'Measuring Local Education Authority performance: a frontier approach', *Economics of Education Review*, **10**, 19–27.

Barrow, M. (1997). 'The New Funding methodology', *Education Economics*, **5**, 135–151.

Bartel, A.P. and F.R. Lichtenberg (1987), 'The comparative advantage of educated workers in implementing new technology', *Review of Economics and Statistics*, **69**, 1–11.

Bassi, L. (1984), 'Estimating the effects of training programs with non-random selection', *Review of Economics and Statistics*, **66**, 36–43.

Battu, H., C.R. Belfield and P. Sloane (1999), 'Overeducation among graduates: a cohort view', *Education Economics*, **7**, 21–38.

Battu, H., C.R. Belfield and P.J. Sloane (2000), 'Overeducation: how sensitive are the measures?', *National Institute Economic Review*, **171**, 82–93.

Battu, H., J. Finch and D. Newlands (1998), 'Integrating knowledge effects into university impact studies: a case of Aberdeen University', University of Aberdeen, mimeo.

Becker, G.S. (1985), *Human Capital*, Chicago: University of Chicago Press for National Bureau of Economic Research.

Becker, G.S. and C.B. Mulligan (1997), 'The endogenous determination of time preference', *Quarterly Journal of Economics*, **CXII**, 729–757.

Becker, W.E. and W.J. Baumol (1996), *Assessing Educational Practices: The Contribution of Economics,* London: Russell Sage.

Bedi, A.S. and N. Gaston (1999), 'Using variation in schooling availability to estimate educational returns for Honduras', *Economics of Education Review*, **18**, 107–117.

Bee, M. and P.J. Dolton (1995), 'The remuneration of school teachers: time series and cross-section evidence', *The Manchester School*, **LXIII**, 1–22.

Behrman, J.R. (1987), 'Schooling and other human capital investments: can the effects be identified?', *Economics of Education Review,* **6**, 301–305.

Behrman, J.R. (1996), 'Measuring the effectiveness of schooling policies in developing countries: revisiting issues of methodology', *Economics of*

Education Review, **15**, 345–364.

Behrman, J.R. and N. Birdsall (1983), 'The quality of schooling: quantity alone is misleading', *American Economic Review*, **73**, 928–946.

Behrman J.R. and N. Stacey (1997), *The Social Benefits of Education,* Ann Arbor, Mich.: Michigan University Press.

Belfield, C.R. (1999), 'The behaviour of graduates in the SME labour market: evidence and perceptions', *Small Business Economics*, **12**, 249–259.

Belfield, C.R. and A. Fielding (2000), 'Measuring the relationship between resources and outcomes in higher education in the UK', *Economics of Education Review*, forthcoming.

Belfield, C.R. and H.R. Thomas (2000), 'The relationship between resources and performance in further education', *Oxford Review of Education*, **26**, 239–255.

Belfield, C.R., A.N. Chevalier, A. Fielding, W.S. Siebert and H.R. Thomas (1997), *Mapping the Careers of Highly Qualified Workers.* HEFCE Research Series, Bristol: Higher Education Funding Council for England.

Belfield, C.R., A.D. Bullock and A. Fielding (1999), 'What determines graduates evaluations of higher education: a retrospective evaluation', *Research in Higher Education*, **40**, 409–426.

Bell, L. (1999), 'Back to the future: the development of educational policy in England', *Journal of Educational Administration*, **37**, 200–228.

Belman, D. and J.S. Heywood (1997), 'Sheepskin effects by cohort: implications of job matching in a signalling model', *Oxford Economic Papers* **49**, 623–637.

Bempah, E.O., M.S. Kaylen, D.D. Osburn and R.J. Birkenholz (1994), 'An econometric analysis of teacher mobility', *Economics of Education Review*, **13**, 69–77.

Benhabib, J. and M. Spiegel (1994), 'The role of human capital in economic development,' *Journal of Monetary Economics*, **34**, 143–173.

Bennett, R., H. Glennerster and D. Nevison (1995), 'Regional rates of return to education and training in Britain', *Regional Studies*, **29**, 279–295.

Betts, J.R. (1995), 'Does school quality matter? Evidence from the national longitudinal survey of youth', *Review of Economics and Statistics*, **77**, 231–247.

Betts, J.R. (1996a), 'Is there a link between school inputs and earnings? Fresh scrutiny of an old literature', in G. Burtless (ed.) *Does Money Matter? The Effect of School Resources on Student Achievement and Adult Success*, Washington, D.C.: Brookings Institution.

Betts, J.R. (1996b), 'What do students know about wages? Evidence from a survey of undergraduates', *Journal of Human Resources*, **31**, 27–56.

Betts, J.R. (1996c), 'Do school resources matter only for older workers?',

Review of Economics and Statistics, **78**, 638–652.

Betts, J.R. (1998a), 'The two-legged stool: the neglected role of standards in improving America's Public Schools', *Federal Reserve Bank of New York Economic Review*, **4**, 97–116.

Betts, J.R. (1998b), 'The impact of educational standards on the level and distribution of earnings', *American Economic Review*, **88**, 266–275.

Bezmen, T. and C.A. Depken (1998), 'School characteristics and the demand for college', *Economics of Education Review*, **17**, 205–210.

Bickel, R. and L. Lange (1995), 'Opportunities, costs and high school completion in West Virginia: a replication of Florida research', *Journal of Educational Research*, **88**, 363–370.

Biggs, M.L. and J. Dutta (1999), 'The distributional effects of education expenditure', *National Institute Economic Review*, July, 68–77.

Bikhchandani, S., D. Hirshleifer and I. Welch (1998), 'Learning from the behaviour of others: conformity, fads and informational cascades', *Journal of Economic Perspectives*, **12**, 151–170.

Birdsall, N. (1996) 'Public spending on higher education in developing countries: too much or too little?', *Economics of Education Review*, **15**, 407–419.

Birdsall, N. and F. Orivel (1996), 'Demand for primary schooling in rural Mali: should user fees be increased?', *Education Economics*, **4**, 279–296.

Bishop, J.H. (1989), 'Occupational training in high school: when does it pay off?', *Economics of Education Review*, **8**, 1–15.

Bishop, J.H. (1996a), 'Incentives to study and the organisation of secondary instruction', in W.E. Becker and W.J. Baumol (eds) *Assessing Educational Practices: The Contribution of Economics*, London: Russell Sage.

Bishop, J.H. (1996b), 'The impact of curriculum-based external examinations on school priorities and student learning', *International Journal of Educational Research*, **23**, 653–752.

Bishop, J.H. (1997), 'The effect of national standards and curriculum-based exams on achievement', *American Economic Review*, **87**, 260–264.

Black, S.E. (1999), 'Do better schools matter? Parental valuations of elementary education', *Quarterly Journal of Economics*, **CXIV**, 577–600.

Blair, J.P. and S. Staley (1995), 'Quality competition and public schools: further evidence', *Economics of Education Review*, **14**, 193–198.

Blaug, M. (1976), 'The empirical study of human capital theory: a slightly jaundiced survey', *Journal of Economic Literature*, **14**, 827–855.

Blaug, M. (1985), 'Where are we now in the economics of education?', *Economics of Education Review*, **4**, 17–28.

Blaug, M. (1992), *The Methodology of Economics*, Cambridge: Cambridge

University Press.

Bleaney, M.F., M.R. Binks, D. Greenaway, G.V. Reed and D.K. Whynes (1992), 'What does a university add to its local economy?', *Applied Economics*, **24**, 305–311.

Blundell, R., L. Dearden and C. Meghir (1996), *The Determinants and Effects of Work Related Training in Britain*, London: Institute for Fiscal Studies.

Blundell, R., L. Dearden, A. Goodman and H. Reed (1997), *Higher Education, Employment and Earnings in Britain*, London: Institute for Fiscal Studies.

Blundell, R., L. Dearden, M. Costas and B. Sianesi (1999), 'Human capital investment: the returns from education and training to the individual, the firm and the economy', *Fiscal Studies*, **20**, 1–23.

Boal, W.M. and M.R. Ransom (1997), 'Monopsony in the labour market', *Journal of Economic Literature*, **XXXV**, 86–112.

Bonesrønning, H. and J. Rattsø (1994), 'Efficiency variation among the Norwegian high schools: consequences of equalization policy', *Economics of Education Review*, **13**, 289–304.

Booth, A.L. and D.J. Snower (1996), *Acquiring Skills: Market Failures, Their Symptoms and Policies*, Cambridge: Cambridge University Press.

Borland, M.V. and R.M. Howsen (1992), 'Students' academic achievement and the degree of market concentration in education', *Economics of Education Review*, **11**, 31–39.

Borland, M.V. and R.M. Howsen (1993), 'On the determination of the critical level of market concentration in education', *Economics of Education Review*, **12**, 165–169.

Boruch, R.F. (1997), *Randomised Experiments for Planning and Evaluation*, Thousand Oaks, Cal.: Sage.

Bosworth, D, P. Dawkins and T. Stromback (1996), *The Economics of the Labour Market*, London: Addison Wesley Longman.

Bound, J. and G. Solon (1999), 'Double trouble: on the value of twins-based estimation of the returns to schooling', *Economics of Education Review*, **18**, 169–182.

Bradley, S. and J. Taylor (1996), 'Human capital formation and local economic performance', *Regional Studies*, **30**, 1–14.

Bradley, S. and J. Taylor (1998a), 'The effect of school size on exam performance in secondary schools', *Oxford Bulletin of Economics and Statistics*, **60**, 291–327.

Bradley, S. and J. Taylor (1998b), 'Cost functions in secondary schools', University of Lancaster, mimeo.

Bradley, S., G. Johnes and J. Millington (1998), 'School choice, competition and the efficiency of secondary schools in England', University of Lancaster, mimeo.

Brasington, D.M. (1999a) 'Joint provision of public goods: the consolidation of school districts', *Journal of Public Economics*, **73**, 373–393.

Brasington, D.M. (1999b), 'Central city school administrative policy: systematically passing undeserving students', *Economics of Education Review*, **18**, 201–212.

Breneman, D.W. (1998), 'Remediation in higher education: its extent and cost', in D. Ravitch (ed.) *Brookings Papers on Education Policy*, Washington, D.C.: Brookings Institution.

Brent, R.J. (1996), *Applied Cost–Benefit Analysis*, Cheltenham, UK: Edward Elgar.

Bressoux, P. (1996), 'The effect of teachers' training on pupils' achievement: the case of elementary schools in France', *School Effectiveness and School Improvement*, 7, 252–279.

Brewer, D.J. (1993), 'Principals and student outcomes: evidence from U.S. high schools', *Economics of Education Review*, **12**, 281–292.

Brewer, D.J. (1996), 'Does more school district administration lower educational productivity? Some evidence on the administrative blob in New York public schools', *Economics of Education Review*, **15**, 111–124.

Bridges, D. and T.H. McLaughlin (1994), *Education and the Market Place*, London: Falmer Press.

Brown, B.W. (1992), 'Why governments run schools', *Economics of Education Review*, **11**, 287–300.

Brown, S. and J.G. Sessions (1998), 'Education, employment status and earnings: a comparative test of the strong screening hypothesis', *Scottish Journal of Political Economy*, **45**, 586–591.

Bullock, A.D. and H.R. Thomas (1997), *Schools at the Centre: A Study of Decentralisation*, London: Routledge.

Burke, S.M. (1999), 'An analysis of resource inequality at the state, district and school levels', *Journal of Education Finance*, **24**, 435–438.

Burtless, G. (1996), *Does Money Matter? The Effect of School Resources on Student Achievement and Adult Success*, Washington, D.C.: Brookings Institution.

Callan, S.J. and R.E. Santerre (1990), 'The production characteristics of local public education: a multiple product and input analysis', *Southern Economic Journal*, **57**, 468–480.

Cameron, S.V. and J.J. Heckman (1998), 'Life cycle schooling and dynamic selection bias: models and evidence for five cohorts of American males', *Journal of Political Economy*, **106**, 2, 262–333.

Cameron, S.V. and J.J. Heckman (1999), 'Can tuition policy combat rising wage inequality?', in M.H. Kosters (ed.) *Financing College Tuition. Government Policies and Educational Priorities*, Washington, D.C.:

AEI Press.

Card, D. and A.B. Krueger (1992), 'Does school quality matter? Returns to education and the characteristics of public schools in the United States', *Journal of Political Economy*, **100**, 1–40.

Card, D. and A.B. Krueger (1996), 'Labour market effects on school quality: theory and evidence' in G. Burtless (ed.) *Does Money Matter? The Effect of School Resources on Student Achievement and Adult Success*, Washington, D.C.: Brookings Institution.

Carmichael, H.L. (1988), 'Incentives in academics: why is there tenure?', *Journal of Political Economy*, **96**, 453–472.

Carnoy, M. (1995), 'Political economy of educational production', in M. Carnoy (ed.) *International Encyclopaedia of the Economics of Education*, New York: Pergamon.

Carnoy, M. (1997), 'Is privatisation through vouchers really the answer?', *World Bank Research Observer*, **12**, 105–116.

Carrington, W. and E. Detragiache (1999), 'How extensive is the brain drain?', *Finance and Development*, June, 46–49.

Case, A. and A. Deaton (1999), 'School inputs and educational outcomes in South Africa', *Quarterly Journal of Economics*, **CXIV**, 1047–1084.

Chadwick, S. (1997), 'Resource dependence in the further education marketplace: considerations for the managers of college mergers', *Journal of Further and Higher Education*, **21**, 305–316.

Chang, C.F. and H.P. Tuckman (1986), 'Price–induced substitution of faculty in academe: does mission make a difference?', *Economics of Education Review*, **5**, 197–204.

Chapman, B. (1997), 'Conceptual issues and the Australian experience with income contingent charges for higher education', *Economic Journal*, **107**, 738–751.

Chressanthis, G.A. (1986), 'The impacts of tuition rate changes on college undergraduate headcounts and credit hours over time: a case study', *Economics of Education Review*, **5**, 205–217.

Chriss, B., G. Nash, and D. Stern (1992), 'The rise and fall of choice in Richmond, California', *Economics of Education Review*, **11**, 395–406.

Chuang, H.L. (1997) 'High school youths dropout and re-enrollment behavior', *Economics of Education Review*, **16**, 171–186.

Chubb, J.E. and T.M. Moe (1988), 'Politics, markets and the organisation of schools', *American Political Science Review*, **82**, 1065–1087.

Clark, A. (1996), 'Job satisfaction in Britain', *British Journal of Industrial Relations*, **34**, 189–217.

Clark, A., A.J. Oswald and P.B. Warr (1996) 'Is job satisfaction U-shaped in age?', *Journal of Occupational and Organisational Psychology*, **69**, 57–81.

Coe, R. and C.T. Fitz-Gibbon (1998), 'School effectiveness research:

criticisms and recommendations', *Oxford Review of Education*, **24**, 421–438.

Cohn, E. (1984), 'Equity effects of the educational finance act in South Carolina', *Economics of Education Review*, **3**, 269–278.

Cohn, E. (1992) 'The impact of surplus schooling on earnings: comment', *Journal of Human Resources*, **27**, 679–682.

Cohn, E. (1997), *Market Approaches to Education*. Oxford: Pergamon.

Cohn, E. and J.T. Addison (1998), 'The economic returns to lifelong learning', *Education Economics*, **6**, 309–346.

Cohn, E. and T.G. Geske (1990), *The Economics of Education*, Oxford: Pergamon Press.

Cohn, E. and W.W. Hughes (1994), 'A benefit–cost analysis of investment in college education in the United States: 1969–1985', *Economics of Education Review*, **13**, 109–123.

Cohn, E. and G. Johnes (1994), *Recent Developments in the Economics of Education*, Cheltenham, UK: Edward Elgar.

Cohn, E. and S. Khan (1995), 'The wage effects of overschooling revisited', *Labour Economics* **2**, 67–76.

Cohn, E., S. Khan and Y.C. Ng (1999), 'Incidence and wage effects of overschooling and underschooling in the United States and Hong Kong', University of South Carolina, mimeo.

Collier, P. and J.W. Gunning (1999), 'Explaining African economic performance', *Journal of Economic Literature*, **37**, 64–111.

Corman, H. (1986), 'The demand for education for home production', *Economic Inquiry*, **XXIV**, 213–230.

Costrell, R.M. (1994), 'A simple model of educational standards', *American Economic Review*, **84**, 956–971.

Costrell, R.M. (1997), 'Can centralized educational standards raise welfare?', *Journal of Public Economics*, **65**, 271–293.

Cronovich, R. (1998), 'Measuring the human capital intensity of government spending and its impact on economic growth across a cross-section of countries', *Scottish Journal of Political Economy*, **45**, 48–77.

Committee of Vice-Chancellors and Principals (CVCP) (1997), *The Impact of Universities and Colleges on the UK Economy*, University of Strathclyde, mimeo.

Daniel, J. (1996), *Mega-universities and Knowledge Media: Technology Strategies for Higher Education*, London: Kogan Page.

Datcher Loury, L. and D. Garman (1995), 'College selectivity and earnings', *Journal of Labor Economics*, **13**, 289–308.

Davis, E. (1998), *Public Spending*, Harmondsworth, Middx: Penguin.

Dean, G.S. and D.E. Gray (1998) 'Funding maximisation within a further education college: a case study', *Journal of Further and Higher*

Education, **22**, 41–48.

Dearden, L. (1998), 'Ability, families, education and earnings in Britain', Working Paper, W98/14: Institute of Fiscal Studies, London.

Dearden, L. (1999), 'The effects of families and ability on men's education and earnings in Britain', *Labour Economics*, **6**, 551–567.

Dee, T.S. (1998), 'Competition and the quality of public schools', *Economics of Education Review*, **17**, 419–427.

De Gregorio, J. (1996), 'Borrowing constraints, human capital accumulation and growth', *Journal of Monetary Economics*, **37**, 49–71.

Department for Education and Science (DES) (1988), *Top-up Loans for Students*, London: HMSO.

Department for Education and Employment (DfEE) (1998a), *Education and Training Statistics for the United Kingdom (1998)*. London: HMSO.

Department for Education and Employment (DfEE) (1998b), 'Education and labour market status of young people aged 16–18 in England: 1992–97', DfEE Statistical Bulletin, 8/98.

Department for Education and Employment (DfEE) (1998c), 'Survey of Information and Communications Technology in Schools 1998', DfEE Statistical Bulletin, 11/98.

Department for Education and Employment (DfEE) (1998d), *The Learning Age*, London: HMSO.

Department for Education and Employment (DfEE) and Office for Standards in Education (OFSTED) (1998), *The Government's Expenditure Plans*, London: HMSO.

DesJardins, S.L., D.A. Ahlburg and B.P. McCall (1999), 'An event history model of student departure', *Economics of Education Review*, **18**, 375–390.

Dick, A.W. and A.S. Edlin (1997), 'Implicit taxes from college financial aid', *Journal of Public Economics*, **65**, 295–322.

Dolton, P.J. (1993), 'The economics of youth training in Britain', *Economic Journal*, **103**, 1261–1278.

Dolton, P.J. (1996), 'Modelling the labour market for teachers: some lessons for the UK', *Education Economics*, **4**, 187–205.

Dolton, P.J. and M. Bee (1985), 'Costs and economies of scale in UK private schools', *Applied Economics,* **17**, 281–290.

Dolton, P.J. and G.H. Makepeace (1990a), 'Graduate earnings six years later: who are the winners?', *Higher Education* **15**, 31–55.

Dolton, P.J. and G.H. Makepeace (1990b), 'The earnings of economics graduates', *Economic Journal*, **100**, 237–250.

Dolton P.J. and M. Robson (1996), 'Trade union concentration and the determination of wages: the case of teachers in England and Wales', *British Journal of Industrial Relations*, **34**, 539–555.

Dolton, P.J. and W. van der Klaauw (1995), 'Leaving teaching in the UK: a duration analysis', *Economic Journal*, **105**, 431–444.

Dolton, P.J. and W. van der Klaauw (1996), 'Teacher salaries and teacher retention', in W.E. Becker and W.J. Baumol (eds). *Assessing Educational Practices: The Contribution of Economics*, London: Russell Sage.

Dolton, P.J. and A. Vignoles (1997), 'Overeducation duration: how long did graduates in the 1980s take to get a graduate job?', unpublished mimeo.

Dolton, P.J. and A. Vignoles (1998), 'The impact of school quality on labour market success in the United Kingdom', University of Newcastle, mimeo.

Dolton, P.J. and A. Vignoles (2000), 'The incidence and effects of overeducation in the U.K. graduate labour market', *Economics of Education Review*, forthcoming

Dolton, P.J., G.H. Makepeace and G.D. Inchley (1990), 'The early careers of 1980 graduates: earnings, earnings differentials and postgraduate study', Department of Employment Research Paper, London: Department of Employment.

Dominitz, J. and C.F. Manski (1996), 'Eliciting student expectations of the returns to schooling', *Journal of Human Resources*, **31**, 1–27.

Downes, T.A. and S.M. Greenstein (1996), 'Understanding the supply decisions of non-profits: modelling the location of private schools', *Rand Journal of Economics*, **27**, 365–390.

Duchesne, I. and W. Nonneman (1998), 'The demand for higher education in Belgium', *Economics of Education Review*, **17**, 211–218.

Duncombe, W., J. Miner and J. Ruggiero (1995), 'Potential cost savings from school district consolidation: a case study of New York', *Economics of Education Review*, **14**, 265–284.

Dundar, H. and D.R. Lewis (1995), 'Departmental productivity in American universities: economies of scale and scope', *Economics of Education Review*, **14**, 119–144.

Duplantis, M.M., T.D. Chandler and T.G. Geske (1995), 'The growth and impact of teachers unions in states without collective bargaining legislation', *Economics of Education Review*, **14**, 167–178.

Dutta, J., J. Sefton and M. Weale (1999), 'Education and public policy', *Fiscal Studies*, **20**, 351–386.

Dynarski, M. (1994), 'Who defaults on student loans? Findings from the national post-secondary student aid study', *Economics of Education Review*, **13**, 55–68.

Eberts, R.W. and J.A. Stone (1995), 'Economics of teacher unionisation', in M. Carnoy (ed.) *International Encyclopaedia of the Economics of Education*, New York: Pergamon Press.

Edwards, J.H.Y., B. Fuller and X. Liang (1996), 'The mixed preschool market: explaining local variation in family demand and organized supply', *Economics of Education Review*, **15**, 149–161.

Eeckhout, J. (1999), 'Educational mobility: the effect of efficiency and distribution', *Economica*, **66**, 317–333.

Egerton, M. (1997), 'The role of cultural capital and gender', *Work, Employment and Society*, **11**, 265–283.

Ehrenberg, R., H. Kasper and D. Rees (1991), 'Faculty turnover at American colleges and universities: analyses of AAUP data', *Economics of Education Review*, **10**, 99–110.

Ehrenberg, R.G. and D.J. Brewer (1994), 'Do school and teacher characteristics matter? Evidence from high school and beyond', *Economics of Education Review*, **13**, 1–17.

Ehrenberg, R.G. and D.J. Brewer (1995), 'Did teachers' verbal ability and race matter in the 1960s? Coleman revisited', *Economics of Education Review*, **14**, 1–21.

Ehrenberg, R.G. and D.R. Sherman (1987), 'Employment while in college, academic achievement and post-college outcomes', *Journal of Human Resources*, **XXII**, 1–23.

Eide, E. and M.H. Showalter (1998), 'The effect of school quality on student performance: a quantile regression approach', *Economics Letters*, **58**, 345–350.

Epple, D. and R.E. Romano (1998), 'Competition between private and public schools, vouchers and peer group effects', *American Economic Review*, **88**, 33–62.

Feinstein, L. and R. Symons (1999), 'Attainment in secondary schools', *Oxford Economic Papers*, **51**, 300–321.

Feldstein, M. (1995), 'College scholarship rules and private saving', *American Economic Review*, **85**, 552–566.

Fels, R. (1996), 'Making US schools competitive', in W.E. Becker and W.J. Baumol (eds). *Assessing Educational Practices: The Contribution of Economics.* London: Russell Sage.

Fidler, B., P. Earley, J. Ouston and J. Davies (1998), 'Teacher gradings and OFSTED inspections: help or hindrance as a management tool?', *School Leadership and Management*, **18**, 257–270.

Fielding, A. (1997), 'On scoring ordered classifications', *British Journal of Mathematical and Statistical Psychology*, **50**, 1–23.

Fielding, A., C.R. Belfield and H.R. Thomas (1998), 'The consequences of drop-outs on the cost-effectiveness of 16–19 colleges', *Oxford Review of Education*, **24**, 487–511.

Figlio, D.N. (1999), 'Functional form and the estimated effects of school resources', *Economics of Education Review*, **18**, 241–252.

Fitz-Gibbon, C.T. (1996), *Monitoring Education: Indicators, Quality and Effectiveness*, London: Cassell.

Fitz-Gibbon, C.T. (1999), 'Education: high potential not yet realised',

Public Money and Management, **19**, 33–40.

Fredrikson, P. (1997), 'Economic incentives and the demand for higher education', *Scandinavian Journal of Economics*, **99**, 129–142.

Freeman, R.B. (1995), 'Demand and supply elasticities for educated labour', in M. Carnoy (ed.) *International Encyclopaedia of the Economics of Education*, New York: Pergamon Press.

Friedman, M. (1997), 'Public schools: make them private', *Education Economics*, **5**, 341–44.

Fuchs, V.R., A.B. Krueger and J.M. Poterba (1998), 'Economists' views about parameters, values and policies: survey results in labor and public economics', *Journal of Economic Literature*, **XXXVI**, 1387–1425.

Fukuyama, F. (1999), *The Great Disruption*, London: Profile Books.

Funding Agency for Schools (FAS) (1999), *Costs and Performance for Grant-Maintained Schools*, York: Funding Agency for Schools.

Gamoran, A. (1992) 'The variable effects of high school tracking', *American Sociological Review*, **57**, 812–828.

Garen, J. (1984), 'The returns to schooling: a selectivity bias approach with a continuous choice variable', *Econometrica*, **5**, 1199–1218.

Gemmell, N. (1996), 'Evaluating the impacts of human capital stocks and accumulation on economic growth: some new evidence', *Oxford Bulletin of Economics and Statistics*, **58**, 9–28.

Gemmell, N. (1997), 'Externalities to higher education: a review of the new growth literature', National Committee of Inquiry into Higher Education.

Gibbs, M., L. Lucas and V. Simonite (1996), 'Class size and student performance: 1984–1994', *Studies in Higher Education*, **21**, 261–273.

Glennerster, H. (1991), 'Quasi-markets in education', *Economic Journal*, **101**, 1268–1276.

Glewwe, P. (1997) 'Estimating the impact of peer group effects on socioeconomic outcomes: does the distribution of peer group characteristics matter?', *Economics of Education Review*, **16**, 39–43.

Glomm, G. (1997), 'Parental choice of human capital investment', *Journal of Development Economics*, **53**, 99–114.

Goldin, C. (1999), 'Egalitarianism and the returns to education during the great transformation of American education', *Journal of Political Economy*, **107**, s65–s94.

Goldstein, H. and L. Spiegelhalter (1996), 'League tables and their limitations: statistical issues in comparisons of institutional performance', *Journal of the Royal Statistical Association*, **15**, 385–433.

Goldstein, H. and S. Thomas (1996), 'Using examination results as indicators of school and college performance', *Journal of the Royal Statistical Society, Series A*, **159**, 149–163.

Grace, G. (1994), 'Education is a public good: on the need to resist the domination of economic science,' in D. Bridges and T.H. McLaughlin, *Education and the Market Place*, London: Falmer Press.

Gramlich, E.M. (1986), 'Evaluation of education projects: the case of the Perry pre-school program', *Economics of Education Review*, **5**, 17–24.

Gray, J. and B. Wilcox (1995), *Good School, Bad School: Evaluating Performance and Encouraging Improvement*, Buckingham: Open University Press.

Gray, J. and B. Wilcox (1996), *Inspecting Schools: Holding Schools to Account and Helping Schools to Improve*, Buckingham: Open University Press.

Gray, J., H. Goldstein, D. Jesson, K. Hedger and J. Rasbash (1995), 'A multilevel analysis of school improvement: changes in school performance over time', *School Effectiveness and School Improvement*, **6**, 97–114.

Green, F., Hoskins, M. and S. Montgomery (1996), 'The effects of company training, further education and the youth training scheme on the earnings of young employees', *Oxford Bulletin of Economics and Statistics*, **58**, 469–488.

Greenberg, D.H. (1997), 'The leisure bias in cost–benefit analyses of employment and training programs', *Journal of Human Resources*, **32**, 413–439.

Greenhalgh, C. and G. Mavrotas (1995), 'The role of career aspirations and financial constraints in individual access to vocational training', *Oxford Economic Papers*, **46**, 579–604.

Greenhalgh, C. and G. Mavrotas (1996), 'Job training, new technology and labour turnover', *British Journal of Industrial Relations*, **34**, 131–150.

Greenwood, D. (1997), 'New developments in the intergenerational impacts of education', *International Journal of Education Research*, **27**, 503–511.

Griffin, P. and P.T. Ganderton (1996), 'Evidence on omitted variable bias in earnings equations', *Economics of Education Review*, **15**, 139–148.

Grogger, A. and E. Eide (1995), 'Changes in college skills and the rise in the college wage premium', *Journal of Human Resources*, **30**, 280–310.

Grogger, J. (1996), 'School expenditures and post-school earnings: evidence from high school and beyond', *Review of Economics and Statistics*, **78**, 628–638.

Groot, W. (1993), 'Overeducation and the returns to enterprise-related schooling', *Economics of Education Review*, **12**, 299–309.

Groot, W. (1994), 'Differences in rates of return by type of education', *Education Economics*, **2**, 209–214.

Groot, W. (1995), 'Type specific returns to enterprise-related training',

Economics of Education Review, **14**, 323–333.

Groot, W. (1996), 'The incidence of, and returns to overeducation in the UK', *Applied Economics,* **28**, 1345–1350.

Groot, W. (1998), 'Empirical estimates of the rate of depreciation of education', *Applied Economics Letters,* **5**, 535–538.

Groot, W. and H. Oosterbeek (1992), 'Optimal investment in human capital under uncertainty', *Economics of Education Review,* **11**, 41–49.

Groot, W. and H. Oosterbeek. (1994), 'Earnings effects of different components of schooling, human capital versus screening', *Review of Economics and Statistics,* **76**, 317–321.

Groot, W. and H.M. van der Brink (1997), 'Allocation and the returns to over-education in the UK', *Education Economics,* **5**, 169–183.

Grubb, W.N. (1993), 'Further tests of screening on education and observed ability', *Economics of Education Review,* **12**, 125–136.

Gyimah-Brempong, K. and A.O. Gyapong (1992), 'Elasticities of factor substitution in the production of education', *Economics of Education Review,* **11**, 205–17.

Haber, S.E. and R.S. Goldfarb (1995), 'Does salaried status affect human capital accumulation?', *Industrial and Labor Relations Review,* **48**, 322–337.

Habeshaw, S., G. Gibbs and T. Habeshaw (1992), *53 Problems with Large Classes: Making the Best of a Bad Job,* Plymouth: TES Books.

Hansen, L.W. (1983), 'Impact of student financial aid on access', in J. Froomkin (ed.) *The Crisis in Higher Education,* New York: Academy of Political Science.

Hanushek, E.A. (1986), 'The economics of schooling: production and efficiency in public schools', *Journal of Economic Literature,* **24**, 1141–1177.

Hanushek, E.A. (1992), 'The trade-off between child quantity and quality', *Journal of Political Economy,* **100**, 84–117.

Hanushek, E.A. (1995), 'Education production functions' in M. Carnoy (ed.) *International Encyclopaedia of the Economics of Education,* New York: Pergamon Press.

Hanushek, E.A. (1997), 'Assessing the effects of school resources on student performance: an update', *Educational Evaluation and Policy Analysis,* **19**, 141–164.

Hanushek, E.A. (1998), 'Conclusions and controversies about the effectiveness of schools', *Federal Reserve Bank of New York Economic Policy Review,* **4**, 1–22.

Hanushek, E.A. and R.R. Pace (1995), 'Who chooses to teach (and why)?', *Economics of Education Review,* **14**, 101–117.

Hanushek, E.A., S.G. Rivkin and L.L. Taylor (1996), 'The identification of school resource effects', *Education Economics,* **4**, 105–25 1996.

Harbaugh, W.T. (1998), 'What do donations buy? A model of philanthropy based on prestige and warm glow', *Journal of Public Economics*, **67**, 269–284.

Harbison, R.W. and E.A. Hanushek (1992), *Educational Performance of the Poor: Lessons from Northeast Brazil*, New York: Oxford University Press.

Harford, J.D. and R.D. Marcus (1986), 'Tuition and US private college characteristics: the hedonic approach', *Economics of Education Review*, **5**, 415–430.

Harmon, C. and I. Walker (1995), 'Estimates of the economic return to schooling for the United Kingdom,' *American Economic Review*, **85**, 1278–1286.

Harris, R. (1997) 'The impact of the University of Portsmouth on the local economy', *Urban Studies*, **34**, 605–626.

Hartog, J. and H. Oosterbeek (1998), 'Health, wealth and happiness: why pursue a higher education?', *Economics of Education Review*, **17**, 245–256.

Haveman, R.H. and B.L. Wolfe (1984), 'Schooling and economic well-being: the role of non-market effects', *Journal of Human Resources*, **19**, 377–407.

Haveman, R.H. and B.L. Wolfe (1995), 'The determinants of children's attainment: a review of methods and findings', *Journal of Economic Literature*, **33**, 1829–1877.

Heaton, C. (1999), 'The equity implications of public subsidisation of higher education: a study of the Fijian case', *Education Economics*, **7**, 153–166.

Hecker, D.E. (1998), 'Earnings of college graduates: women compared with men', *Monthly Labor Review*, **121**, 3, 62–71.

Heckman, J.J. (1999), 'Policies to foster human capital', Cambridge, Mass.: National Bureau of Economic Research, Working Paper 7288.

Heckman, J.J. and J.A. Smith (1999), 'The pre-programme earnings dip and the determinants of participation in a social programme: implications for simple programme evaluation strategies', *Economic Journal*, **109**, 313–348.

Heckman, J.J., A. Layne-Farrar, and P. Todd (1996), 'Human capital pricing equations with an application to estimating the effect of schooling quality on earnings', *Review of Economics and Statistics*, **78**, 562–610.

Heckman, J.J., L. Lochner and C. Taber (1999), 'Human capital formation and general equilibrium treatment effects: a study of tax and tuition policy', *Fiscal Studies*, **20**, 25–40.

Hedges, L.V., R.D. Laine and R. Greenwald (1994), 'Does money matter? A meta-analysis of studies of the effects of differential school inputs on student outcomes', *Educational Researcher*, **23**, 5–14.

Heller, D.E. (1997), 'Student price response in higher education', *Journal of Higher Education,* **68**, 624–659.

Herrnstein, R.J. (1997), *The Matching Law,* Beverly Hills, Cal.: Russell Sage Foundation.

Herrnstein, R.J. and C. Murray (1994), *The Bell Curve: Intelligence and Class Structure in American Life,* New York: Free Press.

Hersch, J. (1995), 'Optimal mismatch and promotions', *Economic Inquiry,* **33**, 611–624.

Heywood, J.S. (1994), 'How widespread are sheepskin returns in education?', *Economics of Education Review,* **13**, 227–234.

Higher Education Funding Council for England (HEFCE) (1995), *A Guide to Funding HE in England,* Bristol: HEFCE.

Higher Education Statistical Agency (HESA) (1996a), *Students in Higher Education 1994/95,* Cheltenham, UK: HESA.

Higher Education Statistical Agency (HESA) (1996b), *First Destinations of Students Leaving Higher Education Institutions 1994/95,* Cheltenham, UK: HESA.

Hoare, A.G. (1995), 'Scale economies in academic excellence: an exploratory analysis of the UK's 1992 research selectivity exercise', *Higher Education,* **29**, 241–260.

Hoenack, S.A. (1994), 'Economics, organizations, and learning: research directions for the economics of education', *Economics of Education Review,* **13**, 147–62.

Hough, J.R. (1994), 'Educational cost–benefit analysis', *Education Economics,* **2**, 93–128.

Hoxby, C.M. (1994), 'Does competition among public schools benefit students and tax-payers?', Cambridge, Mass.: National Bureau of Economic Research, working paper 4979.

Hoxby, C.M. (1996a), 'How teachers unions affect productivity', *Quarterly Journal of Economics,* **CXI**, 671–718.

Hoxby, C.M. (1996b), 'Are efficiency and equity in school finance substitutes or complements?', *Journal of Economic Perspectives,* **10**, 51–71.

Hoxby, C.M. (1999), 'Where should federal education initiatives be directed?', in M.H. Kosters (ed.) *Financing College Tuition: Government Policies and Educational Priorities,* Washington, D.C.: AEI Press.

Inouye, D.K., H.L. Miller and J.D. Fletcher (1997), 'The evaluation of system cost and replicability', *International Journal of Educational Research,* **27**, 137–152.

Jaeger, D.A. and M.E. Page (1996), 'Degrees matter: new evidence on sheepskin effects in the returns to education', *Review of Economics and Statistics,* **4**, 733–740.

James, E. (1987), 'The public/private division of responsibility for education: an international comparison', *Economics of Education Review*, **6**, 1–14.

James, E. (1993), 'Why do different countries choose a different public-private mix of educational services?', *Journal of Human Resources*, **28**, 571–592.

James, E., N. Alsalam, J.C. Conaty and D-L. To (1989), 'College quality and future earnings: where should you send your child to college?', *American Economic Review*, **79**, 247–252.

Jesson, D., D. Mayston and P. Smith (1987), 'Performance assessment in the education sector: educational and economic perspectives', *Oxford Review of Education*, **13**, 249–266.

Jimenez, E. (1986), 'The structure of educational costs: multi-product cost functions for primary and secondary schools in Latin America', *Economics of Education Review*, **5**, 25–40.

Jimenez, E. and J-P. Tan (1987), 'Selecting the brightest for post secondary education in Colombia: the impact on equity', *Economics of Education Review*, **6**, 129–135.

Johnes, G. (1993a), *The Economics of Education*, London: Macmillan.

Johnes, G. (1993b), 'A degree of waste: a dissenting view', *Oxford Review of Education*, **19**, 459–464.

Johnes, G. (1994), 'The determinants of student loan take-up in the United Kingdom', *Applied Economics*, **26**, 999–1005.

Johnes, G. (1997), 'Costs and industrial structure in British higher education', *Economic Journal*, **107**, 727–737.

Johnes, G. (1998), 'Human capital versus sorting: new data and a new test', *Applied Economics Letters*, **5**, 665–667.

Johnes, G. (1999), 'The management of universities', *Scottish Journal of Political Economy*, **46**, 505–522.

Johnes, J. (1997), 'Inter-university variations in undergraduate non-completion rates: a statistical analysis by subject of study', *Journal of Applied Statistics*, **24**, 343–361.

Johnes, J. and G. Johnes (1995a) 'Research funding and performance in UK university departments of economics: a frontier analysis', *Economics of Education Review*, **14**, 301–314.

Johnes, J. and G. Johnes (1995b), 'Neither poison nor panacea', *Economics of Education Review*, **14**, 317–318.

Johnson, G.E. (1984), 'Subsidies for higher education', *Journal of Labor Economics*, **2**, 67–87.

Kane, T.J. (1999), 'Reforming public subsidies for higher education' in M.H. Kosters (ed.) *Financing College Tuition: Government Policies and Educational Priorities*, Washington, D.C.: AEI Press.

Kane, T.J. and C.E. Rouse (1995), 'Labor market returns to two-year and four-year college', *American Economic Review*, **85**, 600–614.

Kang, S. and J.H. Bishop (1989), 'Vocational and academic education in high school: complements or substitutes?', *Economics of Education Review,* **8**, 133–148.

Katz, K. (1999), 'Were there no returns to education in the USSR? Estimates from Soviet-period household data', *Labour Economics*, **6**, 417–434.

Keep, E. (1993), 'The need for a revised management system for the teaching profession', *Education Economics,* **1**, 53–59.

Keep, E. and K. Mayhew (1996), 'Economic demand for higher education: a sound foundation for further expansion?', *Higher Education Quarterly*, **50**, 89–109.

Keep, E. and K. Mayhew (1999), 'The assessment: knowledge, skills and competitiveness', *Oxford Review of Economic Policy*, **15**, 1–15.

Kim, H.Y. (1988), 'The consumer demand for education', *Journal of Human Resources*, **23**, 179–192.

Kodde, D.A. (1985), 'On estimating the impact of tuition on the demand for education from cross-sections', *Economics Letters*, **18**, 293–296.

Kodde, D.A. (1986), 'Uncertainty and the demand for education', *Review of Economics and Statistics*, **67**, 460–467.

Kodde, D.A. and J.M.M. Ritzen (1985), 'The demand for education under imperfect capital markets', *European Economic Review*, **28**, 347–362.

Koshal, R.K. and M. Koshal (1995), 'Quality and economic of scale in higher education', *Applied Economics,* **27**, 773–778.

Koshal, R.K. and M. Koshal (1999), 'Demand and supply of educational service: a case of liberal arts colleges', *Education Economics*, **7**, 121–130.

Koshal, R.K, M. Koshal and B. Marino (1995), 'High school dropouts: a case of negatively sloping supply and positively sloping demand curves', *Applied Economics*, **27**, 751–757.

Kroch, E.A. and K. Sjoblom (1994), 'Schooling as human capital or a signal: some evidence', *Journal of Human Resources*, **29**, 156–180.

Krueger, A.B. (1999), 'Experimental estimates of education production functions', *Quarterly Journal of Economics*, **CXIV**, 497–532.

Kyvik, S. (1995), 'Are big university departments better than small ones?', *Higher Education,* **30**, 3, 295–304.

Lamdin, D.J. (1995), 'Testing for the effect of school size on student achievement within a school district', *Education Economics*, **3**, 33–42.

Lange, T. (1998), *Rethinking Higher Education,* London: Institute of Economic Affairs.

Lankford, H. and J. Wyckoff. (1997), 'The changing structure of teacher compensation, 1970–94', *Economics of Education Review*, **16**, 371–84.

Lee, K. (1997), 'An economic analysis of public school choice plans',

Journal of Urban Economics, **41**, 1–22.

Le Grand, J. (1982), *The Strategy of Equality*. London: George Allen and Unwin.

Leppel, K. (1993), 'Logit estimation of a gravity model of the college enrolment decision', *Research in Higher Education*, **34**, 387–398.

Leslie, L.L. and P.T. Brinkman (1987), 'Student price response in higher education: the student demand studies', *Journal of Higher Education*, **58**, 181–204.

Leslie, L.L. and P.T. Brinkman (1988), *The Economic Value of Higher Education*, London: Macmillan.

Levacic, R. (1998), 'Local management of schools in England: results after six years', *Journal of Education Policy*, **13**, 331–350.

Levacic, R. and D. Glover (1997), 'Value for money as a school improvement strategy: evidence from the new inspection system in England', *School Effectiveness and School Improvement*, **8**, 231–253.

Levacic, R. and D. Glover (1998), 'The relationship between efficient resource management and school effectiveness: evidence from OFSTED secondary school inspections', *School Effectiveness and School Improvement*, **9**, 95–122.

Levacic, R. and J. Hardman (1999), 'The performance of grant-maintained schools in England: an experiment in autonomy', *Journal of Education Policy*, **14**, 185–212.

Levin, H.M. (1992), 'Market approaches to education: vouchers and school choice', *Economics of Education Review*, **11**, 279–286.

Levin, H.M. (1995), 'Cost–benefit analysis' in M. Carnoy (ed.) *International Encyclopaedia of the Economics of Education*, New York: Pergamon Press.

Levin, H.M. and C. Kelley (1994), 'Can education do it alone?', *Economics of Education Review*, **13**, 97–108.

Liebowitz, S.J. and S.E. Margolis (1990), 'The fable of the keys', *Journal of Law and Economics*, **XXXIII**, 1–12.

Liebowitz, S.J. and S.E. Margolis (1994), 'Network externality: an uncommon tragedy', *Journal of Economic Perspectives*, **8**, 133–150.

Light, A. (1998), 'Estimating returns to schooling: when does the career begin?', *Economics of Education Review*, **17**, 31–45.

Lillydahl, J.H. and L.D. Singell (1993), 'Job satisfaction, salaries and unions: the determination of university faculty compensation', *Economics of Education Review*, **12**, 234–243.

Lindley, R. (1991), 'Interactions in the markets for education, training and labour: a European perspective on intermediate skills', in P. Ryan (ed.) *International Comparisons of Vocational Education and Training for Intermediate Skills*, London: Falmer Press.

Lissenburgh, S. and A. Bryson (1995), 'The returns to graduation', London:

Department for Education and Employment.

Lott, J.R. (1987a), 'The institutional arrangement of public education: the puzzle of exclusive territories', *Journal of Public Economics*, **54**, 89–93.

Lott, J.R. (1987b), 'Why is education publicly provided? A critical survey', *Cato Journal*, **7**, 475–501.

Lott, J.R. (1990), 'An explanation for public provision of schooling: the importance of indoctrination', *Journal of Law and Economics*, **XXXIII**, 199–231.

Lowenberg, A.D. and T.D. Tinnin (1992), 'Professional versus consumer interests in regulation: the case of the United States child-care industry', *Applied Economics*, **24**, 571–580.

Luyten, H. (1994), 'School size effects on education in secondary education: evidence from the Netherlands, Sweden and the USA', *School Effectiveness and School Improvement*, **5**, 75–99.

Machina, M.J. (1989), 'Dynamic consistency and non-expected utility models of choice under uncertainty', *Journal of Economic Literature*, **XXVII**, 1622–1694.

Makepeace, G. (1996), 'Lifetime earnings and the training of young men in Britain', *Applied Economics*, **28**, 725–735.

Mancebon, M-J. and E. Bandres (1999), 'Efficiency evaluation in secondary schools: the key role of model specification and of ex post analysis of results', *Education Economics*, **7**, 131–152.

Mane, F. (1999), 'Trends in the payoff to academic and occupation-specific skills: the short and medium run returns to academic and vocational high school courses for non-college-bound students', *Economics of Education Review*, **18**, 417–438.

Manski, C.F. (1989), 'Schooling as experimentation: a re-appraisal of the post-secondary dropout phenomenon', *Economics of Education Review*, **8**, 305–312.

Manski, C.F. (1995), *Identification Problems in the Social Sciences*, Cambridge, Mass.: Harvard University Press.

Manski, C.F. (1997), 'The mixing problem in programme evaluation', *Review of Economic Studies*, **64**, 537–553.

Marlow, M.L. (1997), 'Public education supply and student performance', *Applied Economics*, **29**, 617–626.

Mason, G. (1996), 'Graduate utilisation in British industry: the initial impact of mass higher education', *National Institute Economic Review*, May, 165–171.

McCarty, T.A. and H.E. Brazer (1990), 'On equalizing school expenditures', *Economics of Education Review*, **9**, 251–264.

McGoldrick, K. and J. Robst (1996), 'Gender differences in overeducation: a test of the theory of differential overqualification', *American*

Economic Review, **86**, 2, 280–284.

McMahon, W.W. (1991), 'Relative returns to human and physical capital in the U.S. and efficient investment strategies', *Economics of Education Review*, **10**, 283–296.

McMahon, W.W. (1997a) 'Recent advances in measuring the social and individual benefits of education', *International Journal of Educational Research*, **27**, 453–481.

McMahon, W.W. (1998), 'Conceptual framework for the analysis of the social benefits of lifelong learning', *Education Economics*, **6**, 309–340.

McMahon, W.W. (1999), *Education and Development: Measuring the Social Benefits*, Oxford: Oxford University Press.

McPherson, M.S. and M.O. Schapiro (1991), 'Does student aid affect college enrolment? New evidence on a persistent controversy', *American Economic Review*, **81**, 309–318.

Meer P. van der, and R. Wielers (1996), 'Educational credentials and trust in the labour market', *Kyklos*, **49**, 29–46.

Miller, P., C. Mulvey and N. Martin (1997), 'Family characteristics and the returns to schooling: evidence on gender differences from a sample of Australian twins', *Economica*, **64**, 119–136.

Mincer J. (1997), 'The production of human capital and the life cycle of earnings: variation on a theme', *Journal of Labor Economics*, **15**, S26–S47.

Moen, E.R. (1998), 'Efficient ways to finance human capital investments', *Economica*, **65**, 491–505.

Moll, P.G. (1998), 'Primary schooling, cognitive skills and wages in South Africa', *Economica*, **65**, 263–284.

Monk, D.H. (1987), 'Secondary school size and curriculum comprehensiveness', *Economics of Education Review*, **6**, 137–150.

Moock, P.R. and H. Addou (1995), 'Education and agricultural productivity', in M. Carnoy (ed.) *International Encyclopaedia of the Economics of Education*, New York: Pergamon Press.

Murray, S.E., W.N. Evans and R.M. Schwab (1998), 'Education-finance reform and the distribution of education resources', *American Economic Review*, **88**, 789–812.

National Committee Inquiry into Higher Education (NCIHE) (1997), *Higher Education and the Learning Society*, London: HMSO.

Nonneman, W. and I. Cortens (1997), 'A note on the rate of return to education investment in Belgium', *Applied Economics Letters*, **4**, 167–171.

Noulas, A.G. and K.W. Ketkar (1998), 'Efficient utilisation of resources in public schools: a case study of New Jersey', *Applied Economics*, **30**, 1299–1306.

O'Keeffe, D.J. (1981), 'Curricular yogis and cost–benefit commissars: some thoughts on an economic dimension in curriculum research and policymaking', *Journal of Curriculum Studies*, **13**, 207–214.

Organisation for Economic Co-operation and Development (OECD) (1997), *Human Capital: An International Comparison*, Paris: CERI.

Olson, M. (1982), *The Rise and Decline of Nations*. New Haven, Conn.: Yale University Press.

Oosterbeek, H. (1998a), 'Innovative ways to finance education and their relation to lifelong learning', *Education Economics*, **6**, 219–251.

Oosterbeek, H. (1998b), 'Unravelling supply and demand factors in work-related training', *Oxford Economic Papers*, **50**, 266–283.

Ortmann, A. (1999), 'The nature and causes of corporate negligence, sham lectures and ecclesiastical indolence: Adam Smith on joint-stock companies, teachers and preachers', *History of Political Economy*, **31**, 297–316.

Palme, M.O. and R.E. Wright (1998), 'Changes in the rate of return to education in Sweden', *Applied Economics*, **30**, 1653–1663.

Pascarella, E.T., J.C. Smart and M.A. Smylie (1992), 'College tuition costs and early career socio-economic achievement: do you get what you pay for?', *Higher Education,* **24**, 3, 275–290.

Peltzman, S. (1996), 'Political economy of public education: non-college-bound students', *Journal of Law and Economics*, **XXXIX**, 73–120.

Peterson, P.E. and B.C. Hassel (eds) (1998), *Learning from School Choice*, Washington, D.C.: Brookings Institution.

Phelps, R.P. (1998), 'The effect of university host community size on state growth', *Economics of Education Review*, **17**, 149–158.

Pitcher, J. and K. Purcell (1998), 'Diverse expectations and access to opportunities: is there a graduate labour market?', *Higher Education Quarterly*, **52**, 179–203.

Polachek, S.W. (1975), 'Differences in expected post-school investment as a determinant of market wage differentials', *International Economic Review*, **16**, 451–470.

Polachek, S.W. (1995), 'Earnings over the life-cycle: what do human capital models explain?', *Scottish Journal of Political Economy*, 267–289.

Polachek, S.W. and W.S. Siebert (1993), *The Economics of Earnings*, Cambridge: Cambridge University Press.

Prais, S.J. (1996), 'Class-size and learning: the Tennessee experiment – what follows?', *Oxford Review of Education*, **22**, 399–414.

Prendergast, C. (1999), 'The provision of incentives in firms', *Journal of Economic Literature*, **32**, 7–63.

PREST (1998), *HEI–Industry Links.* HEFCE Research Series: Bristol.

Pritchett, L. (1996), 'Where has all the education gone?', New York: World Bank, mimeo.

Pritchett, L. and D. Filmer (1999), 'What education production functions really show: a positive theory of education expenditures', *Economics of Education Review*, **18**, 223–240.

Psacharopoulos, G. (1995), 'Returns to investment in education: a global update', *World Development*, **22**, 1325–1343.

Psacharopoulos, G. (1996a), 'Economics of education: a research agenda', *Economics of Education Review*, **15**, 339–344.

Psacharopoulos, G. (1996b), 'Public spending on higher education in developing countries: too much rather than too little', *Economics of Education Review*, **15**, 421–422.

Ram, R. (1989), 'Can educational expansion reduce income inequality in less-developed countries?', *Economics of Education Review*, **8**, 185–195.

Ram, R. (1995), 'Intercountry and intracountry inequalities in school enrollments: a broad international perspective', *Economics of Education Review*, **14**, 363–372.

Rauch, G.E. (1993), 'Productivity gains from geographic concentration of human capital: evidence from the cities', *Journal of Urban Economics*, **34**, 380–400.

Rees, D.I. and H.N. Mocan (1997), 'Labor market conditions and the high school dropout rate: evidence from New York State', *Economics of Education Review*, **16**, 103–109.

Rizzo, J.A. and R.J. Zeckhauser (1992), 'Advertising and the price, quality and primary care of physician services', *Journal of Human Resources*, **27**, 381–421.

Robinson, P. (1995), 'Qualifications and the labour market: do the national training and education targets make sense?', London School of Economics: Centre for Economic Performance, Working Paper 736.

Robst, J. and K. Cuson Graham (1999), 'The effect of uncertain educational requirements on education and wages', *Applied Economics*, **31**, 53–63.

Romer, P.M. (1994), 'The origins of endogenous growth', *Journal of Economic Perspectives*, **8**, 3–22.

Ross, K. and R. Levacic (1999), *Needs-based Resource Allocation in Education via Formula Funding of Schools*, Paris: UNESCO.

Rothschild, M. and L.J. White (1990), 'The university in the marketplace: some insights and some puzzles', in C. Clotfelter and M. Rothschild (eds) *Studies of Supply and Demand in Higher Education*, Chicago: University of Chicago Press.

Rothschild, M. and L.J. White (1995), 'The analytics of pricing in higher education and other services in which customers are inputs', *Journal of Political Economy*, **103**, 573–586.

Rouse, C.E. (1998a), 'Schools and student achievement: more evidence from the Milwaukee parental choice problem', *Federal Reserve of New York Economic Policy Review*, **4**, 56–65.

Rouse, C.E. (1998b), 'Private school vouchers and student achievement: an evaluation of the Milwaukee parental choice program', *Quarterly Journal of Economics*, **CXIII**, 553–602.

Runde, J. (1998), 'Assessing causal economic explanations', *Oxford Economic Papers*, **50**, 151–172.

Sander, W. (1995), 'Schooling and smoking', *Economics of Education Review*, **14**, 23–33.

Sattinger, M. (1995), 'Search and the efficient assignment of workers to jobs', *International Economic Review*, **36**, 283–302.

Schultz, T.P. (1999), 'Health and schooling investments in Africa', *Journal of Economic Perspectives*, **13**, 67–88.

Shachar, R. and B. Nalebuff (1999), 'Follow the leader: theory and evidence on political participation', *American Economic Review*, **89**, 525–547.

Shleifer, A. (1998), 'State versus private ownership', *Journal of Economic Perspectives*, **12**, 133–150.

Siebert, W.S. (1985), 'Development in the economics of human capital', in D. Carline, C.A. Pissarides, W.S. Siebert and P.J. Sloane. *Labour Economics*, London: Longman.

Slavin, R.E. (1999), 'How can funding equity ensure enhanced attainment?', *Journal of Education Finance*, **24**, 519–528.

Slavin, R.E., N.A. Madden, L.J. Dolan and B.A. Wasik (1996), *Every Child, Every School*, California: Corwin Press Inc.

Sloane, P.J., H. Battu and P. Seaman (1996), 'Overeducation and the formal education/experience and training trade-off', *Applied Economics Letters,* **3**, 511–515.

Smart, J.C. (1988), 'College influences on graduates' income levels', *Research in Higher Education,* **29**, 41–59.

Smet, M. and W. Nonneman (1998), 'Economies of scale and scope in Flemish secondary schools', *Applied Economics*, **30**, 1251–1258.

Smith, A. (1776), *An Inquiry into the Nature and Causes of the Wealth of Nations*, London: Methuen.

Sonstelie, J.C. (1982), 'The welfare costs of free public schools', *Journal of Political Economy*, **90**, 794–808.

Southwick, L. and I.S. Gill (1997), 'Unified salary schedule and student SAT scores: adverse effects of adverse selection in the market for secondary school teachers', *Economics of Education Review*, **16**, 143–153.

Sparkes, J. and A. West (1998), 'An evaluation of the English nursery voucher scheme', *Education Economics*, **6**, 171–184.

Spence, M. (1973), 'Job market signalling', *Quarterly Journal of Economics*, **87**, 353–374.

Sperling, J. (1998), 'The American for-profit university: a model for the information economy', *Economic Affairs*, **18**, 11–16.

Stampen, J.O. and A.F. Cabrera (1988), 'The targeting and packaging of student aid and its effect on attrition', *Economics of Education Review*, **7**, 29–46.

Stanley, G. and P. Reynolds (1994), 'The relationship between students' level of achievement, their preferences for future enrolment and their image of universities', *Higher Education*, **27**, 85–93.

Steuerle, C.E. (1996), 'How should government allocate subsidies for human capital?', *American Economic Review*, **86**, 353–357.

Stevens, M. (1994), 'A theoretical model of on-the-job training with imperfect competition', *Oxford Economic Papers*, **46**, 537–562.

Stevens, M. (1999), 'Human capital theory and UK vocational training policy', *Oxford Review of Economic Policy*, **15**, 16–32.

Stevenson, L. and J. Stigler (1986), 'Mathematics achievement of Chinese, Japanese and American children', *Science*, 693–699.

Sullivan, D.H. and T.M. Smeedling (1997), 'Education attainment and earnings inequality in eight nations', *International Journal of Education Research*, **27**, 513–525.

Sutherland, S. (1992), *Irrationality*, Harmondsworth, Middx: Penguin.

Temple, J. (1999), 'A positive effect of human capital on growth', *Economics Letters*, **65**, 131–134.

Theobald, N.D. and R. Gritz (1996), 'The effects of school district spending priorities on the exit paths of beginning teachers leaving the district', *Economics of Education Review*, **15**, 11–22.

Thobani, M. (1984), 'Charging user fees for social services: education in Malawi', *Comparative Education Review*, **28**, 402–423.

Thomas, H.R. (1990), *Education, Costs and Performance: A Cost-effectiveness Analysis*, London: Cassell.

Thomas, H.R. and J. Martin (1996), *Managing Resources for School Improvement: Creating a Cost-effective School*, London: Routledge.

Tight, M. (1996), 'The re-location of higher education', *Higher Education Quarterly*, **50**, 118–135.

Toutkoushian, R.K. (1998), 'Sex matters less for younger faculty: evidence of desegregate pay disparities from the 1988 and 1993 NCES surveys', *Economics of Education Review*, **17**, 55–71.

Tsang, M.C. (1987), 'The impact of underutilization of education on productivity: a case study of the U.S. Bell companies', *Economics of Education Review*, **6**, 239–254.

Tsang, M.C. (1988), 'Cost analysis for educational policymaking: a review of cost studies in education in developing countries', *Review of Educational Research*, **58**, 181–230.

Tucker, I.B. (1987), 'The impact of consumer credentialism on employee and entrepreneur returns to higher education', *Economics of Education Review*, **6**, 35–40.

Tyler, J.H., R.J. Murnane and J.B. Willett (2000), 'Estimating the labor market signaling value of the GED', *Quarterly Journal of Economics*, **CXV**, 431–468.

Usher, D. (1997), 'Education as a deterrent to crime', *Canadian Journal of Economics*, **30**, 367–384.

Varian, H.R. (1999), *Intermediate Microeconomics*, New York: W.W. Norton.

Varian, H.R. and C. Shapiro (1999), *Information Rules*, Boston, Mass.: Harvard Business School.

Verdugo, R.R. and J.M. Schneider (1994), 'Gender inequality in female-dominated occupation: the earnings of male and female teachers', *Economics of Education Review*, **13**, 251–264.

Verry, D.W. (1987), 'Educational cost functions', in G. Psacharopoulos (ed.) *Economics of Education, Research and Studies*, New York: Pergamon Press.

Verstegen, D.A. and R.A. King (1998), 'The relationship between school spending and student achievement: a review and analysis of 35 years of production function research', *Journal of Education Finance,* **24**, 243–262.

Wahlberg, H.J. (1998), 'Uncompetitive American schools: causes and cures', in D. Ravitch (ed.) *Brookings Papers on Education Policy*, Washington, D.C.: Brookings Institution.

Waterman, C. (1984), *Economic Theory of the Industry*, Cambridge: Cambridge University Press.

Weale, M. (1992), 'Externalities from education', in F. Hahn (ed.) *The Market: Practice and Policy*, Basingstoke: Macmillan.

Weale, M. (1993), 'A critical evaluation of rate of return analysis', *Economic Journal*, **103**, 729–737.

Weiss, A. (1995), 'Human capital versus signalling effects of wages', *Journal of Economic Perspectives*, **9**, 133–154.

West, E.G. (1970), *Education and the State*, London: Institute of Economic Affairs.

West, E.G. (1991), 'Public schools and excess burdens', *Economics of Education Review*, **10**, 159–169.

West, E.G. (1997), 'Education vouchers in principle and practice: a survey', *World Bank Research Observer*, **12**, 83–103.

White, J. (1994), 'Education and the limits of the market', In D. Bridges and T.H. McLaughlin (eds) *Education and the Market Place*. London: Falmer Press.

Winkler, D.R. (1984), 'The fiscal consequences of foreign students in public higher education: a case study of California', *Economics of Education Review*, **3**, 141–154.

Winkler, D.R. and T. Rounds (1996), 'Municipal and private sector response to decentralization and school choice', *Economics of Education Review*, **15**, 365–376.

Winston, G.C. (1999), 'Subsidies, hierarchy and peers: the awkward economics of higher education', *Journal of Economic Perspectives*, **13**, 13–37.

Witte, J.F., T.D. Sterr and C.A. Thorn (1995), 'Fifth-year report: the Milwaukee parental choice program', University of Wisconsin, mimeo.

Wolfe, B.L. and S. Zuvekas (1997), 'Nonmarket outcomes of schooling', *International Journal of Educational Research*, **27**, 491–502.

Woodhall, M. (1991), 'The economics of education and the education of policy-makers: reflection on full-cost fees for overseas students' in G.K. Shaw (ed.) *Economics, Culture and Education: Essays in Honour of Mark Blaug*, Aldershot: Edward Elgar.

Woodhall, M. (1995), 'Student loans', in M. Carnoy (ed.) *International Encyclopaedia of the Economics of Education*, New York: Pergamon Press.

Woods, P.A., C. Bagley and R. Glatter (1998), *School Choice and Competition: Markets in the Public Interest?*, London: Routledge.

World Bank Indicators (1999) *World Bank Indicators and International Data*, Washington D.C.: World Bank.

Wozniak, G.D. (1987), 'Human capital, information and the early adoption of new technology', *Journal of Human Resources*, **22**, 101–112.

Zanzig, B.R. (1997), 'Measuring the impact of competition in local government education markets on the cognitive achievement of students', *Economics of Education Review*, **16**, 431–441.

Zarkin, G.A. (1985), 'Occupational choice: an application to the market for public school teachers', *Quarterly Journal of Economics*, **C**, 409–446.

Zweifel, P. and R. Eichenberger (1992), 'The political economy of corporatism in medicine: self-regulation or cartel management?', *Journal of Regulatory Economics*, **4**, 89–108.

Index

achievement functions, 75–76
administration, costs, 135
assessment systems, 79–82, 147

barriers to entry, 146
brain drain, 25, 204
budgeting, 174

capacity effects, 85, 87
cartels, 149
Chicago Summer Bridge Program, 79
class size, 114–115
    cost-effectiveness, 98
    reduction, 11
cognitive partitioning, 59
community effects, 138
competition in schooling, 107, 145–146,
    152
    evidence, 151–153
Comprehensive Employment and Training
    Act, 218
cost–benefit analysis, 10
cost-effectiveness, 7
cost-plus formulae, 174
costs,
    cost functions, 8, 84–85
    measurement, 10
    multi-product, 86
    per-student evidence, 84
crime, 194–195
customer–input technology, 87–89

data envelopment analysis, 77–78

deadweight loss effects, 180–183
decentralisation, 150
demand for education, 49–51, 54–55
    capital constraints, 65
    income effects, 56–58
    interest rate effects, 62–65
    normal good, 55
    price effects, 55–56
democracy, 196, 198

economic growth, 199–203, 205
economies of scale, 108–111
economies of scope, 108–112
education enterprises, 73–75
efficiency,
    external, 7, 11
    internal, 6
effort levels, 187
elasticity of substitution, 25, 140–141
enrolment decisions,
    evidence 53
    information, 49, 53–54
equity effects, 203, 213
exclusive territories, 147, 154, 166
expansion of education systems, 57
expenditures,
    international data, 3
    per-student, 5
    trends, 4
experimental research, 12–13, 32
externalities, 193
    calculation, 197–198
    evidence, 198

factor substitution, 140–141
fiscal rate of return, 167–168
fixed-price formulae, 174
formula funding, 172–174
franchising, 176
funding education, 170–171

government intervention, 164
government provision, 164–165
grants, 160

happiness, 194
health, 194, 204–205
Herfindahl index, 151
higher education subsidies, deadweight
    loss, 184–185
household inputs, 136
human capital,
    ability effects, 18–20, 22
    depreciation, 22
    earnings effects, 17–18
    life-cycle model, 17

incentives, 79, 187
income elasticity of demand, 58
independent study, 134
inspection grades, 102–103
internal efficiency, 73–74

Job Training Partnership Act, 218

length of school year, 11
loans, 159–161

macro-economic effects, 201–203
macro-economic rate of return, 167
management of education, 134–135
market analysis, 9, 92–93
marketisation, 150–151
mergers, school districts, 150
merit goods, 165
Milwaukee Parental Choice Program, 158–
    159

minimum efficient scale, 115
mixing problem, 13
monopolies in education, 147
multi-level modelling, 178
multiplier, 12

network effects, 82
non-completion,
    costs of, 115–116
    determinants, 69
    effect on earnings, 43–44
    enrolment effects, 66–68
non-pecuniary benefits, 193–194, 199
Nursery Voucher scheme, 157–158

OFSTED, 177
over-education,
    calculation, 35–36
    definition, 35
    effects on earnings, 39–40
    effects on firms, 40
    effects on productivity, 39
    evidence, 37–38

parental investments, 136–137
participation rates,
    opportunity costs, 31
    wage effects, 23–25
peer effects, pricing, 92
peer inputs, 138–140
performance indicators, 176–179
Perry Pre-school Program, 197
physical capital, 25, 196
physical inputs, 135–136
policy, 212–213
political effects, 179–180
price discrimination, 147–148
price elasticity of enrolment, 57
private schooling, 153
privatisation, 154–155
production functions, 73–77, 103–6
    modelling, 9
purchaser–provider split, 173

quasi-markets, 149–150

rate of return, 11
    calculation, 27–28
    estimates, 28–31, 61–62, 119
    inference, 31–33, 119
    policy, 168, 169
    private, 18
remediation, costs of, 117
resource effects,
    achievement, 97–98
    earnings, 99–101
    performance, 102–103
revenues, education enterprises, 87–89

school-effectiveness, 108, 178
schooling–work trade-off, 134
screening/signalling,
    evidence, 43–44
    models, 40–42
sheepskin effects, 43–44
size effects, 113–114
skill-biased technology change, 25–26
social benefits, 165
social rates of return, 166–167
    evidence, 167
sorting, 42–43
South African education, 106, 143,
    172
standards in education, 78–82
STAR trial, 13, 98
strategic oligopoly, 148
streaming/tracking, 138–139
student inputs, 133–134
subsidies, 170–172
supply of education, 52–53

tax bases, 171, 175
tax distortions, 181, 184

teachers, 121–132
    demand for, 121–123
    earnings, 121–125
    effects, 128–130
    incentives, 131–132
    market, 126–128
    performance, 130–131
    supply, 124–126
teaching,
    adverse selection, 123
    barriers to entry, 123
    expenditure on, 121–122
    unions, 129–131
Teaching and Higher Education Act, 168
tenure, 131
tracking/streaming, 138–139
training, 20–23
    evidence, 21, 33–34
    transferable, 21–22
trust, 196
twins, 32

uncertainty,
    effects on earnings, 53
    enrolment decisions, 49, 52
unionisation, teaching, 129–131

vocational courses, earnings effects,
    101–102
vouchers, 154–156
    evidence, 156–158

wealth effects, 51, 57–58, 59–61, 63,
    65, 176
welfare burdens, 180–181

x-inefficiency, 186–189

years of schooling, data, 4